ROYAL HISTORICAL SOCIETY
STUDIES IN HISTORY 73

THE ENGLISH ORDNANCE OFFICE 1585–1625

THE ENGLISH ORDNANCE OFFICE 1585–1625

A CASE STUDY IN BUREAUCRACY

Richard Winship Stewart

THE ROYAL HISTORICAL SOCIETY
THE BOYDELL PRESS

© Richard W. Stewart 1996

All Rights Reserved. Except as permitted under current legislation no part of this work may be photocopied, stored in a retrieval system, published, performed in public, adapted, broadcast, transmitted, recorded or reproduced in any form or by any means, without the prior permission of the copyright owner

First published 1996

A Royal Historical Society publication
Published by The Boydell Press
an imprint of Boydell & Brewer Ltd
PO Box 9 Woodbridge Suffolk IP12 3DF UK
and of Boydell & Brewer Inc.
PO Box 41026 Rochester NY 14604–4126 USA

ISBN 0 86193 233 1

ISSN 0269–2244

British Library Cataloguing-in-Publication Data
Stewart, Richard W.
  The English Ordnance Office, 1585–1625 : a
  case study in bureaucracy. – (Royal Historical Society
  studies in history ; v. 73)
  1. Ordnance Board – History 2. Military supplies –
  History – 16th century 3. Great Britain – History,
  Military – 1485–1603
  I. Title II. Royal Historical Society
  942'.01
  ISBN 0861932331

Library of Congress Catalog Card Number: 95–47553

The paper used in this publication meets the minimum requirements
of American National Standard for Information Sciences –
Permanence of Paper for Printed Library Materials, ANSI Z39.48–1984

Printed in Great Britain by the publisher

Contents

		Page
Acknowledgements		vii
Abbreviations		ix
Preface		xi
1	Introduction	1
2	The ordnance office: officers, artificers, management and finances	6
3	Administrative tensions, corruption and reform	33
4	Ordnance supplies and suppliers: the great ordnance	63
5	Gunpowder and saltpetre	80
6	Handguns, 'habilliments of war' and the arms merchants	96
7	The wider ordnance establishment	111
8	Conclusion	141
Appendixes		
1	Ordnance office personnel and salaried artificers, 1585–1625	151
2	Craftsmen and suppliers to the ordnance office, 1593–1603 and 1620–5	155
3	Sample supply lists: army and navy	162
4	Ordnance supply items: prices 1574, 1593, 1625	166
5	Estimated ordnance office expenses in selected years	167
Bibliography		171
Index		177

The Society records its gratitude to the following whose generosity made possible the initiation of this series: The British Academy; The Pilgrim Trust; The Twenty-Seven Foundation; The United States Embassy's Bicentennial funds; The Wolfson Trust; several private donors.

Acknowledgements

The truth of the assertion that all scholastic work results from a collective effort only becomes clear when one actually tries to assemble a coherent analysis out of a jumbled mass of evidence, advice and possibilities. The guidance and assistance of other scholars is ultimately just as important to the equation as is the location of the proper documents and sources. It is not possible to thank all of those whose assistance has made this book a reality.

However, I do wish to acknowledge a few specific institutions and people. I want to thank the helpful staffs of the Public Record Offices at Chancery Lane and Kew, and those of the British Library Manuscripts Reading Room and the Hampshire Record Office in Winchester. Maija Cole and William Bidwell of the Yale Center for Parliamentary History provided invaluable hints on how to navigate the labyrinth of parliamentary sources. The staff of the Institute of Historical Research in London were very courteous and helpful. The chairmen and members of the Tyacke–Lake–Starkey Tudor History seminar at that institute provided stimulation for ideas and sources. Much valuable advice was given to me while in London by the late Professor Sir Geoffrey Elton, by Nicholas Tyacke, Ian Roy, Peter Lake, Mark Kishlansky, Linda Levy Peck, Victor Stater, Joanna Mattingly, David Hebe and many others. For financial support while carrying out research in London and while writing, I would like to thank Yale University, the Fulbright program and the American Society of Arms Collectors.

I owe a special debt to a number of scholars who have given freely of their time in reading my various drafts. Foremost among them is Professor Conrad Russell who shared his immense knowledge of Tudor and Stuart England with me in the course of numerous seminars, lectures and correspondence. Our occasional disagreements on the mechanics of the dissertation process should not hide our fundamental agreement on the historical process or my debt to him for sharing so many insights with me. I also wish to thank Dr Linda Colley, whose excellent advice and eternal patience helped clarify my prose and ideas immeasureably. I am extremely grateful too for the timely advice and wide-ranging perspectives of Dr Paul Kennedy; his courtesy and support was of great benefit to me. Dr John Boswell, Director of Graduate Studies at Yale, was equally supportive and his timely assistance gave my morale a critical boost at a trying stage in my work. His recent death was a tremendous loss to Yale and to the entire historical profession. I wish to thank Professor Geoffrey Parker for his invaluable advice and generous support to an admirer of his own work on logistical problems in early modern Europe. Dr David Underdown also gave freely of his time and advice, and my attempts to grapple with the problems of bureaucracy and corruption owe much to his perceptive reading and comments. Sir Geoffrey Elton further encouraged me in this study at a timely juncture. His passing leaves two generations of Tudor and Stuart students in mourning for his wisdom, insight and guidance. Lastly, I wish to thank Mark Charles Fissel, who allowed me to publish two articles on the ordnance office in action in a collection of essays he edited, and Brian Sullivan, who encouraged me to keep working on this book despite the conflicting pressures of full-time work for the US government. That I did not always chose to take the advice of these scholars at all times means that those errors in fact or interpretation which remain are now my own responsibility.

Lastly, I wish to extend my deep thanks and gratitude to my wife, Lynn, whose talents in many areas of historical writing and research greatly exceed my own. This book is dedicated to her.

Richard Winship Stewart
1995

Abbreviations

AO	Audit Office Accounts
APC	*Acts of the privy council*
BIHR	*Bulletin of the Institute of Historical Research*
BL	British Library
CJ	*Journals of the House of Commons*
CSP Carew	Calendar of the Carew manuscripts
CSPD	*Calendar of state papers, domestic*
CSPD Add.	*Calendar of state papers, addenda*
CSP, Ireland	*Calendar of state papers relating to Ireland*
CSP, Foreign	*Calendar of state papers, foreign*
EHR	*English Historical Review*
HMC	Historical Manuscripts Commission
LJ	*Journals of the House of Lords*
PRO	Public Record Office
SP	State Papers
WO	War Office Records

Preface

This book examines the procedures and tensions involved in the procurement, maintenance and supply of weapons and munitions to the English armies from 1585 to 1625 – and their political implications. This is a period which encompasses a number of distinct phases. It opens with England's preparations for war with Spain, the result, most immediately, of English military involvement in the Netherlands, continues through that war and through the even more dangerous – in land war terms – rebellion in Ireland which did not end until after the death of Elizabeth I. Since it is often as instructive to view a military establishment (especially military supply) in times of peace as it is in war, the story then extends through the long and corrosive (for military preparedness) peace of James I until the initiation of some rearmament in the 1620s. The discussion ends with the renewal of war in 1625, a war which went badly with the launching of two disastrous expeditions, to Cadiz in 1625 and to Rhé in 1627.

From war, to peace, to war again, the arms establishment and policies of England are traced with a view to answering certain key questions in late Tudor and early Stuart politics and government. How expensive was war in the new age of gunpowder? How did the government cope with buying, storing, issuing and controlling arms and armaments in war and peace? How did early modern bureaucracies function? What was the nature of office-holding in virtually the only permanent military establishment in England in the Tudor and early Stuart periods? How pervasive was corruption and mismanagement in this era before the creation of anything approaching a rationalised bureaucracy?

In an attempt to answer these questions, or at least to place them in their proper contexts, this study seeks to integrate political, financial, industrial, administrative and military concerns in order to highlight the workings of the arms supply network in war and peace. The organisation of that network and its functioning in support of the military policies of Elizabeth I and James I over time are analysed in order to provide a comparative judgement of its efficiency. Particular attention is paid to the expansion of the military supply bureaucracy and related industries during the war with Spain from 1585 to 1604 and to their collapse during the twenty years of peace which followed, a collapse with ominous implications for the renewal of war in 1625.

Although some attention is paid to the vitally important but well-studied militia system in the counties, the bulk of this work is concerned with the problems of an early modern bureaucracy and its working relationships both with the privy council and with the various arms manufacturers and suppliers of England. The focus is on the size and complexity of the permanent arms supply establishments of the ordnance office and the armoury, their administrative problems, which include corruption, and the status of the basic arms and munitions industries of England.

This study of an early bureaucracy shows that the personal nature of early modern office-holding and the lack of any means by which routine procedures might be institutionalised was crucial to the success or failure of the Tudor and Stuart arms supply network. In a wider sense, the ultimate success or failure of that network had greater implications in areas of national prestige and finance. During the wars of Elizabeth, it slowly developed the ability to supply a large military establishment but could not preserve that expertise during peace. Later, the Stuart ordnance office lapsed into corruption, mismanagement and waste which crippled its ability to function when called upon in 1625. The costs of war – financial, political, economic – were heavy, but the costs of unpreparedness for war were to have even more serious consequences in a formative period in the development of English arms and military establishments.

1

Introduction

On 19 June 1588, while anxiously awaiting news of the sailing of the Spanish Armada, Lord Admiral Howard aboard the *Ark Royal* wrote a short note to Secretary Walsingham. Howard complained that, while he was glad his ships had been resupplied with food for another month at sea, he had hoped that it would have been for two months. In undoubted exasperation with his queen, who was as renowned for her parsimony as for her courage, he commented bitterly, 'for the love of God, let not her Majesty care now for charges'.[1] His wish was not fulfilled for even in this, one of the major crises of her reign, Elizabeth kept her eye on her treasure and went to great lengths to pay only for those military supplies she deemed essential in prosecuting the war with Spain. It would not be going too far to say that the cost of war horrified Elizabeth. She saw enormous quantities of money expended with few tangible results to show for it.[2] Armies were expensive to raise, costly to supply, and tended to melt away whether or not they came in contact with any enemy. Her commanders in the field were seemingly not as aware as she was of the cost of their military operations; their concern was focused on getting more men and more supplies. However, Elizabeth was sensitive to the cost of it all and to the fact that financial strain could be almost as destabilising to a kingdom as defeat in battle. To paraphrase a truism, war has always been too important and costly to be left to the generals. As I. A. A. Thompson has said in his work, *War and government in Habsburg Spain 1560–1620*, 'War was by far the severest test that faced the sixteenth-century state.'[3]

Historians have long recognised the critical effects of war upon the emerging nations of early modern Europe. However, they have tended to avoid focusing on many of the specific administrative problems which resulted from the growth of an increasingly professional military and the complex supply network which developed out of the need to sustain that establishment. By

---

[1] CSPD, Eliz. I, 1581–90, 490; *State papers relating to the defeat of the Spanish Armada anno 1588*, ed. J. K. Laughton, London 1894, 211.
[2] For the financial impact on Elizabethan strategic planning see R. B. Wernham 'Elizabethan war aims and strategy', in S. T. Bindoff, J. Hurstfield and C. H. Williams (eds), *Elizabethan government and society: essays presented to Sir John Neale*, London 1961, 340–68. See also his *After the Armada: Elizabethan England and the struggle for western Europe 1588–1595*, Oxford 1984, 415–16.
[3] I. A. A. Thompson, *War and government in Habsburg Spain 1560–1620*, London 1976, 1.

concentrating upon the battles, and the diplomacy which sought to capitalise on them, historians, with a few notable exceptions such as Thompson, Geoffrey Parker, C. G. Cruickshank and Ian Roy, have generally avoided the more mundane aspects of military supply. There remains the need to examine various aspects of the development of the logistical supply systems of early modern armies. Without a successfully administered network, especially during a time of growth in the numbers of types and the complexity of weapons' systems, success in the field was often problematical. It would not be going too far to state that success or failure on the battlefield of sixteenth-century Europe was directly proportional to the degree of effectiveness of the military supply lines and the administrative methods used to ensure the flow of food, clothing, weapons and pay to troops in the field. Geoffrey Parker has dealt best with the critical nature of the supply lines serving the Spanish army in the Low Countries in his work *The army of Flanders and the Spanish road*.[4] His work is a vital first step for anyone studying military problems of the sixteenth or early seventeenth centuries.

A new and particularly important element in the logistical requirements of early modern armies, which set them apart from their late medieval counterparts, was the increasing numbers and sophistication of the firearms, armaments and munitions which had to be supplied. Rapid growth in the use of firearms – from great artillery pieces down to small handguns – on the battlefields of Europe forced governments to pay more attention to the supply needs of their armies. Arms and munitions had to be ordered well in advance of any planned conflict. Then they had to be ordered from a wide variety of sources, manufactured, carefully tested for quality, then stored, maintained and issued to the troops. Those governments that were most cost-conscious, amongst which must be numbered Elizabeth's England, even held to the faint hope that these expensive weapons would be returned after an expedition or war. Governments began to establish new bureaucracies at central armouries and some local storehouses to handle this process. They were forced to set up complex administrative procedures to deal with a whole range of new military supplies: gunpowder, artillery, handguns, lead shot and siege trains. In these developments it is possible to discern the beginnings of what has become a hallmark of a modern army: a complex and sophisticated supply bureaucracy.

The study of all of the elements in the arms supply network of England in the early modern period poses too great a problem. Some artificial limitations have to be imposed. There were few aspects of the military or political world of early modern England which were not affected by the increasing size and cost of the military establishment. This was especially true from 1585 to 1604 when England was at war with Spain, the greatest power in Europe. However, even during England's relatively peaceful years from 1604 to 1625, the cost of

---

[4] Geoffrey Parker, *The army of Flanders and the Spanish road 1567–1659*, Cambridge 1972.

maintaining some level of military readiness was not negligible. Numerous aspects of the political world of Tudor and Stuart England were affected by the supply of arms and the bureaucracy which grew up around it. The arms bureaucracy did not 'wither away' in peacetime. Administrative tensions continued and, if anything, grew worse both within the office and within the general political culture. There were many well-publicised cases of corruption and, if the evidence is to be believed, such cases proved more costly in peacetime than in war. In war, waste is inevitable and often overlooked in the immediate scramble to supply matériel to the active forces. In peacetime, there are no such over-riding considerations and the administrative organs of the state have fewer excuses for fiscal impropriety.

Nor were the problems of military supply restricted to the bureaucracy of central government. The counties had a share both in the procurement of military supplies, and in paying for them, especially in the case of individual weapons and clothing. The cost of these weapons and the procedures for storing them was of continuing interest to the county community and often resulted in local tensions which could spill over into parliamentary debates. The concern of county elites with the cost, use, export or procurement of military supplies, and with the militia, was a constant feature of seventeenth-century parliaments.[5] The supply of arms and gunpowder was thus as much a political as a military problem. Given that one of the main 'triggers' of the conflict between king and parliament in 1642 was the control of the militia of the kingdom, it would be hard to overstress the long-term potential impact of disputes over arms and the militia. Thus several specific controversies in the counties over the establishment of centralised county armouries and the dispatch of inspectors and patentees into the counties to examine county arms stores will be considered.

Close examination of the role of the state in the growth of a military bureaucracy will also clarify some of the issues surrounding the slow, but by no means sure, centralising tendencies of the early modern state and the wide ramifications of that process for England from the last years of Elizabeth I to the start of the reign of Charles I. It is likely that the resulting tensions did not evaporate during the later period of Charles's 'personal rule' (1629–40), but rather continued to plague the Stuart political scene. However, it would be overstating the case to say that such a process was in any way 'inevitable' or that systemic and regular pressures forced centralisation along certain paths in a smooth or continuous process. The contrary was the case; the gradual centralisation of the arms bureaucracy, mirroring similar developments in other early modern bureaucracies, occurred only slowly and

---

[5] See especially L. O. J. Boynton, *The Elizabethan militia 1558–1638*, London 1967, and A. Hassell Smith, 'Militia rates and militia statutes', in Peter Clark, N. R. N. Tyacke and G. R. Alan (eds), *The English commonwealth 1547–1640: essays presented to Joel Hurstfield*, New York 1979, 93–110.

erratically, responding to specific problems. Once those problems were resolved, the urge to centralise disappeared with them.

In terms of the overall military supply establishment, moreover, the point must be made that compared with food and pay, arms supply was the least important supply requirement for an early modern military force. The regular flow of replacements, pay and food were absolutely essential if an organised army was to be maintained; battles could be fought with little more than sharpened sticks if all the other elements of an army were in place. Arms also seem to have made up a smaller portion of the estimated expenses for a military operation than did food costs or wages. Arms were, on the whole, durable goods which could theoretically be passed on to replacement troops when the original users died. However, for this to happen, military commanders needed to create a host of stricter administrative controls on officers and men in the field. The need for greater control of weapons, especially firearms, and for more intensive training of troops if they were to be effective in the use of the new weapons, is an important element of Michael Roberts's now famous 'military revolution'.[6] The consequences of the 'arms revolution' for military training need not detain us here, but they should be kept in mind during discussions of the wide impact of weapons on the state and its military. The monetary cost of weapons was relatively slight, but the need for training and stricter controls of men and weapons ensured that the growing use of firearms was changing the way in which wars were fought in Europe in the early modern period.

The supply of arms in early modern England also played a key role in the growth of bureaucracy and of the power of the state. From 1585 to 1603, under pressure of war, the size, complexity of procedures and duties of the English ordnance office, the key office for the supply of a host of military items, expanded to meet the increasing requirements of England's military establishment. This expansion was far from being rationally planned or executed but was an almost accidental consequence of the purchase through the office of increased quantities of war matériel. The number of official clerks in the office grew, and the duties of the officers became clearer through the performance of those duties. With charges of mismanagement or corruption being made, office reformers gradually came to perceive how the office ought to function, and to write about it. The official and unofficial descriptions of how the office was supposed to operate were increasingly contrasted with the reality of how the office did function. Developing realisation of how a bureaucracy should work was made possible in large part because of the pressing need for a better, more efficient office to supply the military. War has often been seen as a key element in the growth of the modern nation state. The

---

[6] Michael Roberts, *The military revolution 1550–1660*, Belfast 1956. See also Geoffrey Parker, *The military revolution: military innovation and the rise of west, 1500–1800*, Cambridge 1988.

INTRODUCTION

systems devised for the supply and maintenance of – and accountability for – a wide range of munitions was a small but important part of that gradual trend towards a more rational and bureaucratic organisation of the resources of the state.

A warning must be posted at this point concerning the nature of the evidence. Any claim to comprehensiveness in presenting a total picture of the English arms supply system must certainly founder upon the rocks of incomplete evidence and excessive expectations. Most records of the ordnance office, the main central organ of government arms supply, do not begin until 1594. Earlier records are scattered, poorly organised and incomplete. Those that do exist are often internally inconsistent and do not easily mesh with the equally untrustworthy declared accounts of the lieutenant of the ordnance. The other central agency for arms procurement was the office of the armoury which was gradually sliding into insignificance. Its records deteriorated as its role dwindled. Nor would complete central accounts, even if they did exist and were more accurate, tell the entire story. The counties bore a large part of the financial and administrative burden of arms supply for the militia and for the levies for overseas service and it would almost be possible to tell a different tale of arms procurement methods and procedures for each county. Yet, despite the diversity and complexity of these sources, it should be possible to examine many of the key elements in the beginnings of a permanent, centralised, military arms supply establishment. Such an attempt must be made if the role of government and the military in early modern society is to be understood.

2

The Ordnance Office: Officers, Artificers, Management and Finances

'the negligent and unarmed are always a prey to the vigilant and powerful' – Sir Ferdinando Gorges (1607)

The English office of the ordnance had been in existence since the early 1400s but underwent a major expansion of its role and level of activity during the mid sixteenth century. It had initially been part of the privy wardrobe, but became distinct and separate from the wardrobe and from the master of the armoury by 1485.[1] Originally consisting only of a master, a clerk and a yeoman, it grew dramatically under Henry VIII until by the early part of the reign of Elizabeth it consisted of some seven minor officers, eight clerks, twelve artificers and twenty labourers under the supervision of a master of the ordnance, often a major court official. The growing threat of war with Spain in 1585 created the need both for an expanded domestic arms industry and for a more effective means of administering the procurement, transport and issuance of those arms. Any such expansion relied heavily upon the performance of the key officers of the ordnance.[2]

The ordnance office, located in the Tower of London, was responsible for most English arms purchases in the Tudor and Stuart periods. Its administrative offices were probably near the chapel of St Peter ad Vincula and in the White Tower itself. The master of the ordnance, as one of the perquisites of his job, maintained an official residence in the Brick Tower.[3] Most arms and ordnance supplies were kept in the storehouses of the nearby Minories property directly adjacent to the Tower. It was here, at least from 1566, that the office had the space available for storing the increasing quantities of firearms, ordnance, gunpowder and other military supplies needed for this chief arsenal of the realm. Since the ordnance had to share the Tower with the armoury, the mint and the prison, it needed the warehouses in the

---

[1] R. Ashley, 'The organisation and administration of the Tudor office of the ordnance', unpubl. BLitt diss. Oxford 1973, 14–30.
[2] For a complete list of ordnance officers and personnel see appendix 1.
[3] O. F. G. Hogg, *The royal arsenal: its background, origin and subsequent history*, 2 vols, London 1963, i. 66.

Minories for its bulky supplies.[4] The heavy ordnance itself was often left out on Tower Wharf, its weight being its best protection from theft. The more dangerous items, such as gunpowder, saltpetre, camphor and other flammables, were generally kept inside the Tower precincts for safety. Most of the rest of the ordnance supplies were stored in the Minories and the offices which dealt with the receipt, maintenance and issue of the bulk of the supplies were also there.

The ordnance office also maintained smaller storehouses at Deptford, Woolwich, Rochester and Chatham which were primarily used for naval supplies. In addition, there were small stores of ordnance in numerous castles and forts throughout the realm with which the officers of the ordnance were at least indirectly concerned. The largest and most important of these were: Berwick and Newcastle, responsibility for which was delegated to the master of the ordnance in the north; the office of the ordnance in Dublin, under the control of the master of the ordnance for Ireland; and some small general storehouses in Portsmouth, Dover and Rochester. The ordnance office and this handful of 'sub-offices', run by a few procurement 'professionals', formed almost the entire permanent army supply establishment in early modern England. In fact, with the exception of a handful of royal guards and a small garrison in Ireland, the ordnance office constituted virtually the only permanent army establishment of the period. As such, it provides an interesting case study of early modern office-holding, procedures, organisation, cost and corruption. The ordnance office was an early bureaucracy concerned as much with its own survival, salaries and perquisites as with maintaining an appropriate level of supply effectiveness.

The ordnance office can be seen as an unrationalised bureaucracy in that its organisation and management had evolved slowly over time and not from any preconceived plan. Its evolution was the result of specific circumstances rather than arising from any conscious urge on the part of the crown to organise an office out of nothing to fulfill a fully elaborated and recognised need. Although Weber's ideal of a bureaucracy as a rational, impersonal, specialised, hierarchical body with specific, highly elaborated tasks probably never existed or ever will exist, his model of an ideal bureaucracy remains the standard by which all bureaucracies can be judged. While doing so, of course, care must be taken not to force such ideal standards on to the bureaucracy of Tudor and Stuart England and thus warp our understanding of it in its own terms. Yet only by holding up an ideal will comparisons and measurements of effectiveness make sense. The standard rule to be followed throughout this work will be whether or not the bureaucracy was effective in accomplishing its set tasks and what specific 'dysfunctional' areas inhibited its effectiveness.

---

4   Idem, *English artillery 1326–1716*, Woolwich 1963, 71–2. The Minories were named after the religious order of Sorores Minores (the little sisters) and was purchased by the crown in September 1563: Edward M. Tomlinson, *A history of the Minories*, London 1907.

A prime example of dysfunctional behaviour is office corruption which in itself is resistant to standardised definition. This will be dealt with in chapter 3.

It is necessary to begin by discussing the officers of the ordnance, their functions and personalities. For, in a very real sense, early modern bureaucracies were so far from being rationalised that offices were more extensions of the individual personalities holding office than strictly delineated functional areas of responsibility. Corporate identity – viewing the office and not the man – was so rare as to be remarkable whenever it did occur.

Officers and artificers

The head of the ordnance office was the master, sometimes called the master-general, of the ordnance. (For a complete list of all ordnance officers during this period see appendix 1.) He was generally a major court figure and was seldom involved in the daily functioning of the office. In common with most Elizabethan office-holders, he was not well paid. His salary was only £151 11s. 8d. per year, paid out of the household funds.[5] (See table 1 for other salaries.) The master of the ordnance in 1585 was Ambrose Dudley, earl of Warwick, who had been granted that office in 1560. In 1585, the office was regranted to him, in survivorship with Sir Philip Sidney.[6] It is doubtful whether Sidney took a very active role in the management of the ordnance office since he was also appointed governor of Flushing and in 1586 was mortally wounded near Zutphen, leaving the office to Warwick's sole charge again.[7]

After the death of the earl of Warwick in 1590, the office was left vacant until the appointment of the earl of Essex in 1597.[8] While the majority of Essex's activities in the next few years revolved around court politics and his Irish adventures, he was not an inattentive master until he went to Ireland in 1599. The warrant books of the office for his years in the post show that each warrant for supplies to be issued from the office in those busy years passed through the earl's hands. He generally included his own warrant certifying that it was proper to act upon it.[9] Essex was relieved of his office as master of the ordnance (as well as the positions of privy councillor and earl marshal) in

---

[5] PRO, SP 12/221/12–13, book of crown offices [n.d.].
[6] *CSPD Eliz. I, 1581–90*, 254 (21 July 1585).
[7] Warwick's tenure was not without its share of problems and accusations of malfeasance in office. His estate was charged with owing £2,005 to the ordnance office around 1602. This sum was forgiven his widow, the countess of Warwick, in that year and was included 'in her general pardon': *CSPD Eliz I, 1601–3*, 278–9, petition of the countess of Warwick [1602?].
[8] Hogg, *English artillery*, 48.
[9] PRO, WO 55/451, warrants relating to stores, 1598–1601. For some of Essex's accounts see ibid. AO 1/1833/11.

OFFICERS AND ARTIFICERS

Table 1
Salaries of ordnance officers and artificers

Master general	*£151 11s. 8d.
Lieutenant general	72
Lieutenant's clerk	20
**Deputy lieutenant	50
Clerk of the ordnance	71
Surveyor of the ordnance	56
Keeper of the stores	48
Clerk of the deliveries	18 5s.
Master gunner of England	70
Proofmaster	24
Clerks	20
Keeper of the small guns	50
Furbishers	12
Keeper of the rich weapons	20
Messenger	20
Plumber	12
Bowyer	12
Master smith	12
Carpenter	12
Wheeler	12
Fletcher	12
Cooper	12
Labourers	10

* all salaries are per year
** only in existence from approximately 1600–2

June 1600 after his return from Ireland against the queen's express commands.[10]

The mastership of the ordnance was again vacant until 1603 except for the unusual and temporary appointment of Sir Walter Raleigh as master 'for her highnes presente Important services' in February 1601. He was apparently appointed so that he could organise and receipt for the ordnance supplies rushed to the court at Whitehall during the Essex 'demonstration' that month.[11] However, this appointment can be considered the equivalent of being a 'master of the ordnance for the field', which was a common office

---

[10] HMC, *Salisbury*, x. 178, Sir Gelly Merricke to the earl of Southampton, 11 June 1600. Both men later took part in Essex's revolt, armed demonstration or coup in February 1601.
[11] PRO, WO 55/1629, 295, 14 Feb. 1601. The supplies included four field artillery pieces, 2,400lbs. of gunpowder, 100 muskets, 100 calivers and 200 pikes. The ordnance was ordered by the earl of Nottingham, lord admiral, on a warrant dated 14 Feb. 1601. See also WO 55/451, for a copy of the warrant.

created especially for each military expedition. Raleigh was not properly registered as having been granted the office, nor did he continue as master once the emergency was over.

The next master of the ordnance was Charles Blount, Lord Mountjoy, whose fame rests more on his suppression of Tyrone's rebellion in Ireland than on his short tenure in the ordnance office. He returned from Ireland in 1603 and was created earl of Devonshire and master of the ordnance on 13 August of that year. He did not enjoy his reward for long for he died in 1606. Apparently his tenure was not profitable. His declared accounts, taken after his death, list an inventory of 'unserviceable and decayed iron (caste & forged) small gonnes, etc.' which Devonshire 'assumed' control of shortly after he took over the office. He was apparently granted the right (and profit) of selling this ordnance, worth some £1473 3s. 2d., by the privy council. However, after his death the council changed their minds and required his widow to return any unsold pieces and all the money collected, £1,279, to the ordnance office and then to the exchequer.[12] Despite this change of heart, the master's office was often seen more as a reward for faithful service than as an administrative responsibility; it was an office for courtiers, not civil servants.

This practice changed somewhat in 1608 with the appointment of Baron Carew of Clopton (Sir George Carew until 1605) on 27 June 1608. He held the office until his death in 1629.[13] Carew was an unusual appointment in that he had extensive experience in ordnance administration and management at several levels within the military establishment before becoming master. He had served as the master of the ordnance in Ireland from 1588 to 1592 before being brought back to London as lieutenant of the ordnance in 1592. He served in that important office, and as master of the ordnance in the field during the Cadiz expedition in 1596, until his appointment as master in 1608. Since there were many periods between 1592 and 1608 when there was no master of the ordnance, Carew's expertise and powerful court connections (it was Burghley who brought him back from Ireland and he remained a close friend and confidant of Sir Robert Cecil for many years) were invaluable.[14] In addition, his service as lord president of Munster during

---

[12] PRO, E 351/2613. Inventory was taken Jan.–Feb. 1604 on a warrant dated 29 Dec. 1603. The disposal of unserviceable property was apparently a common practice of at least one past master. The earl of Warwick had disposed of large quantities of supplies between 1568 and 1582. According to an auditor, Warwick apparently 'bestowed all theise parcells amongst his good friends, wellwillers and servants, being a progative of his office and used by his predecessors and by divers others that have Office of the charge as well abrode as in court': ibid. E 101/532/3.

[13] *CSPD James I, 1603–10*, 442, grant for life, 27 June 1608. He was created earl of Totnes in 1626 and is buried in Trinity Church, Stratford-on-Avon in the Clopton chapel. The excellent relief work on the tomb shows cannons, powder, shot, flags and cannonballs as a tribute to his long identification with the ordnance office.

[14] For Carew's accounts in Ireland see PRO, E 351/2609. For the Cadiz expedition see E 351/2611, 2612.

Tyrone's rebellion added greatly to his reputation. On at least one occasion in a letter from Ireland, the attorney general, Sir John Davis, referred to him as 'the most understanding gentleman of artillery in this kingdom'.[15]

Carew's tenure as master of the ordnance, consisting as it did mostly of service during time of peace, was unremarkable in most respects. However even his level of experience and reputation for fair dealing did not guarantee ordnance office efficiency or probity.[16] There were numerous corruption scandals during his tenure. Nor was Carew's own conduct in office, particularly as a client of Cecil, free from disparagement by his rivals. Lord Treasurer Buckhurst, earl of Dorset, was reported to have said of Carew, 'that Sir George Carye was an errant knave and had deceaved yo[ur] Ma[te] of a hundred thowsand poundes, and no man coulde tell wch waie it was gone'.[17] However, this isolated and unsubstantiated charge seems to have had no effect on Carew's career or standing at court.

The post of master of the ordnance had its share of duties and cannot be considered solely as a sinecure, but the real business of the office was supervised on a day-to-day basis by the lieutenant of the ordnance. This officer was expected to be in virtually daily attendance, for which he was paid £72 per year out of the ordinary allowance for the office.[18] One of his key duties was accounting for all the money which was paid into the office by the exchequer and which was then paid out to its various suppliers.[19] The lieutenant was allowed a clerk at £20 per year and, through him, was expected to pay all the bills.[20] The lieutenant was to maintain the official ledger books and supervise the surveys and inventories of the equipment. His duties also included paying the salaries and travel fees of junior officers and permanent artificers, and

---

[15] HMC, *Salisbury*, xii. 46, Davis to Cecil, 6 Feb. 1602.
[16] See ch. 3 for the Dallison scandal.
[17] BL, MS Royal 18A LIX, fo. 4, charges against Carew's conduct in Ireland, 24 July 1610. This was reported third hand after Dorset's death. Even if Carew were flagrantly dishonest, sums of money which could permit peculation on such a scale did not flow through his hands at any time, or in total, during his years of public service, whether in Ireland or elsewhere. It is possible that this letter refers to Sir George Carey (Carew was often spelled as Carey) who, as treasurer-at-war in Ireland, was often accused of fiscal impropriety.
[18] PRO, SP 12/255/64. According to this document, this allowance was set at £72 in 1563. Like so many other government salaries of the period, it remained at the same level despite the increase in duties.
[19] The accounts for the lieutenant are virtually complete from at least 1578 until the Civil War (Sir Robert Constable's accounts from 1588 to 1591 are missing) and are excellent sources for the *official* amount of money spent on ordnance supplies and administration. The fact that they were drawn up 10 to 20 years after the fact means they should not be believed uncritically: PRO, E 351/2623–2655; AO 1/1836–1841 (duplicates).
[20] See instructions to the ordnance office, signed by Burghley and Mildmay, 1572: BL, MS Harl. 309, fo. 53. The lieutenant was to pay the craftsman in the presence of the surveyor of the office and the clerk of the ordnance. Suppliers were lucky to be paid quarterly; the unlucky ones waited years.

generally supervising the personnel.[21] He can truly be said to have run the ordnance office.

The duties of the lieutenant of the ordnance were by no means easy. Supervision of a busy office with several strong-willed and often quarrelsome officers was not always a pleasure. One letter from Sir George Carew to Sir Robert Cecil in June 1594, two years after he took the post, clarifies the often unsettled nature of the office:

> By the favour of your father, with your help unto her Majesty, I was removed from my place in Ireland to the office which now I hold. To discourse unto you all my griefs were exceeding tedious, for I do not pass a day without new occasions and with infinite repentance for leaving my office there, which was of good profit, and where I lived quietly in sufficient content, to wear my days in this troublesome place where I have at no time found either profit or ease; and therof you [can] not marvel, the allowances being so small as they are and, which is worse, my fellows in office so corrupt and of such malicious spirits as but in hell I think their matches can hardly be found.[22]

Despite his complaints, Carew stayed in the job until moving up to the master's post in 1608. Others who held the job between 1590 and 1625 included Sir Robert Constable (1588–91), Sir Roger Dallison (1608–15) and Sir Richard Morrison (1616–25).[23]

There were times, of course, when the lieutenant had to be absent from his post and the crucial nature of his office was such that no single subordinate officer was considered capable or senior enough to perform his duties. However, it was necessary that one individual should be held fiscally accountable for all the exchequer payments to the office. This situation arose in 1600 when Carew was appointed lord president of Munster. He decided to appoint a deputy from outside the normal ordnance staff to fill his position on a temporary basis. His choice happened to fall upon his uncle, George Harvey, who was appointed deputy in February 1600 and was directed 'provisonally to supply that roome . . . as farr forthe as yf Sir George Carewe himselfe were personally here'.[24] Harvey was paid £50 per year, directly out of

---

[21] In addition, on at least one occasion, the lieutenant was expected to be able to fill in for the lieutenant of the Tower during his absence: CSPD James I, 1603–10, 446 (6 July 1608).

[22] HMC, Salisbury, iv. 555, Carew to Cecil, 14 Sept. 1595. His plea for some other employment fell on deaf ears. Another letter of complaint to Cecil in Sept. 1595 begins with comments about 'this unquiet office, wherein is small profit and infinite vexations' and ends with a plea 'that he may be removed he cares not whither': ibid. v. 377.

[23] For Dallison's grant of office see PRO, SP 14/60/75, and CSPD James I, 1603–10, 444, 1 July 1608. The grant included responsibility for the ordnance office at Berwick-upon-Tweed (at a salary of 100 marks a year) which up until this point had been a separate office, the master of the ordnance for the north, held by Sir Richard Musgrave. For Morrison see CSPD James I, 1611–18, 342 (1 Jan. 1616). See appendix 1 for a complete list of ordnance personnel.

[24] APC 1599–1600, 33.

the exchequer rather than out of the ordinary quarter's allowance of the office.[25] While he was to be held accountable for the sums of money sent to the office by the exchequer, many of the lieutenant's usual duties and responsibilities were to be shared with one of the clerks, Richard Paulfreyman (or Palfreyman), who also held the office of keeper of the small guns.[26]

The appointment of a deputy lieutenant of the ordnance was one instance of the creation of a temporary post. There was another temporary office which defied classification even at the time. This was the office of yeoman of the ordnance. In the early ordnance office, there was doubtless an official post of yeoman but by the 1590s the job was no longer on the payroll. The yeoman's duties, to oversee the transport of munitions from the Tower to the consumer were by 1590 almost entirely performed by conductors appointed specifically for that task by the lieutenant. However, during his time as deputy, Harvey discovered that an unused privilege is not necessarily a lapsed one. He apparently arranged for the conducting of munitions himself on the sensible ground that 'the former yeoman refused to execute that service, saying that he had been a leader of men and did scorn to be a leader of carts'.[27] However, the yeoman at the time (whose name was not mentioned) claimed the privilege of arranging for this service and doubtless expected to receive whatever the non-salaried fees would be for arranging the movement of supplies and the allocating of freight contracts. To buttress his claim, he turned to witnesses within the office such as Stephen Bull, master gunner of England, the surveyor and clerk of the ordnance and John Bagnoll, clerk, who had been in his office for thirty-six years. Faced with all this, Harvey capitulated. He explained to the council that he had not been aware of a problem 'thinking it was the lieutenant's place, but now satisfied, only desires your warrant, whereby the yeoman may proceed in the service'.[28]

Below the major posts of master and lieutenant (or deputy lieutenant) of the ordnance, existed a second tier. These offices were those of clerk of the ordnance, surveyor of the ordnance, keeper of the stores, clerk of the deliveries and master gunner of England.[29] The officers filling these posts were

---

[25] PRO, E 403/1693, fo. 4, 21 Feb. 1601. See also the appropriate quarter books of the office: WO 54/3 1600–2.
[26] PRO, E 403/2560, fo. 209, 10 Feb. 1600. The wording of this exchequer document seems to indicate that Paulfreyman was to be the *de facto* deputy and substitute for Carew in the running of the office while Harvey was merely to be the man appointed to receive the £6,000 per year on the dormant privy seal (11 Dec. 1587) for the ordinary expenses of the ordnance. The orders of the privy council, Harvey's position as signer of the warrants for the release of any stores, and his actions in the office prove otherwise. However, Paulfreyman is referred to occasionally as the 'sub-treasurer' of the office.
[27] HMC, *Salisbury*, x. 457.
[28] Ibid. The office of yeoman of the ordnance continued to exist but only in a peripheral capacity and no mention is made of it in the official quarter books despite occasional references to the position in the delivery books: PRO, WO 49/31, fo. 11; SP 12/237/114.
[29] Ibid. WO 54/1–10.

considered to be the 'principal' officers of the ordnance to whom, according to a report in 1618, the government of the office was 'anciently committed'.[30] There was probably a rough hierarchy of positions, but it is very difficult to establish any definite 'pecking order' at this level. This was a major failing of the bureaucracy of the ordnance office throughout this period, as it was of most of the bureaucratic organisations of early modern England. Each office-holder had his own notions of personal prestige and power which were as much concerned with his own perceived personal status as with any consideration of the office as separate from the man. Thus it was very rare to find any officer who agreed to subordinate himself to the larger organisation or to any rationalised system of precedence. Each officer had his own tenacious hold on his post, which was generally held for life unless gross malfeasance could be proved, and his own conception of the duties of the office which few lieutenants and no colleagues in the office could successfully dispute. It would be hard to overstress the pervasiveness and pernicious effect of the view of office as personal property. Modern attempts to create a rationalised bureaucracy, imperfect in execution though they are, continue to have difficulty in coping with individuals whose strong personalities affect the nature of their offices. Any attempt at creating a functioning bureaucracy was impossible as long as an office was viewed as a personal possession rather than as an administrative responsibility. In a damning summary of the ordnance office, one perceptive student of the ordnance has written:

> The ordnance was a weak spot in Elizabethan administration. Each of the principal officers was appointed under a separate patent to carry out the traditional duties of his office, and each, to prevent 'poaching' on his preserves, spent a considerable amount of time and ingenuity in defending what he considered to be his rights and privileges against his colleagues. There was little or no loyalty for the organisation as a whole and of corporate spirit there was none.[31]

If one had to superimpose some degree of order upon this administrative chaos, one would have to cast the clerk of the ordnance in the role of *primus inter pares*. Initially he had been chiefly responsible for making out indentures for issuing supplies and taking the lists of the remains of supplies coming back into the office. However, over time these responsibilities devolved upon the clerk of the deliveries and the surveyor of the ordnance. The clerk of the ordnance was thus left with the responsibility for the permanent books of the office which were created every quarter based on the journals and indentures of each of the subordinate offices responsible for a specific supply action. In

---

[30] Ibid. SP 12/237/110–17, a partial copy of answers to Cranfield's report on the ordnance office. This document is in a collection of miscellaneous documents relating to the Admiralty from 1590 into the reign of Charles I. This particular document is from 1618.
[31] Hogg, *Royal arsenal*, i. 45.

addition, according to one of the numerous lists of office duties of the time, he was to keep his own separate journal of all the items coming into the stores. This was to be just one of three separate journals of receipt kept within the office, the other two being those maintained by the surveyor of the ordnance and the master of the ordnance's own clerk.[32] The clerks of the ordnance were William Paynter (1554–95), Sir Stephen Riddlesden (1595–1603), John Riddlesden (1603–7) and Francis Morice (1608 to the end of the period under discussion).

The surveyor of the ordnance, probably the next ranking officer, controlled the quality of the materials brought into the stores, kept journals of all items received and maintained duplicate journals of all issues and deliveries. In addition, at least during the tenure of John Linewray (1602–6), the surveyor was also instrumental in assisting the lieutenant in 'sniffing out' internal corruption and graft.[33]

The keeper of the stores supervised the maintenance procedures of the 'great stores' (heavy ordnance, gunpowder, gun carriages etc.). He also kept a journal of the supplies on hand in the entire office. The clerk of the deliveries, on the other hand, only maintained a journal of the items issued out of his own office and kept a list of the recipients of the supplies who were to be held responsible for them. This seems to indicate that the post of clerk of the deliveries was probably a relatively junior one despite its being authorised an additional clerk at £10 per year and despite the office being held by at least one knight, Sir Robert Johnson (1602–10, from 1604 with his son Robert Johnson, Jr). The duties were relatively menial and the clerk does not seem to have been entrusted with keeping the numerous 'master' journals and ledgers as were the other officers.[34]

The last of the ordnance offices in the second tier was that of master gunner of England, a post held by Stephen Bull (1578–89), Stephen Bull, Jr (1589–1607), William Bull (1607–10), William Hammond (1610–23) and John Reynolds (1623–38).[35] The master gunner's duties were many and his

---

[32] BL, MS Harl. 168, fos 161–2, 'Orders to be Observed and kepte within the office of the Ordinaunce', July 1589. In 1584, 1589, 1596, 1597, 1598, 1601 and 1618–20 there were major attempts to reform the administrative procedures of the office. Each attempt demonstrated a determination to eliminate corruption by increasing the complexity of the system by means of overlapping ledgers, journals and books. In the words of one student of the Tudor ordnance office 'The intention seems to have been to frustrate dishonesty by administrative complexity': Ashley, 'Tudor Office', 101.

[33] HMC, *Salisbury*, xi. 551, 'Particular services effected in the office of the Ordnance by John Linewray', undated, probably 1601. For Linewray's involvement in uncovering abuses and corruption see ch. 3.

[34] In 1606 Sir Robert Johnson even complained about his office as one 'fitter for my gen[tleman]-clerke, than for me' and asked for a place 'more agreeable to my breeding': Magdalene College, Cambridge, MS Pepys 2878, fos 120–1, 16 Jan. 1606. My thanks to Dr Linda Levy Peck for allowing me to read her transcript of this letter.

[35] Hogg, *English artillery*, 276.

unique position as artillery technician gave him a level of expertise with firearms unmatched by the other officers. He was responsible for the training and certifying of all gunners in the kingdom (both land and sea), for proofing (testing) the heavy ordnance, for maintaining the artillery garden north of the Tower where the shooting took place, and for proofing the gunpowder and small handguns. In addition, he was supposed to keep a roster of all the trained gunners in England and a list of all the ordnance in all the forts, blockhouses and ships of the kingdom along with an account of their state of readiness.[36] While it is to be doubted whether each of the master gunners of England performed all of these duties in a comprehensive manner, he was expected to be, and in most cases was, the crown's chief technical expert on all aspects of artillery. The master gunner was paid £70 per year for performing these duties and often simultaneously held the post of proofmaster for an additional £24 per year.[37] His office was far from being a sinecure, and, of the officers who regularly received riding fees in addition to their salaries, the master gunner of England was second only to the well-travelled purveyors of timber in the amount of travel money received.[38]

The key officers of the ordnance were primarily responsible for receiving, issuing, maintaining and accounting for the war matériel and supplies and for the money sent from the exchequer to pay for them. However, it should come as no surprise that they required an ever increasing clerical staff to deal with the expansion of the office from the beginning of the war with Spain to the death of Elizabeth. Even with the coming of peace in 1604, the ordnance, like most bureaucracies, remained at its wartime size, thus proving the old adage that bureaucracies are easy to expand but difficult to shrink.

When Sir George Carew took over as lieutenant in 1592, there were seven clerks drawing salaries in the office, despite the fact that only five were authorised to be paid out of the ordinary.[39] Carew immediately cut the staff back to the authorised size and eliminated some additional riding fees and allowances which had been added on to the books over time by the clerk of the ordnance, William Paynter, and the keeper of the stores, Thomas Bedwell. This was but a temporary pruning, however, and by 1603, there were nine clerks on the rolls.[40] The clerical staff expanded further during the years

---

[36] Ibid. 121–2.

[37] PRO, WO 54/1–10. His salary of £94 per year was thus more than that of the lieutenant of the ordnance. He also was given the use of a house in the artillery gardens, near where he exercised the 'scholars' in gunnery.

[38] In 1599 Francis Carter and Robert Gore, purveyors, received £24 for the year's riding charges and travel fees. Stephen Bull received £14 10s. while the wheelers and carpenters received only £8 10s. The recurrence of exactly these figures in 1600, 1601 and 1602 (at least) seems to indicate they were regular supplements to the officer's income rather than exact measures of travelling in performance of official duties: PRO, WO 49/24, 25, 26, 28.

[39] Ibid. SP 12/255/64, first ordnance office allowances, [1595?].

[40] Ibid. WO 54/4.

of peace even though there was no need for more clerks and by 1624 there were ten clerks on the rolls. It is possible that the number of official clerks increased to match the number of temporary and therefore unofficial clerks who had probably been brought in during time of war to deal with the press of business. However, the fact remains that the official public payroll for clerks increased even when there was no particular need for their services. Salaries for the clerkships varied, sometimes depending upon the individual, with the lieutenant's clerk and the clerk of the deliveries being paid £18 5s. and the other clerks £20 per year.[41]

The expansion in the number of clerks in the office was not the only growth to have occurred in the Elizabethan ordnance office even before the wartime build-up of the 1580s. The changing nature of warfare prompted the creation of a new office sometime after the middle of the sixteenth century. The English military establishment during the reign of Elizabeth faced the need to purchase and maintain ever increasing quantities of small firearms including the harquebus, the caliver and the musket, all expensive items.[42] Inevitably, as more were required, so the administrative requirements of the office increased. To meet this need, the office of keeper of the small guns (also called keeper of the small stores) was created by at least 1576 with a salary of £50 per year.[43] The post was held by William Fowkes (or Fookes) from 1595 to 1597, Henry Halder from 1597 to 1599, Richard Paulfreyman (or Palfreyman) from 1599 to 1610, and then by his son, James Paulfreyman, from 1612 to 1625.[44] Richard Paulfreyman held the office at the same time as drawing his clerk's salary of £20 per year. Even after his promotion to clerk to the master of the ordnance in 1608, he kept both offices until his death in 1609.[45] The work of the office of small guns seems to have been accomplished despite this pluralism. This was probably because the real work of the office was done by the two furbishers employed at £12 per year whose duties included scouring, oiling and carrying out minor repairs on the handguns.

---

[41] *CSPD James I, 1611–18*, 205 (4 Nov. 1613); PRO, WO 54/8. The discrepancy in pay scales cannot easily be explained unless the lieutenant's clerk (William Cudnor from at least 1594–1603) also received some money from the lieutenant.

[42] For example, the purchase of over £139,000 of small arms and armour in the 1560s by Sir Thomas Gresham presented the ordnance office with a dramatically increased store of firearms. See Gresham's declared accounts on these transactions in PRO, E 351/26. The money spent also covered transportation, insurance and 'Rewards to searchers and officers for quyet passinge', probably bribes to customs officials. My thanks to Doug Bisson who brought this document to my attention.

[43] Ibid. E 351/2623. This declared account of 1578–81 lists £31 14s. owed to Nathaniel Partridge for weapons repair carried out by him as office-holder. In 1598, when the office was granted to Henry Halder, it was listed at a salary of 10d. per day, but the quarter books still list his salary at £12 10s. per quarter or £50 per year: *CSPD Eliz. I, 1598–1601*, 65, docquet, 24 Jun. 1598; PRO, WO 54/1, 2.

[44] Ibid. WO 54/1–10.

[45] Richard Paulfreyman is one of the 'social success stories' of the office. He began as a clerk and by 1598 is referred to as 'gentleman': ibid. WO 49/21.

Major repairs were contracted out to the various gunmakers dwelling near the Tower.

The office of keeper of the rich weapons was another office which was often held in conjunction with a different post in the ordnance. Paying £20 per year, it was held by William Ridge from at least 1595 until 1614 or 1615, simultaneously with the post of furbisher, then by Nedtracy Smart until 1621 when Thomas Powell took over.[46] The primary duties of the keeper of the rich weapons seem to have been the storage and maintenance of the 'guilt' (gilded) javelins, ceremonial halberds and other weapons of such craftsmanship or metalwork that they were kept separate from the normal issue weapons.

In addition to these minor posts, there was also the position of messenger of the office with a salary of £20 per year. The messenger seems to have worked hard for his money as he was constantly being employed in carrying warrants, indentures, open letters of purveyance and other messages around London and between the Tower and the other ordnance storehouses in Chatham, Rochester, Portsmouth, Deptford and Woolwich. He was also occasionally called upon to perform some extraordinary duties, such as in February 1601 when the messenger, one Moses Winchell, was employed by Deputy Lieutenant Harvey to carry warnings of the activities of the earl of Essex to the 'gonners and Laborers at the Tower and the Court and for providinge everie night a watch of gonners & laborers ever since the apprehension of Th'erle of Essex'.[47] In addition to his salary he was paid a small *per diem* allowance on the road and was regularly reimbursed for his boat and horse hire.

While the ordnance office relied heavily upon the existence of civilian contractors and merchants for many of the supplies it required (see chapter 4), it also kept a few key artificers on a permanent salary, a form of retainer, for the daily performance of a wide variety of tasks and supply functions.[48] There was a proofmaster, although this was often a job held by the master gunner of England as a perquisite at a salary of £24 per year, and the actual work was therefore mostly done by his assistant.

There were also other craftsmen on retainer: a plumber to provide lead and cast shot; a blacksmith for nails and ironwork; a carpenter for chests, gunstocks, carts and carriages; a wheeler to make wheels; a fletcher for arrows; a cooper to make barrels and casks; and a bowyer to craft bows and bowstrings. All these craftsmen were paid £12 per year out of the ordinary allowance of the ordnance office, and were also paid for their labour on any items they built at the direction of the office. The raw materials for many items such as timber or iron ore were often provided from the office stores.

---

[46] Ibid. WO 54/110. Neither Smart nor Powell, however, were granted the other post of furbisher while they held their office.
[47] Ibid. WO 49/26, 27, end of quarter's riding charges, 24 Mar. 1601.
[48] See appendix 2 for a complete list of artificers from 1585 to 1625.

The bowyer and fletcher, being the older crafts, had small workshops in the Tower itself, but the majority of the artificers worked in the Minories.[49]

Labourers, some twenty in number, complete the list of ordnance office personnel. They were paid £10 per year for stacking the supplies in the storehouses, loading them onto carts or placing them onto lighters which would then take them out to larger, ocean-going ships. They were also called upon to take supplies to the Rochester or Chatham storehouses. Relatively faceless individuals, only a few men stand out of the crowd, such as John Tree the elder. He was probably foreman over the other labourers and he earned a little extra every year by 'taking up', or arranging, for hoys to come to the wharf to pick up supplies and by providing hay for wadding when the great ordnance in the Tower fired salutes. One should not ignore Henry Gotobed either, who, in addition to his unusual name, was possessed of unusual ambition which took him from the lowly post of labourer in 1606 to that of furbisher by 1616.[50] Such mobility was not common even if the latter post was probably classed at the same general level as that of labourer. Labourers generally remained labourers, while artificers were similarly restricted to their crafts. Only an examination of the personnel in the clerk's offices and in the junior supervisory positions can reveal the possibility of administrative mobility, and even then such moves were more the exception than the rule.

To summarise, the office of the ordnance maintained a substantial number of officers, clerks and artificers whose duties remained remarkably constant during times of war or peace. In effect, the ordnance office was almost the only centralised military establishment in England, other than the Admiralty, which remained in existence even in peacetime. It was a relatively cheap establishment, costing only £6,000 per year, paid out of the ordinary of the exchequer. This sum, if carefully managed, could have ensured the regular purchase of small amounts of war matériel in addition to covering office payroll expenses. Officers were available to carry out regular basic supply procedures in order to maintain at least a rudimentary ability to supply England's military forces in the event of conflict. They should at least have been able to provide an 'institutional memory' of the supply procedures necessary to outfit a land or sea force. The ordnance office was virtually the only central storehouse for the realm and the responsibilities of the officers in peacetime included the supervision and the regular supply of numerous storehouses, castles and forts in England and Ireland. This alone should have kept them prepared to perform their basic functions: supplying the English armies with weapons and gunpowder during war. As we shall see, it did not.

---

[49] In the case of the master smith of the ordnance, however, his forge was in the Mint which led to some disputes with the officers there in 1606 as to whether that shop belonged to the ordnance office or to their own smith. It was located near the powder storehouse in the White Tower: HMC, *Salisbury*, xxiv. 86–7; xviii. 249, 267.
[50] PRO, WO 54/5,7.

Office management

The administration of the ordnance office generally centred around the lieutenant (or his deputy), the surveyor, the clerk of the ordnance and the keeper of the stores.[51] These officers were primarily responsible for the level of efficiency of the ordnance in the procurement, storage, issuance and accountability of the war supplies managed by the office.

The first step in any supply system was for the military forces to request supplies. Then, before filling the order, the ordnance office needed to determine the current stock of each of the items requested. If enough was not to hand, the officers would receive warrants listing how much had to be procured. Another factor was that the officers would then have to determine how much additional supply had to be ordered to replenish the stores to meet future needs. The obvious answer to these requirements would have been for the ordnance office to develop a regularised inventory procedure in order to keep track of how much was in the store, how much had been issued and how much was needed. Indeed, this type of inventory did occur occasionally. The instructions of the earl of Warwick in 1589 to the lesser ordnance officers and the directions given to the earl of Essex in 1597 stressed the need for a general survey in order to discover the exact state of the office before any further supply was made.[52] This strongly indicates that no regular inventory or survey procedure had yet been implemented. The numerous special commissions, surveys and investigations into abuses throughout this period seem to indicate that this valuable tool for efficient management was not adopted until the 1620s.

The establishment of some form of regular survey was occasionally discussed. Several times, especially during the war years, Lord Burghley, Sir Robert Cecil or other members of the privy council would comment on the need to establish a 'staple' or basic equipment and matériel level in the Minories and Tower which would be closely monitored and regularly surveyed. At least as early as 1586, Burghley was jotting down notes to himself about the establishment of provincial staples, especially in the port towns of Portsmouth, Southampton and Yarmouth but also in numerous county towns. Sir John Peyton, lieutenant of the Tower, recommended in 1596 that there be established 'a royal store and a provincial one, the former to be at the Queen's charge and proportionable to her dignity and state and the other

---

[51] Ibid. SP 12/237/114, a partial copy of the answers of the ordnance officers to Cranfield's report on the ordnance [1618]. This is one document among several dealing with the Admiralty from 1590 through the reign of Charles I. According to the report, the office was 'aunciently centered' on these key personnel.

[52] Ibid. SP 12/228/20, orders and directions for the better governance of the office of the ordnance by the earl of Warwick, 18 Nov. 1589. See also SP 12/262/105, instructions from the queen to the earl of Essex on his appointment to the office of the ordnance, 7 Apr. 1597.

at the charge of the subject, in regard of his own defence'.[53] Under this arrangement, every time a major issue of equipment was dispatched out of any of the storehouses, the ordnance officers would automatically arrange with contractors and merchants for resupply in an effort to keep the stores fully charged, 'wch nowe wanteth by reason that ther is to muche of some thinges & to lyttle of some more needefull provisions'.[54] But no systematic programme to create staples was undertaken, although there was a continuing interest in decentralising the ordnance stores to a certain degree by improving the storehouses at Portsmouth, Deptford, Chatham and Rochester. Only at the Tower and, to a lesser extent, in the ordnance office in Ireland, was there any major attempt to provide a staple, and even in London one does not find the administrative policies enacted for such an initiative to succeed.[55]

In order to establish a regular staple the ordnance office needed two things: a regular (and large) supply of money and a commitment to rationalised supply procedures. Both of these prerequisites were, on the whole, lacking. In the former instance, the ordnance was always kept on a very short regular allowance of £6,000 per year and even this small payment dried up between 1617 and 1620. As for regular surveys, the office did not begin to take regular annual inventories until 1620 and then only after a serious corruption scandal and the investigation of the office by yet another special commission.[56]

There were exceptions to the lack of an inventory procedure, in the case of two items: gunpowder and brass ordnance. In the latter case, the inventory requirement was probably due to the high financial value of each piece of ordnance (upwards of £80 each) and the crown's interest in knowing how many of these 'strategic' weapons were on hand. Regular inventories of gunpowder, on the other hand, were recognised as critical because of its essential role in the defence of the kingdom and the obviously disastrous consequence should it ever run too low. For example, after the near disaster of the Armada of 1588, the crown began requiring virtually monthly inventories of gun-powder during 1588 and 1589, and almost annual ones during

---

[53] *CSPD Eliz. I, 1595–7*, 179–80, Sir John Peyton's statement on the preparations of the Spaniards, Feb. [?] 1596. The royal store at the Tower was certainly in existence at this time, and Peyton perhaps meant that a larger and more regular staple should be established.
[54] PRO, SP 12/269/44, instructions for the better service of the ordnance, undated, probably May 1596. Other recommendations included making the officers swear oaths to perform their duties faithfully, not to contract with artificers without the knowledge of the lieutenant and to ensure the regular auditing of the surveyor's books by the exchequer.
[55] There are occasional hints in the records that someone at the ordnance was thinking of maintaining a staple. In April 1589 the ordnance declared that the stores needed an additional 188 lasts of gunpowder to bring them up to the desired 'staple' of 300 lasts. There is very little evidence that this was a continuing requirement.
[56] For some key inventories before 1620 see PRO, SP 12/187/73 (for 1567–82); SP 12/177/25 (for 1585); E 101/64/19 (for 1588); WO 55/1659 (for 1589–91); BL, MS Royal 17A XXXI (for 1603); PRO, WO 55/1676 (for 1609); and WO 55/1680 (for 1617–24).

the later war years.⁵⁷ Even then it is possible that this was in response to a crisis situation and not a result of any conscious urge to rationalise an administrative system. However, the frequent surveys of powder supplies and the regularity with which Burghley's scribbled notes include many cryptic comments on gunpowder provision, seem to indicate that administrators at the highest levels recognised the need for such exact knowledge at least of these military resources of the kingdom.

Given that gunpowder and brass ordnance were exceptions to the lack of a rational inventory policy, it seems as if the ordnance office as a whole did not see the need for yearly, general inventories of all supplies. In part this was because they were expensive and time-consuming operations, but it was also because embarrassing shortages might be discovered. If the office bookkeeping procedures had been as accurate as they should have been, the clerks could have kept a running total of supplies brought into or issued out of the office. This did not occur, however, as neither the indenture nor delivery books were accurate enough to serve this purpose. At least in this instance, the administrative methods of the ordnance office were seriously flawed; without exact knowledge of the contents of the stores and a recommended supply level, or staple, effective management of the ordnance would remain an elusive goal. Only after the investigation into the office by a special commission headed by Lionel Cranfield in 1618 does one find such yearly surveys actually occurring.⁵⁸ The receipt books and internal records of the office from 1620 to 1625 include major inventories and running totals of supplies received and issued.⁵⁹

Once it had been determined, or assumed, that more of a particular item was needed for the stores, the privy council or the lord admiral would initiate a warrant for the ordnance officers to obtain the necessary supply. Without this warrant, generally confirmed by the master of the ordnance if there was one, no supplies were to be issued.⁶⁰ The warrant would further specify whether the items were to be paid for out of the ordinary allowance of the office or out of some extraordinary fund. If the order was for supplies for a

---

⁵⁷ By 1640 powder inventories were being taken on a monthly basis: *CSPD Charles I, 1640*, 4, 105, 258, 439.

⁵⁸ Michael B. Young, 'Illusions of grandeur and reform at the Jacobean court: Cranfield and the ordnance', *Historical Journal* xxii (1979), 53–73. This is a very persuasive article which covers a great deal of important ground while providing considerable evidence that much of the success of the special commission was not due to Cranfield but to Sir John Coke's leadership of the earlier naval commission.

⁵⁹ PRO, WO 55/1678, 1680; WO 49/50, 52, 53.

⁶⁰ All the instructions issued to the ordnance officers over the years were very insistent that no supply was to be initiated by the ordnance officers themselves without a specific warrant from at least six of the privy councillors or the lord admiral for naval items: ibid SP 12/269/44, instructions for the better service of the ordnance, [1598?]. See also SP 12/262/105, instructions from the queen to the earl of Essex on his appointment to the office of the ordnance, 2 Apr. 1597.

foreign expedition or the supply of a fleet, the goods were generally paid for on a privy seal. The ordinary allowance could not handle such large-scale purchases. Gunpowder was an exception to this practice since the contracts with the powdermakers were for regular, monthly supplies of fixed amounts at fixed rates. No special warrants were required. The powder was still paid for by money which went through the lieutenant's hands, but the powdermakers presented their indentures directly to the treasury before money under a special privy seal was paid to the lieutenant of the ordnance.[61]

Once the ordnance officers received the warrant for the supply of an item, they would then authorise an artificer within the office or an outside contractor to provide it. In the case of gunpowder and such items as muskets or match, this would be an outside contractor or merchant. But if the item were gun carriages or iron nails or powder casks, salaried artificers in the Minories could make it. The merchant or craftsman would procure or build the item in question at an agreed price and would then bring it into the office for testing. The surveyor of the ordnance was supposed to check the quality of all goods brought into the office. This was accomplished by ensuring that all weapons and ordnance were thoroughly proofed by the master gunner of England and his assistant proofmasters and that all other goods met office standards.[62] If the items were approved, the surveyor provided the supplier with an indenture. This was a double copy of the list of supplies provided which was cut in half by a wavy line called an indent. The office would keep one half of the indenture for its records, while the supplier would keep the other half as proof that he was owed a certain amount of money for the items provided. The craftsman was supposed to present this copy of the indenture at the end of the quarter in order to get paid.

The approved supplies were then moved into the various storehouses in the Tower or Minories where they would be entered on to the books of the keeper of the stores and the surveyor of the ordnance. Once in the storehouses, office personnel or contractors were responsible for keeping the iron items clean, dry and oiled, and were to keep strict account of them at all times. Routine maintenance would be performed on all firearms by the furbishers in the office of the small guns and by the craftsmen themselves for

---

[61] The switch to regular and direct payments out of the exchequer did not occurr until 1599 and was a source of some complaint by the ordnance officers: ibid. SP 12/274/89, remembrances exhibited by the lieutenant of the ordnance to secretary Cecil concerning the 'late Patent' of the gunpowder makers, 31 Aug. 1599. The last paragraph of this document is interesting in that it includes an attack on Sir John Davies, surveyor of the ordnance, who was supposedly interfering with the duties of John Linewray, clerk of the deliveries, in the making of 'true' certificates of receipt. Thus the complaint about how the powder was to be paid for was probably an element in their intra-office power struggle.
[62] The standards for weapons and gunpowder were clearly established, but for the other items the office was not so particular. Proofing generally included testing armour for strength, sometimes firing pistols into it to see if it were 'pistol-proof', and test firing all firearms with two shots each.

pikes, bows and arrows, gun carriages, halberds or other items. The heavy ordnance (especially the iron ordnance) was left on the wharf. From there it could most easily be lifted onto lighters by cranes on the wharf before being sent down the Thames to naval or merchant ships. The small amount of rust that accumulated in the interval does not seem to have impaired the condition or serviceability of the heavy ordnance. As for other, less sturdy, items such as muskets, pikes or gunpowder, no instructions are extant which describe how they were to be maintained. Presumably each craftsman or officer knew how to scour and varnish the metal parts and replace the wooden parts of each item when necessary.[63] Only in the case of gunpowder, a delicate commodity, does there seem to have been an agreed procedure for maintenance. Most of the gunpowder contracts stipulated that the contractors would rework any powder which became damp within a five-year period as long as the powder had not been issued.

The issue of supplies followed many of the same procedures as receipt of items into the store. Upon receipt of the necessary warrant from the privy council or lord admiral, through the master of the ordnance (if the office was not vacant), the lieutenant would direct the keeper of the stores and the surveyor to assist the clerk of the deliveries in issuing the supplies. The surveyor, whose responsibility for quality authorised him to be present at any time during the process, was to certify that the warrant was correct and adequate and then to verify that the person receipting for the item was authorised to do so. In the case of supplies for ships, only the master gunner of that ship was to be held responsible for the use and safe return of the supplies, and it was his signature on the indent that was required. In the case of supplies for land forces, the master of the ordnance in the field (each expedition or field army had such an officer) was held to be ultimately responsible for all supplies, although the items were often indented with a conductor who was to carry the matériel into the field. Copies of all such indentures were preserved by the clerk of the deliveries as proof of a supply action, by the keeper of the stores as proof of relief of responsibility for the items and by the surveyor of the ordnance for accounting purposes.[64]

Ordnance finances

The problems involved in discovering the actual amount of money spent on ordnance during war or peace are so great that often little more than an

---

[63] Given reports in 1625–7 of pikes which broke in two in the soldiers' hands and muskets without touch-holes, one must doubt whether the artificers or officers really followed their own guidelines. For the shortcomings of the Cadiz and Rhé expeditions see Stephen J. Stearns, 'The Caroline military system, 1625–1627: the expeditions to Cadiz and Re', unpubl. PhD diss. Berkeley 1967.

[64] PRO, SP 12/237/114, Cranfield's report on the ordnance, [1618].

educated guess may be made. The accounts of the lieutenant of the ordnance bear little relationship to the indenture books of the office which adds to the confusion.[65] Contemporaries could often not get to the bottom of the accounting methods used by the ordnance office in order to discover exactly how much was spent and for what. This was particularly true in the Jacobean period: accounting procedures then have been described as being 'designed to bemuse rather than to enlighten'.[66] However, even a rough guess at the amount of money going through the office, when combined with some of the administrative measures taken to manage the finances of the ordnance office, may give us some idea of the extent of the office's money problems.

The ordnance office faced two major financial difficulties in this period: external problems, i.e. how much money it had to spend, and internal ones, i.e. what it did with the money it was given. By definition, external problems were outside its control but still had a direct impact on office efficiency. On the other hand, inefficient use of the money it received was often the direct fault of its own officers or their management practices. Both sources of problems must be analysed if a full picture of the administrative difficulties of the ordnance office is to be provided.

The overlapping of responsibilities within the ordnance office did not provide the best climate for efficient management. This should not have been the case with finance. With very few exceptions, all the money which was to be spent on supplies went through the hands of the lieutenant of the ordnance or his deputy. The lieutenant alone was held accountable for the money sent to the office. This was true of the ordinary allowance of £6,000 per year and of the extraordinary privy seal payments. Even the payment to the powdermakers for gunpowder on a special privy seal eventually went through the hands of the lieutenant. Since his accounts were audited by the well-established auditors of the exchequer, careful accounting and exact lists of expenditure should have made it possible to keep track of all ordnance expenses, both for the maintenance of the office, for supplies and for special large purchases. However, as the Dallison incident indicates, this was far from being the case. The major discrepancies in his accounts show how far the ordnance office was from anything approaching modern accounting procedures. The lack of an effective auditing procedure was not the sole fault of the ordnance office and the problems which resulted were not too different from those affecting the other offices of state. However, the ordnance officers exacerbated the general lack of fiscal sophistication by their internal debt mechanism.

---

[65] See appendix 5 for a table of estimated ordnance office expenses in selected years.
[66] Menna Prestwich, *Cranfield: politics and profits under the early Stuarts: the career of Lionel Cranfield, earl of Middlesex*, Oxford 1966, 249. There are also problems with missing accounts. For many years either the accounts of the lieutenant are missing (such as the Constable years) or else the indenture books are missing or incomplete.

The ordnance office maintained an almost constant floating debt on the office's books in the manner of a modern revolving charge account, although with no provision for interest.[67] This debt was created by the conscious habit of running up heavier bills per quarter than either their allowance or the privy seals could cover. Then, in an almost futile attempt to reduce that debt, the oldest indentures would be paid first and the newer ones would then wait another quarter or two to be paid. This form of short-term debt management does not seem to have been too harmful to relations with contractors, since few debts were allowed to remain unpaid for more than two quarters during the war years of Elizabeth. However, it was an obvious temptation to the ordnance officers. During the peak war years from 1595 to 1602, internal office debt averaged around £1,000 per quarter. Merely by failing to pay suppliers off completely every quarter, the office was able to roll the debt over to the next quarter. After the conclusion of peace in 1604, the debt level declined to an average of £560 per quarter through to 1607. The accounts of Sir George Carew in 1604 show that in that year the office did not owe anything to any of its suppliers.[68] This financial retrenchment, along with limited expenditures on any military supplies, continued until 1608 when Carew left his post as lieutenant and moved up to become master of the ordnance. From that point until 1613 the debt increased to an average of £1,326 per quarter.[69] Once again it can be seen that the individual holding the office made a tremendous difference in office effectiveness and honesty. The office debt increased almost immediately under Carew's successor, the corrupt Sir Roger Dallison.

Dallison managed to run up debts of at least £13,000 during his tenure from 1608 to 1613, which had to be paid off by special privy seals issued to his successor, Sir Richard Morrison.[70] To be sure, most of Dallison's problems stemmed from his own corrupt dealings, but much of the money he embezzled had been given to him as lieutenant of the ordnance to pay the craftsmen (see chapter 3). The system literally threw temptation in his way and even complaints by suppliers and the other officers did not alert the government to what was going on. Instead, the office carried the debt on its own books at over £3,000 per quarter. In financial management terms it is possible to see

---

[67] When Sir John Hawkyns was managing the navy, he would pay some merchants immediately after deducting 3d. per £. Many suppliers preferred that to a lengthy wait for the full amount. Under the corrupt administration of Sir Robert Mansell, patentee and courtier, it was more common to deduct the 3d. per £ and then not pay the suppliers at all: Michael Oppenheim, *A history of the administration of the royal navy and of merchant shipping in relation to the navy from MDLX to MDCLX with an introduction treating of the preceding period*, n.p. 1896, repr. 1961, 192

[68] PRO, AO 1/1838/39, declared accounts of Sir George Carew, 1604.

[69] Ibid. WO 54/1–10. Some quarter books are missing, including most for 1614–16.

[70] Virtually all the sources agree on the figure of debt, but between 1618 and 1624 there are other indications that something approaching to £25,000 was paid to Morrison to settle Dallison's old debts. See appendix 5.

that administrative mechanisms to pay contractors and craftsmen lacked built-in checks and provided ample opportunity for inefficiency if not outright corruption. In this instance, only prompt and regular auditing procedures could have encouraged probity in office. Personal honesty was a critical factor in the financial management of the office since there was apparently no effective check on the power of the lieutenant. The reputation of the office suffered immeasurably from Dallison's corrupt dealings. Suppliers who were not paid for their items soon stopped bringing more into the office. Financial mismanagement and corruption had brought the arms supply system to a standstill.

The Dallison case was an exceptional example of financial mismanagement of the ordnance office; none the less some merchants and artificers were not paid for many years. For example, a warrant from the early reign of James I lists several dozen craftsmen who were still owed money, some £1,707, from when Sir Robert Constable was lieutenant (1588–91).[71] Furthermore, in the lieutenant's accounts of the 1620s, especially in the accounts of Dallison's successors who had to pay many of his bills, are lists of unpaid bills from 1608 and 1612. It seems that even in peacetime it was not uncommon to delay paying the suppliers for several years. There were also some complaints of failure to pay debts during Elizabeth's wars. One document from December 1592 lists nearly 100 large and small craftsmen and merchants owed over £4,000 by the ordnance office.[72]

Corruption and embezzlement often lay at the root of failure to pay the office suppliers rather than any systemic or organisational problem. The office procedures, if followed, would have dealt with bills in a reasonably prompt fashion. There were some other instances of failing to pay suppliers for goods brought into the office, not all of which can be traced back to corrupt practices by the office personnel. However, these often seem to have been due to disputes over the quality of the item or to the loss of an indenture by the craftsman or the office. Without the indenture, proof of provision was difficult and with the privy council constantly on the look-out for false provision and corruption, it often took years to resolve these disputes. For example, in 1592, Peter Gill, one of her Majesty's gunfounders of brass ordnance, was accused of owing the office some £1,112 5s. 2d. This was the value of the copper and tin which had been issued to him to make brass ordnance. However, ordnance weighing much less than the amount of metal (minus normal wastage of metal during casting) was returned to the office. As a result of this discrepancy, Gill's indentures were frozen until 1595; the ordnance office stopped paying him for any of the other, legitimate, supplies

---

[71] PRO, SP 15/36/89, list of debts left unpaid by Sir Robert Constable, lieutenant of the ordnance in the late queen's time [1604?].
[72] Ibid. SP 12/243/96, accounts of Powell, Painter and Bedwell and the debts owed to suppliers of the ordnance office, December 1592.

that he brought into the office until they were satisfied with his accounting for the metal.[73] It seems that most of the individuals who were owed substantial sums of money were either large scale merchants or else artificers who maintained a semi-official relationship to the office. Men such as Randall Symmes, a major arms merchant, Simon Furner, a merchant of rope and match, John Heybourne, Her Majesty's pikemaker, or Martin Hopkins, the master smith of the ordnance, were more commonly kept waiting for their money for an additional quarter while smaller, independent craftsmen were not. They were doubtless better able to afford a short term debt without running into the cash-flow problems of the smaller, or non-salaried operators. In addition, the larger craftsmen, especially the ordnance manufacturers and the arms merchants, often had no other legal outlet for their products and were in a sense captive suppliers.

The internal financial mismanagement of the ordnance office, especially in the Dallison years, resulted in a new approach. Smarting from the Dallison scandal, a new policy was instituted in 1618 after all the debts of the Dallison years had been paid. The internal failure of the ordnance office to police itself led to more direct management of the ordnance by the treasury commissioners who replaced the disgraced Suffolk.[74] One of their main goals was to reduce the deficit in the ordinary, or the regular expenses of the crown, for the household expenses, the wardrobe, the navy and the ordnance. Naturally, the ordnance was a target for savings and the commissioners stopped paying most of the ordinary allowance of the office in an attempt to save money and reduce the crown's deficit.[75] From 1618 until 1626, the ordinary allowance of £6,000 per year was not paid. Only an average of £2,000 per year was paid on the privy seal dormant which authorised ordinary expenditure. Everything else, all supplies and maintenance costs for the office, was to be paid for by privy seal. This policy was obviously intended to keep the lieutenant of the ordnance on a short financial leash, but its long-term consequences were little short of disastrous.

It is not difficult to understand why the removal of the ordinary allowance for the office was harmful. A small and regular budget could have been more effectively managed than a large infusion of cash after several years of penury. The regular trickle of £6,000 per year into the office under an honest lieutenant would probably have meant, as it had under Elizabeth, that the stores could have been enlarged slowly and better maintained into the bargain. Orders would have been placed with suppliers and craftsmen and paid for on a quarterly basis; officers and suppliers alike would have been actively

---

[73] Ibid. E 101/67/24, Gill's account of metal issued to him versus amount of ordnance returned, 1588–92. See also WO 54/1.

[74] The commissioners of the treasury in 1618 were Sir Francis Bacon, Fulke Greville, Sir Edward Coke, Sir Robert Naunton, Archbishop Abbot and Sir Julius Caesar. They were joined by Cranfield in 1619: Prestwich, *Cranfield*, 219–21, 242.

[75] Ibid. 247–8

employed and the system would have functioned more smoothly with regular use. In addition, the quality control measures of the ordnance would have been more efficient since smaller quantities of goods would be brought in on a more regular basis. Maintenance procedures also undoubtedly suffered without a regular allowance for repairs. Officers' salaries were still paid under the new system, but there was virtually no extra money from 1618 to 1621 for any other routine maintenance or purchases. Even the unpleasant experience of trying to provide large quantities of arms at short notice in 1621, when it seemed that England would intervene in the continental wars, did not reverse the policy of feast or famine for the office. What money was directed to the ordnance office was earmarked for special purchases to prepare for the abortive expedition to the Palatine. The payment of the full ordinary allowance of £6,000 per year was not resumed until 1626.[76] In addition to the administrative problems, the suppliers of war matériel needed a regular market, even if that market was small, in order to survive. Neither ordnance officers nor suppliers nor the nation as a whole was well served by the failure to pay the regular allowance for the office on a yearly basis.

The policy was justified by the commissioners as necessary in order to save money for the crown. They claimed to have reduced the expenses of the ordnance from £34,000 to £21,000 per year, thus saving the crown some £13,000 annually. These figures are a gross exaggeration. A glance at the ordnance expenditures from the start of James's reign (see appendix 5) shows that at no time did the ordnance office spend more than £13,000 per year, the size of the purported savings. In order to get even close to the figures claimed by the commissioners, one must go back to 1599 when, at the height of a major war, Elizabeth's ordnance office spent around £26,500 in one year. If the commissioners were using that as their starting point, then the office was indeed reduced from spending around £30,000 per year to spending close to an average of £5,000 per year. This would have been a large saving, but the way in which it was figured was hardly honest. The claim of savings in the ordnance of £13,000 per year, or the even larger figure of £20,000 saved per year cited in 1621 cannot be taken seriously.[77] The Jacobean ordnance office from 1603 to 1617 spent, on the average, only £9,000 per year, less the £13,000 embezzled by Dallison. Even if one adds the additional money spent to pay for Dallison's corruption, the office only spent an average of £10,000 per year. From 1618 to 1621, on the other hand, it spent £44,600, or an average of £11,150 per year. It is difficult to see where any savings at all, let alone £20,000 per year, could be claimed.

---

[76] See the declared accounts of Sir William Heydon, father of Sir John Heydon in PRO, E 351/2654. The ordinary payments to the office began in 1626, but were retroactively paid to 1624. Since the money was not put into the office until 1626, the latter date probably reflects the yearly financial status of the office more accurately.
[77] See also *Commons debates 1621*, ed. Wallace Notestein, Francis H. Relf and Hartley Simpson, 7 vols, New Haven, Conn. 1935, ii. 8–9; iv. 4.

If the claims of the commissioners of the treasury were grossly inflated, can it still be said that by reducing the ordinary expenditure of the office from £6,000 to an average of £2,000 per year then at least some savings were obtained? The answer must, in the long run, be no. In all, the ordnance office still spent some £112,000 between 1617 and 1625, an average of £12,500 per year. Most of this expenditure was concentrated in the years 1621, 1624 and 1625. Over 50 per cent of the total was spent in just one year on the privy seal authorising the spending of the parliamentary subsidy of 1624: £65,000 was spent from 1624 to 1625. The savings achieved by the commissioners' short-sighted policy were illusory since more money had to be spent in a shorter period of time in order to prepare for war. The lack of a regular allowance hurt office preparedness during peacetime and left it in a position where massive expenditure was needed in a short space of time to make up for the deficiencies. The poor condition of the ordnance office stores in 1624 was a direct result of this policy. Stores were low, the purchase of gunpowder had declined, and Lionel Cranfield, one of the main reformers in the treasury commission and now lord treasurer and earl of Middlesex, was attacked in the Lords for his arrogance and mismanagement.[78]

Cranfield's personal greed and his complicity in the short-sighted abolition of the ordinary allowance left the office in poorer condition in 1624 than it had been in 1617 after Dallison's depredations. A major survey of the office in 1624 (the 'Grand Proportion') showed that the office required an infusion of some £51,696 4s. 2d. in ordnance supplies to bring the stores up to a suitable level.[79]

This catalogue of insufficiency condemns the policy of management by privy seal. We will never know whether the sole cause of the woeful state of the office was the lack of a regular allowance to support routine maintenance and to assure the regular flow of supplies into the office. However, it is suggestive that the ordnance stores were in better shape while a regular allowance was being paid. This fact, combined with the supposition that small, regular infusions of supplies and cash would keep the arms supply system functioning better than occasional, massive expenditure, strongly indicates that the failure to pay the ordinary allowance was a specific instance of financial mismanagement by central government.

The wider question of whether the government could afford to maintain a regular arms system, even at the bargain rate of £6,000 per year, can only be touched upon here. The financial resources of the English government in the

---

[78] Prestwich, *Cranfield*, 395, 451–2, 456–8. While reducing the ordnance office to this state, and arranging for similar 'savings' on the wardrobe at the same time, Cranfield managed to increase his own income by at least £6,000 per year: Young, 'Illusions of grandeur', 70.
[79] PRO, WO 55/1680. Some £15,980-worth of gunpowder alone was deemed necessary for the stores along with £1,441-worth of axes, £2,528 for gun carriages, £1,220 for small arms and £15,022 for cannon shot.

early modern period have been the subject of much debate in recent years, much of it focusing upon Stuart extravagance as opposed to Tudor frugality. It is instructive to note that most historians seem to use these terms fairly consistently when characterising the fiscal policies of the two dynasties. The pioneering, and still largely unsuperseded work on the financial problems of early modern England even has chapters and sub-chapters entitled 'The frugal years' for the early reign of Elizabeth and 'The extravagance of the Stuart court' for the early years of James I.[80] This is not the place to discuss the complicated financial situation of the two monarchs, but one conclusion seems clear. Elizabeth and her ministers, by a means of a variety of loans, benevolences, subsidies and fiscal economies, managed to find the money to maintain an unprecedented military establishment for use against the greatest power in Europe while suppressing an extensive rebellion in Ireland. The state was in debt at her death (Salisbury's figure of £600,000 is probably accurate) but it managed to pay its bills and keep fighting. James I, on the other hand, despite keeping England at peace for most of his reign and despite the debt-reducing policies of the earl of Salisbury, was in debt to the tune of £800,000–£900,000 by 1618 with the deficit increasing every year.[81] The corruption of Lord Treasurer Suffolk and the short-sighted and personally-enriching tactics of Cranfield, together with with the personal extravagance of James I must have played a part in this debt explosion. James's government was chronically short of money and the expedients used to raise funds – impositions, purveyance, feudal dues – were so unpopular that any additional expenses on 'unnecessary' military supplies during peacetime must have seemed foolish. When the time came to generate even larger sums for war, the weak financial base of the crown was not strong enough to bear the additional expense without increasingly drastic measures.

Even given the poor financial condition of late Jacobean government, it is still hard to see why the government, which managed to support the rapacious appetites of Cranfield and then the duke of Buckingham, could not come up with the small sum of £6,000 per year for the ordnance. That small regular payment, when added to an occasional infusion of a few thousand pounds per year for special occasions, would have left the office in much better shape than it was in 1624. It is probably no coincidence that the period between 1617 and 1624, which saw the office decline to the point where over £50,000 was required to bring the stores up to an acceptable level, also saw only an average of £2,000 per year being paid out of the ordinary. If the full ordinary had been paid for those years, the ordnance would have spent an additional £32,000 on supplies, and would probably have spent it more effectively by spreading it out over a number of years. The shortfall in 1624 would then have been only £18,000-worth of supplies. Such

---

[80] Frederick C. Dietz, *English public finance 1558–1641*, New York – London 1932.
[81] Ibid. 149–50

a sum would have been well within reach of even James's government during its preparations for war in 1624. As it was, the government had to spend some £65,000 in 1624 and 1625 anyway, and there is some doubt as to whether this money was well spent since it was disbursed in such a hasty fashion. James's government did not lack the money to keep the ordnance office stores up to a sufficient level: rather it unwisely spent what it had. It dumped a large sum of money on the office at the proverbial last minute instead of spreading it out by making a small regular payment over a number of years during peace. The cost of war in the early modern period was great but sometimes the lack of preparedness during peacetime was, in the long run, more expensive.

The responsibility for this must in part be attributed to the internal organisation and administration of the office. However, another key element is the fact that within the ordnance office and between the office and the court were personality clashes, cases of blatant corruption, and other administrative dysfunctions. Tensions within the office, its problems with corruption, and the various remedies suggested to deal with them are the topics to which we now turn.

3

Administrative Tensions, Corruption and Reform

> The heavens themselves, the planets, and this center,
> Observe degree, priority, and place,
> Insisture, course, proportion, season, form, office, and custom, in all line of order.
> – Shakespeare, *Troilus and Cressida*, act I, scene iii, 85

The internal administrative procedures that the ordnance office adopted (or had forced upon it during periodic shake-ups) varied greatly from decade to decade, but some of the means of managing the process of arms supply were relatively consistent throughout the later Tudor and early Stuart period. However, these procedures were not without tension. It is therefore useful to examine some instances of stresses within the office which resulted from management problems and from the nature of office-holding in early modern England, before going on to investigate charges of corruption made against the ordnance office and the reform proposals which attempted to deal with this continual problem. Even well-organised bureaucracies can suffer administrative set-backs as a result of occasional lapses into corrupt practices. The ordnance office during the last years of Elizabeth and even more so under the reign of James I was only marginally effective even in the best of circumstances. It was even less successful when handicapped by corrupt practices. Thus the office and the entire government paid a high price for their failure to prevent corruption from occurring or to uncover corrupt personnel promptly. The attempts at reforming the office, like most of the other contemporaneous reform attempts in the wardrobe, the navy and the household, were largely doomed to failure.

Administrative tensions

The complexity of the supply process and the overlapping systems of indentures, ledger books and official responsibilities were meant to prevent fraud and deceit but in many cases merely increased the chances that officers could get away with financial wrongdoing. The very complexity of the system of checks and balances created its own loopholes for the clever and industrious cheat. In addition, even when the system worked fairly well (that is, when it was not openly corrupt) its complexity and the nature of office-holding in the early modern period led to many tensions. There were problems within the office involving personality clashes, patronage disputes and the reversion of office. A brief look at each of these areas may help to clarify the nature of bureaucracy in the early modern period when government administrative methods were at a formative stage.

The nature of bureaucracy has been much discussed by social scientists and historians. The influence of Max Weber on general theories of bureaucracy has been particularly powerful. In broad terms, his concepts of the characteristics of a bureaucracy are of an organisation with clearly delineated areas of responsibility, official precedence, central direction and written records. It is further characterised by being staffed by professional functionaries using rational principles of management. Underlying it all would be a merit-based system for recruiting new members and disciplining wayward ones. The entire Weberian bureaucracy, an ideal construct to be sure, thus relies upon a rational conception of man: nineteenth-century man as well. It also relies upon a rational belief, often misplaced, in the ability of the state systematically to recruit, train, place, pay and retain a professional civil service.[1] The actual performance of any bureaucracy in history has, of course, generally departed from the Weberian ideal, but the goal of increased efficiency by the elaboration of offices and responsibilities has remained a valid one for states over time. Bureaucracy remains an essentially rational and artificial construct.

Historians find a great deal to argue with in Weber's conception of bureaucracy; they argue even more about its applicability in any given historical circumstance and time. Constructs have a way of never quite fitting real events and personalities. Certainly few English historians agree on just how closely the offices and administration of Tudor and Stuart England approached that ideal. Elements of a rational bureaucracy can be discovered in virtually every governmental organisation throughout the period. However, the question remains of just when, if ever, the rational elements can be said to predominate over the traditional and personal elements.

G. R. Elton, in his seminal works on Tudor England, states that the period from 1530 to 1540 was crucial in the evolution of English office-holding. He declares that 'The plain fact is that Henry VII ascended the throne of a medievally governed kingdom, while Elizabeth handed to her successor a country administered on modern lines.'[2] Elton's argument is that this transformation occurred due to the modification of traditional household government along the modern lines of a bureaucratic organisation – a revolution in

---

[1] *From Max Weber: essays in sociology*, ed. and trans. H. H. Gerth and C. Wright Mills, New York 1958. See also G. E. Aylmer, *The king's servants: the civil service of Charles I, 1625–1642*, London – Boston, 1961, 1974, 455–63.

[2] G. R. Elton, *The Tudor revolution in government*, Cambridge 1953, 1974, 3. Though much criticised and modified over the years, the central argument for a quantum leap in administrative techniques in the Cromwellian years of Henry's reign still seems strong.

government. By 1540, he argues, the household type of administration was largely replaced by 'rational bureaucratic methods and instruments'.³ While admitting that there was still a long way to go for the English state in the creation of a fully-fledged bureaucracy, Elton considers that by the mid-Tudor period most of the basic elements of that structure were in place.

Linda Levy Peck, on the other hand, sees the early Stuart period as crucial in the formation of a rationalised bureaucracy. Her work on the patronage and politics surrounding the career of the earl of Northampton has highlighted the fact that 'Jacobean government remained intensely personal and was far from being a rationalised bureaucracy.'⁴ She sees the beginnings of such a bureaucracy, however, as resulting from the reform commissions of Northampton which, despite his unsavoury reputation for favouritism, seem to have accomplished a great deal towards exposing corrupt individuals and practices. In direct opposition to Weber, who years earlier saw warfare as a chief cause of the centralisation of the state and the growth of bureaucracy, she has further stated that these peacetime commissions were the main driving force, at least in the English case: 'While historians have often focused on warfare as the stimulus to rationalisation of bureaucracy, these initiatives began during the Jacobean peace.'⁵

Nevertheless, as G. E. Aylmer has pointed out, English government under Charles I continued to be based on patronage networks and the conception of an office as personal property, so much so that no bureaucracy in the modern sense existed. However, in many important respects he sees that it was moving in that direction. In fact, Aylmer states that in many respects one could consider the English government to have been organised on bureaucratic lines for some years: 'With its elaborate and highly formalised procedure, the copiousness of its written records, the jealousies of its department divisions, its hierarchy, and its specialisation, English central government had been thoroughly bureaucratic for a very long time.'⁶

How long a time, apparently, remains a matter of dispute. It behoves any student of Tudor and Stuart government to examine the details of early administrative practice in order to throw light on how and when the transformation into a rationalised bureaucracy occurred. The Elizabethan period was certainly one of the critical periods in this transformation because it incorporated substantial elements both of a rational conception of office with a personal one. As Wallace MacCaffrey has said of Elizabethan government: 'The practice of the Elizabethan administration mingles confusedly the notion of a professional, paid public service with that of personal service to the

---

³ Ibid. 415.
⁴ Linda Levy Peck, *Northampton: patronage and policy at the court of James I*, London 1982, 215.
⁵ Ibid.
⁶ Aylmer, *King's servants*, 461.

monarch.'[7] A look at the ordnance office, in time of war and peace during the early modern period, should provide a number of indications of how this 'mixed administration' worked.

Roles and responsibilities

One of the key characteristics of any bureaucracy is the clear delineation between the roles of officers and the responsibilities of their office. In the ordnance office, duties often overlapped or were divided in such a way as to blur essential lines of authority. This was not always a bad thing. In some instances the interlocking responsibilities of the ordnance officers served the valuable function of preventing the issuance of items with insufficient or inaccurate warrants. However, without clear lines of authority, officer was sometimes pitted against officer.

In May 1593, for example, Sir George Carew, lieutenant of the ordnance, complained that the surveyor, with the co-operation of the keeper of the stores, had cancelled and returned some warrants for supply that Carew had issued. While Carew admitted that it was his fault that the warrants had not been correctly entered in the office books, he complained bitterly about the challenge to his authority implicit in the surveyor's actions:

> That which grieveth me is the contemptible dealing of the keeper of the store, who (if he be an officer) is but to keep and deliver, and not to comptroll or equal his authority with mine, who (until her Majesty make a master) am the first in the office. Heretofore in the like unrespective manner he hath often used me, which I have swallowed; but if this pass smoothly with him I shall receive the Queen's fee and deserve but little. . . . If there were anything in my warrant defective, upon his request I would have amended it; but to return it in this indecent manner I hope you will conceive as I do, that he hath much forgotten himself.[8]

In this indictment one can sense an internal power struggle as well as a dislike of what we would view as a useful double-checking of authority: an internal review of the warrant for issuing supplies. Carew attacked both the standing of the surveyor in the office (if he be an officer), the personality of the surveyor (his 'unrespective' and 'indecent manner'), and the very position of the surveyor as part of the administrative checks and balances of the office. This incident serves once again to point out that office-holding in the late sixteenth and early seventeenth centuries was still a struggle of personality and individual power versus administrative systematisation and

---

[7] Wallace T. MacCaffrey, 'Place and patronage in Elizabethan politics', in S. T. Bindoff, J. Hurstfield and C. H. Williams (eds), *Elizabethan government and society*, London 1961, 95–126.
[8] HMC, *Salisbury*, iv. 315, Carew to [Burghley?], 16 May 1593.

rationalisation. Personal prestige and status were so bound up in the office that every attempt to provide anything close to a modern 'checks and balances' took on the appearance of a personal challenge. The uneasy balance between personal prestige and official duty remained an inherent flaw in the administration of the ordnance office throughout the early modern period.

An even more serious clash within the office broke out in March 1600 and continued to affect the administration of the ordnance until it was resolved by the unusual circumstances surrounding the self-destruction of the earl of Essex. In a sense, this dispute can be seen to demonstrate in microcosm the tensions which permeated the late Elizabethan world, involving as it did personal honour, frustrated ambition and political patronage. The immediate cause of the problem was the lack of official authority held by the deputy lieutenant of the ordnance, George Harvey, when he filled in for his nephew, Sir George Carew, from 1600 to 1603 while Carew was lord president of Munster. But at its root lay an unspoken challenge to what could be called a new and still immature conception of office-holding.

The controversy began on 13 March 1600 when Harvey and Richard Paulfreyman, the subtreasurer and clerk, met the other officers of the ordnance to discuss an unwarranted payment of £20 per year to John Lee, the keeper of the stores.[9] Apparently Paulfreyman was the first to object to this payment. Almost immediately Sir John Davis, surveyor of the ordnance, allegedly called Paulfreyman 'saucy companion' and stated that his allegations were 'an indignity not to be endured by the officers'.[10] Why Davis intervened is not clear, but he may partly have been motivated by envy that a mere clerk had been appointed as subtreasurer of the office rather than he himself who had excellent court connections. Davis owed his position in the ordnance office to his relationship with the earl of Essex. He had served with him in France, Portugal, Cadiz and on the Islands voyage, and had been appointed surveyor at his behest.[11] In addition, Davis may have objected to Paulfreyman's claims to higher social status since from 1598 he had been signing his letters as 'R. Paulfreyman, gent.'. Claims to gentility nearly always grate on social superiors.

As an Essex appointee, Davis probably felt that he could challenge Paulfreyman and Harvey directly and he continued to do so. The next day, in the presence of Harvey and the lieutenant of the Tower, Davis objected to Paulfreyman's attendance at an office meeting. Claiming that Paulfreyman

---

[9] This allowance was apparently to be in addition to the authorised £40 per year salary the keeper drew, and had been entered on the quarter books (now missing) in 1591 during the time between the appointments of Sir Robert Constable and Sir George Carew as lieutenants of the ordnance: Ashley, 'Tudor ordnance', 137–40.
[10] HMC, *Salisbury*, x. 100–1, Harvey to Cecil, 4 Apr. 1600. Sir John Davis, or Davies, should not be confused with Sir John Davies, solicitor-general and attorney-general for Ireland and a correspondent of Sir Robert Cecil.
[11] BL, MS Add. 6177, fo. 55.

'was no officer', he and two of his henchmen physically ejected the unfortunate subtreasurer from the room.¹² Davis even referred to Harvey as 'but a deputy' and later that day refused the deputy's order to accompany the clerk of the ordnance to Chatham to take the remains of four ships.

Despite Davis's obvious combativeness and insolence, no action was taken against him and he was free to continue his obstructive ways. In November 1600 Harvey again complained to Cecil that Davis was attempting to run the office as his own patronage network. Calling Davis 'a shepstar's son, hatched in Gutter Lane' Harvey reported that Davis objected to the patronising of Thomas Aldridge, deputy wheelwright under William Smeaton:¹³

> Davis objects without reason to Aldridge, and countermand's [my] orders. Davis plots that no man shall serve her Majesty in the office but himself, and such as depend on him. If this is affected the office will be brought to 'the old course' of Rowland and Painter's services [two particularly corrupt ordnance officers of the 1580s] wherein her Majesty lost and was deceived almost £100,000.¹⁴

Once more we see Davis attempting to take advantage of his strong position in the office as an appointee of Essex. Even though Essex was then temporarily out of favour, neither he nor his clients expected that state of affairs to be of long duration. Davis appears to have had all the arrogance and disdain for authority that so often drove Essex and his cronies to the brink of, and then beyond, danger. Davis's ambition to run his own patronage network was so strong that he brooked no interference from any rivals. As long as personal ambition and the arrogance of a claim to protection by reason of a powerful patron existed, there was no chance of even a semblance of a 'rational' civil service. That no such system was yet in existence is demonstrated by the fact that there was no mechanism to force Davis to toe the line. Only the supreme folly of Davis's participation in the comic opera of the downfall of Essex removed him from his post and placed him in a cell in the Tower not far from his old offices; offices in which both Harvey and Paulfreyman could perhaps be seen going about their labours with self-satisfied smiles at that new turn of events.¹⁵

---

¹² HMC, *Salisbury*, x. 100–1. See also Hogg, *Royal arsenal*, i. 51–3. One of Davis's bully boys was William Scott, clerk in the office who was later involved in the Essex revolt along with his master and patron.
¹³ HMC, *Salisbury*, x. 399, Harvey to Cecil, 28 Nov. 1600. A 'shepstar' was a type of starling, but the exact meaning of a 'shepstar's son' must be left to the imagination.
¹⁴ Ibid.
¹⁵ For the examination of Sir John Davis in the Tower see *CSPD Eliz. I, 1598–1601*, 547–8. Davis was pardoned by Cecil a year later: BL, MS Add. 6177, fo. 74, letter of thanks to Sir Robert Cecil, 6 Feb. 1602. Davis never gave up trying to return to some kind of office, asking to supervise the production of gunpowder and saltpetre in Feb. 1602, improve the quality of match in the office or be appointed to a new office of comptroller of the ordnance: HMC, *Salisbury*, xii. 58–9, 492, 542–3, Davis to Cecil.

Disputes such as the one between Davis and Harvey were not easily resolved, nor was the damage limited to these two offices in the ensuing bureaucratic battles. John Lee and Richard Paulfreyman continued to fight along the battle lines established by their superiors, splitting the office into two obviously hostile camps. John Lee accused Paulfreyman of lying and usurping the office of the keeper of the small guns and instigated a general enquiry into his activities. According to Paulfreyman's answer to the charges, Lee had accused him of drawing an excessive salary and charging the merchants who dealt with the office poundage between four and six pence per pound for items purchased by the office. This type of 'handling-charge' was not unusual in this period, and only if excessive was it regarded as unusual or corrupt. In his counter-attack, Paulfreyman admitted that he did take this small poundage from the merchants, but justified it by claiming that it did the merchants no hurt (since they 'have great gain by the Queen') and the practice 'only' brought him £100 per year. Then Paulfreyman charged Lee, who also held the office of deputy master of the armoury under his cousin, Sir Henry Lee, with making money out of a shipment of swords which had recently been sent to Ireland. He also reiterated his accusation that Lee's allowance of £20 per year had been illegally paid to him in the years between the death of Constable and the arrival of Carew.[16]

In none of the charges and counter-charges of these individuals is there enough evidence to pronounce judgement. However, the obvious existence of the conflict split the office into two factions, resulted in a long standing war among the officers and seriously affected the functioning of the office. The appointment of a deputy had probably been meant to preclude just such disputes as had occurred. However, no deputy, however knowledgeable, could wield the same authority as a regularly appointed, fully empowered lieutenant. And even then it might not have been possible to force so strong a personality into official obedience; the notion of the office as personal property precluded the use of the ultimate sanction of loss of position without which no civil service can function effectively.

Appointment and reversion

The way in which officers were appointed in the Tudor and Stuart period and the practice of reversion of offices were other weaknesses in the administrative organisation of the ordnance office. However, these problems were generally outside the control of the officers.[17] Without a civil service appointment system, there was no recognised way of ensuring that qualified

---

[16] Ibid. xi. 560; xii. 191, 656; xiv. 152. The struggle continued until at least June 1602 and probably until Lee left the office, under a cloud, in 1604.
[17] For office-holding definitions and the best study of reversion methods in Stuart England see Aylmer, *King's servants*, 69.

personnel filled the various positions in the ordnance office. Reversions, by means of which the rights to an office after the departure or decease of the present holder, were obtained, were in the gift of the king, and owed much to patronage connections and little to merit. As such, impending vacancies in the ordnance were filled on the *ad hoc* basis familiar to all students of patronage networks. Thus Sir John Davis used the earl of Essex to obtain his job as surveyor of the ordnance. It is likely that his rival, Richard Paulfreyman, rose in office due to his connections with Harvey and Carew who were definitely part of the Cecil patronage network.

Complicating this system was the almost hereditary nature of many of the offices, a result of their being considered effectively personal property. Many of the sons or close relatives of ordnance personnel seem to have had a place made for them in the office. Richard Paulfreyman shared his office with his son James as keeper of the small guns, the Bull family held a virtual monopoly on the master gunner's office for thirty years. Even the lieutenant, Sir George Carew, made his uncle George Harvey his deputy. In several other instances, there were probably hereditary principles at play. When Sir Robert Johnson (clerk of the deliveries) died in 1620, the office passed to Edward Johnson. Sir Robert had shared his office with his son Thomas until the latter's death in 1605 or 1606 and it is not unlikely that the identical last name of his successor in 1620 was not a coincidence although definite proof is lacking.[18]

The transmission of offices probably also occurred in some of the lesser offices with Martin Hopkins, Jr succeeding his father as a furbisher, and John Tree the younger obtaining a job as labourer in the office thanks (doubtless) to his father's influence.

Relatives of ordnance officers seem to have had some advantage in gaining office, but there were no guarantees. In 1595 Carew was unable to obtain the post of keeper of the stores for his uncle despite his position. He had to wait until 1600 for the temporary post as his deputy.[19] However, John Lee was appointed office of keeper of the stores in that year, perhaps in part because he was a close relative (probably a cousin) of Sir Henry Lee, master of the armoury.

There were, of course, occasions when offices were not passed to relatives and outsiders were able to obtain the reversion. Reversions within the ordnance office were granted by the monarch in the manner usual to late Tudor and early Stuart government with one major difference. The posts available in the ordnance generally required the officer or artificer to be in residence and to perform the duties of the office in person. In the case of the artificers' posts, one had to be a well-qualified craftsman in the particular trade before

---

[18] HMC, *Salisbury*, xviii. 3, earl of Devonshire to earl of Salisbury, sometime before 25 Mar. 1606.
[19] 'Touching his place [Thomas Bedwell, keeper of the store], I did formerly entreat you for my uncle, whom I know to be a very fit man for an accomptant office': ibid, v. 191, Carew to Lord Burghley, 8 Apr. 1595.

entering into the position. For other higher ranking positions such as surveyor or keeper of the stores, the management skills required were more considerable than those necessary for a large number of government positions. When this is added to the fact that the officers in the ordnance did not get paid very well, it is not surprising that competition for appointment to the ordnance was not particularly keen. There were perquisites to the offices, however, both legal and illegal ones, so there was some competition. With competition comes confusion and one occasionally finds multiple reversions causing difficulties.[20] One such example from 1624 may help point out the confusion and perils of the scramble for office in early Stuart England.

In May 1624 Sir Ralph Sydenham wrote to Secretary Conway, asking him to obtain a note from the king which would assure him the reversion of the office of surveyor of the ordnance, held at that time by Richard Kaye. Sydenham claimed in this letter that a reversion had been granted to him to take effect on the death of the former surveyor (Sir John Kaye, probably a relative of Richard Kaye) but that the king had forgotten about it and granted the office to Richard. Probably as a result of Conway's prompting, the king ordered that no reversion be made without his approval since he remembered the promise and was 'still wishful to favour' Sydenham despite his resolutions not to grant any more reversions. However, in November of the same year, Sir John Coke claimed that the reversion was actually to go to a Mr Read who had agreed with Mr Kaye for the purchase of the office.

Outright purchase of an office was rare in the ordnance office, and allusion to it in official correspondence rarer still. There was mention of a price for an office in 1601, when a William Smith wrote to Cecil on the 9 February claiming that he had talked with Sir John Davis just the week before and had received 'from his own mouth' a price for the office of surveyor. Showing rather morbid haste – Davis had only just been arrested for his role in the Essex demonstration – Smith begged Cecil that the now vacant office be granted to him. Prices for office did exist and could be mentioned even at the highest levels of government although in this case no exact sum was quoted.[21] He further claimed that Sydenham had obtained his reversion on misinformation since Kaye had the earlier reversion but that since Read was already an old man, Sydenham's early succession to the office was probable. Normally such multiple reversions were frowned upon, but, as Coke summed up, 'this being an exchange of an officer [Read was obviously switching with

---

[20] Aylmer, *King's servants*, 96–106. Aylmer's many examples of complicated reversion problems between 1625 and 1640 vividly demonstrate the truth of his contention that the 'granting of reversions was not always a straightforward matter'.
[21] HMC, *Salisbury*, xi. 37. Patronage was often more important than money in gaining an office, even in the case of posts for which some 'professional qualifications' were required. The outright sale of office was probably more common under James I than Elizabeth: Aylmer, *King's servants*, 76–7.

Kaye, for a price], not the death or removal of one, Sir Ralph Sydenham's claim of reversion is not thereby affected'.[22]

The confusing path to office in the early Stuart period was one strewn with pitfalls. Holding the reversion to an office promised little more than a firm possibility of actually securing it. However, there seems little doubt that the mechanism for finding new personnel at all levels certainly did not ensure that the ordnance office would obtain the best qualified personnel to run its complex supply process.

In sum, we can see by these examples of administrative tensions and faults in the system for appointment that the nature of office holding in the early modern period lay at the root of many of the problems involved in managing the ordnance office. Influence, personal prestige, patronage and the poor delineation of responsibilities disrupted what was at best a cumbersome system of military supply. In addition, the complex nature of the supply process and the lack of effective enforcement or supervisory techniques also insured that there was plenty of scope for those who were primarily interested in private profit. It was not possible to supervise individuals whose idea of office was virtually inseparable from their own notions of personal status and power.

Corruption and reform

> 'O! that estates, degrees and offices
> Were not deriv'd corruptly, and that clear honour
> Were purchas'd by the merit of the wearer.'
> – Shakespeare, *The Merchant of Venice*, act II, scene ix, 39

Even a reasonably efficient and rational bureaucracy has difficulty in preventing illegal activities. The fact that the ordnance office in the early modern period was not efficiently ordered and rationalised led to many instances of shady practice and outright corruption.

The definition of corruption has always been a historical problem. Charges of corruption abound in the early modern period but they were often rooted in the political battles of the time rather than in demands for greater morality in government. At the same time, modern notions of corruption seldom apply in the period before the establishment of a civil service system. The overt use of patronage and favour or the common seventeenth century practice of purchasing a reversion to an office would all be condemned by modern political scientists yet none excited much substantive complaint at the time. Complaints about patronage were generally objections to the person appointed rather than the means. Yet it is necessary to define and use the concept of corruption in order to hold individuals in government to some

---

[22] *CSPD James I, 1623–5*, 251, order by the king on the reversion, 21 May 1624. See also ibid. 397, Sir Ralph Sydenham to Secretary Conway, [May] 1624.

standard if their relative effectiveness in office is to be assessed. Corruption was a fact of life in Tudor and Stuart politics and administration.

While the term corruption often falls victim to relativism, perhaps the most useful discussion of the problem of definition is contained in Joel Hurstfield's essay on political corruption.[23] Hurstfield rejects both the despair at setting any standards of the relativists and the moral rigidity of the historians who judge the past according to their own standards. His working definition of corruption, which I will use, is that corruption occurs when undue influence or personal gain interferes with the public interest. The use of patronage or the taking of small gifts, if it does not lead to damage to the public interest, is not automatically judged as being corrupt. Corruption is an appropriate term, according to Hurstfield, 'where gifts are accepted while holding judicial office; where state revenues are directed into private purses; where appointment and advancement in the public service are by favouritism, or for reasons other than the public interest'.[24] The use of public money for private purposes, although common in the early modern period, must be judged as corrupt because in no way can it be considered as serving the public interest. The lack of an appropriate salary for a post explains why such behaviour was common but does not excuse it. Likewise, the use of favouritism to obtain an office – the term having all the overtones of appointing unqualified personnel to sinecures – was a corrupt practice although the general system of patronage was not. Patronage was a common system of rewarding clients and filling offices which, if used carefully, was often a beneficial way of mixing personal loyalties with public service.[25] As Linda Levy Peck has shown, the correct use of patronage was of great value to the bureaucracy and the crown in the age when there was no reasonable alternative.

The patron–client relationship was the chief means by which the crown won the loyalty of powerful subjects, integrated regional elites and local governments into the state and staffed its administration. Lacking coercive institutions such as a standing army or a paid local bureaucracy by which to impose their will, the Tudors had successfully made the court the centre of power, offering honour, privilege and office in exchange for service and obedience.[26] The patronage system was the centrepiece of this new development.

---

[23] 'Political corruption in modern England: the historian's problem', in his *Freedom, corruption and government in Elizabethan England*, Cambridge, Mass. 1973, 137–62.
[24] Ibid. 162.
[25] See MacCaffrey, 'Place and patronage', 103.
[26] Peck, *Northampton*, 24, 147. Peck's effective rehabilitation of Northampton and his use of patronage does not deflect her from a commitment to 'the modern western definition of corruption' which opens up a host of problems for her final conclusions that Northampton was more of a reformer than historians have considered him to be. See also MacCaffrey, 'Place and patronage', 96.

The opposite side of patronage was favouritism, which perverted the system by appointing individuals whose qualifications were slight or nonexistent. According to Hurstfield such a practice could not be considered in the public interest and must be adjudged corrupt where found. Hurstfield's definition has the additional effect of forcing the historian to examine the facts of each accusation of corruption and to assess the evidence according to the universal standard of whether the public interest was served by such behaviour or not. How does such an examination of corruption alter our view of the ordnance office?

The ordnance office has always had an 'unsavoury reputation' for poor management and corruption. Michael Oppenheim, in his study of the administration of the Royal Navy, referred to that office in the 1630s as one which 'still retained that evil pre-eminence in sloth and incapacity it had already earned and had never since lost'.[27] In his massive study of the Caroline civil service, G. E. Aylmer further characterised the ordnance officers as, 'slovenly, idle, incompetent, corrupt and often fraudulent'. However, he goes on to say that 'several of the heaviest charges against them remain unproven'.[28]

How much corruption was there in the ordnance office at the time? Which administrative practices increased the potential for corruption? What form did these abuses take? How did the government attempt to deal with such corruption and to what degree were reform attempts successful? Even if some of the evidence on corruption is sketchy, such questions must be asked in order to provide the clearest picture of administrative practices in an early modern bureaucracy.

The administration of the ordnance office had plenty of inherent problems which often led to office friction, inefficiency and complaints. In some instances, office procedures almost seemed to lend themselves to abuse. For example, the division of duties within the office placed most of the responsibility for making out indentures for supplies which were purchased on the shoulders of the clerk of the ordnance and the keeper of the stores. In 1601 there were well-documented allegations that these two officers were often in collusion and that many items 'supposed to be bought with her Ma[jesty's] mony and brought into her highnes store Where noe such matter was, but the mony converted to there own uses'.[29] The complaint was that many

---

[27] Oppenheim, *Royal navy*, 158, 289.
[28] G. E. Aylmer, 'Studies in the institutions and personnel of English central administration 1625–42', unpubl. DPhil diss. Oxford 1954, 113. While Aylmer's comments are about the later ordnance office, they can also be taken as indicative of the behaviour of officers under Elizabeth and James I.
[29] BL, MS Sloane 871, fo. 129, copy of Mr Linewray's book for reformation of abuses in the office of the ordnance, [1601]. The charges were made against William Paynter, clerk of the ordnance and Thomas Bedwell, keeper of the stores. Even if one assumes that Linewray's charges were exaggerated, there seems little doubt that 'a number of grave deceptions were practiced': H. C. Tomlinson, *Guns and government: the ordnance office under the later Stuarts*, London 1979, 5–6.

supplies brought into the office were provided 'by them who are to Accompt for her Ma[jesty's] monny paid into the said office, and thereby doe discharge themselves even as they themselves liste'.[30]

In other words, the officers were selling supplies to their own office, certifying (to themselves) that their provisions were correct and then authorising payments to themselves. Even after these false indentures had been brought to light, the clerks of the office continued to bring supplies into the office, especially ships 'emptions' (miscellaneous supplies of rope, oil, canvas, lead, nails etc.). Clerks such as Tristram Slader, Thomas Lincon, Richard Haynes, Richard Lenthall and William Scott provided as much as £360-worth of naval supplies per year in order to supplement their incomes.[31] The amount of money flowing to the clerks as suppliers was substantial, yet there were only a few complaints at the time. The modern notion of 'conflict of interest', where it is not considered proper for a government official to be directly involved in providing goods or services to his own office was obviously not strongly held in this period. But the provision of supplies by ordnance officers was only potentially a corrupt practice. In this the ordnance office was not unique; virtually all the offices of the period would fail this test. However, the temptation for personal gain was also matched by administrative procedures which made corruption possible.

The poor division of responsibility, the continuous temptation of illegal gain due to a failure to comprehend the dangers of conflict of interest, the poorly arranged procedures for financial accountability and the nature of office holding in the sixteenth and seventeenth centuries all led to many real abuses within the office and even more imagined ones. Even contemporary reform commissions – and there were many throughout this period, notably in 1596, 1597, 1598, 1601 and 1618–20 – were baffled by the true extent of the abuses within the office. They were also confused, as are all modern students of the office, when they attempted to identify reasons for its ineffectiveness. It was simply very difficult to decide who was corrupt and how they accomplished their corrupt acts.

Administrative procedures of the period may have contained the potential for abuse and corruption, but we must determine how often and in what form actual corruption occurred. To do so, it is necessary to examine some of the many attacks upon the ordnance office in order to gain a sense of the size of the problem. At the same time, we must be very careful not to assign modern ideas of administrative principles to Tudor and Stuart officials while still holding them up to at least contemporary standards of morality and perform-

---

[30] BL MS Sloane 871, fo. 132, copy of Linewray's book.
[31] PRO, WO 49/23, 26. In 1599 identifiable naval supplies purchased by the office cost £782; in 1601 such items cost £460. In those years the clerks were responsible for £360- and £138-worth of the supplies, respectively. The amount of supplies brought in for each ship was not huge – an average of between £6 and £30 per ship. However, these small sums added up in the course of a year.

ance. In addition, we shall look briefly at the reform attempts in the household, the wardrobe and the navy to help us place the ordnance office in context.

Complaints of corruption, as distinct from proven instances of it, abound throughout the early modern period. In 1582 John Powell, about to be made surveyor of the ordnance, documented some £10,474 which he claimed had been detained corruptly by the ordnance officers for supplies of all sorts which were indented for but never brought into the office.[32] No accusations were made against individuals by name in this book of information but there is no doubt, based upon later evidence, that William Paynter, clerk of the ordnance, was one of those implicated. Even so, Paynter remained in office until 1595 and even counter-attacked Powell in 1589 by declaring that he, Powell, was the corrupt influence in the office.[33] This may have been true, since Powell was accused by Carew in 1593 with helping the keeper of the stores, Thomas Bedwell, to cover up many corrupt practices.[34] Powell was discharged from his office the same year, 1595, that his old rival Paynter died.[35] According to a report from 1601, the ordnance office was defrauded of £60,000 during the Paynter years, although this was undoubtedly an exaggeration.[36] However, the constant attempts at office reorganisation and the regular charges and counter-charges of corruption within the office indicate that there was something seriously wrong that defied contemporary analysis.

It became painfully apparent over the years that attempts at administrative reform of the office had little positive effect.[37] Neither complex administrative reorganisation nor regular reports to the exchequer were enough to halt abuses within the ordnance office. Even attempts to ensure honesty by forcing officers to put up a bond did not seem to work. When John Lee took over as keeper of the stores in November 1595, he was forced to take out

---

[32] Ibid. SP 12/157/43, 'A brief collection of such somes of money as hathe ben proved against the officers of the Ordnannce upon the book of Information exhibited by John Powell', [1582?]. According to this book, the large sum was 'confessed by the said officers and confirmed in the book of Informacion under the hande of the right Honorable the Lord High Tresawrer of England and Sir Walter Myldmay Comyssioners appoynted in that behalf'. If the officers admitted to £10,000, the real sum was probably even higher.

[33] Powell apparently disproved the charges in the presence of Sir Robert Constable, the lieutenant, and declared that Paynter deserved whipping for his false report. Hogg says of Paynter that he was by all accounts 'a scurvy Knave': *Royal arsenal*, i. 45.

[34] HMC, *Salisbury*, iv. 315, Sir George Carew to Mr Beadwell, 15 May 1593.

[35] Ibid. x. 86, Paynter to Cecil, 30 Mar 1600. However, William Paynter's son, Anthony, applied for the office of surveyor of the ordnance in 1600 boldly claiming that he had 'been brought up in that office'. If his bid had been accepted, it seems probable that his upbringing would have led to a repetition of his father's behaviour.

[36] HMC, *Salisbury*, xi. 551, particular services effected in the office of the ordnance by John Linewray, [1601].

[37] PRO, SP 12/175/97, orders set down for the government of the office by Ambrose, earl of Warwick, [1584]. See also BL, MS Harl. 168, fos 161-2; PRO, SP 12/262/105, 268/13, 269/44.

a bond for £3,500 to guarantee his good behaviour in office.[38] These bonds apparently had little effect; they were ultimately forfeited due to the 'greate damage losse and inconvenience' which occurred during Lee's tenure in office. However, it was not until 1618 that the collection of the bonds was granted to one Patrick Murray in consideration of his (unstated) service to the crown. He was to have the responsibility of collecting the bonds, but there is no evidence one way or the other of his degree of success in obtaining cash for the paper guarantees.[39]

There were many other proposals suggesting ways to restrain corrupt behaviour in office. Those made in 1598, 1601 and 1618 are valuable in providing an overall assessment as well as in indicating what types of practices were considered to be corrupt, while attempts at reform in other selected crown offices provide useful comparative material.

First let us look at the proposals made in 1598 by an unidentified reformer with, apparently, a great deal of inside information. The depth of his knowledge indicates that he was an officer in the ordnance. It should also alert us to a common danger in assessing reform proposals in Tudor and Stuart England: they were often 'covers' for attempts at personal gain or elements in an internal office power struggle.

The 1598 report

The 1598 reform project was addressed to the ordnance commissioners. Basically, it can be divided into seven sections of complaints followed by the reformer's suggested remedies. The first, most general, complaint was that 'through ignorance or ambition of some Th'officers whoe (not knoweinge or forgettinge theire owne place have derogated from others and arrogated unto themselves much more then is due unto them)' have made the ordnance office 'Stranglie caried and Confused'.[40] The recommended cure for such ignorance or arrogance was to create distinct job descriptions for each office and thus, in essence, rationalise each office according to function. This would reduce the friction and contention between the officers which, as we have seen, regularly disrupted the office.

The next problem discussed was the poor organisation and mismanagement of the 'great stores' under the control of the keeper of the stores, Mr John Lee. Lee, as part of his running battle with Richard Paulfreyman, had used his authority to prevent Paulfreyman from assuming his duties as keeper

---

[38] Ibid. SP 39/9/106, sign manual, 30 July 1618. More than thirty of his friends and relatives, including Sir Henry Lee, each stood £100 in bond in surety for him; to this was added his own personal bond for £500.
[39] See also BL, MS Sloane 871, fo. 141, copy of Linewray's book, which was included in a collection of documents on ordnance reform with material up to 1627.
[40] PRO, SP 12/268/13, project for ordnance office reform, [July?] 1598.

of the small guns in order to usurp the functions for himself. Moreover, Lee was already over-committed and was charged with allowing the keys to the stores to be kept by his servants one of whom was supposedly 'a very lewd man'. To settle the first of these problems, the reformer recommended that the keeper of the small guns be established by patent as had previously been the case under Henry Halder. As to Lee's mismanagement, rather than recommending his dismissal for incompetence (a drastic solution seldom carried out in the bureaucracy of the time), it was recommended that two special keys be made up for the stores, one to be given to an appointee of Lee and one to an appointee of the commissioners. Both keys, presumably, would be needed before the stores could be opened. This 'dual key' control system might have helped restrict unaccompanied, possibly corrupt, access to the stores if it had been adopted, but it spoke little for Lee's honesty.

The third reform proposal dealt with the problem of the office's gunpowder store. It was recommended that the gunpowder patentee be paid by the lieutenant of the office as had previously been the case, rather than directly by the exchequer in order to insure a quality product. The reformer also complained that the powder was being stored with the match in the storehouses in such great stacks that the old powder was on the bottom and was thus never used until it was damp and unserviceable. He recommended for security purposes that a new powderhouse be built in the White Tower and that extra space be allowed for a better rotational system to ensure that the older powder was used first.

The fourth recommendation was that a staple be established of all the principal munitions which was to be automatically replenished. In addition, the storehouse at Rochester was to be expanded and used for this purpose for naval supplies since, according to Riddlesden, clerk of the ordnance, there were no storerooms large enough at Chatham.

The next problem to be addressed was the failure to pay the merchants, artificers and craftsmen promptly. The reformer accused the suppliers of taking advantage of the time-lag between supply of items and receipt of payment for those items as an excuse to raise their prices. The cure for this was to pay them on a monthly basis which would, supposedly, bring prices down. No mention was made of the fact that the craftsmen or merchants were in any way justified in their price increases due to the lax method of payment. The reformer saw price rises as vaguely unethical tricks which were only partly justified by the failure of the ordnance officers to pay the craftsmen promptly. Even this knowledgeable observer was not able to comprehend the economic forces which would necessitate some financial penalty or price increase because of the government's failure to pay its bills promptly, let alone the play of supply and demand in the marketplace.

The sixth and last general section of complaints was a direct attack on the self-interest and corruption within the office. The appointment of George Hogge as clerk of the deliveries in succession to his father, Brian Hogge, despite his lack of any skill in the office, came under direct attack. The writer declared that the six years of work which had been done by John Linewray to reform that office was now being undone by Hogge's appointment as joint clerk of deliveries with Linewray. The recommendation was that one or the other individual be appointed to hold the office, and there is no doubt that the reformer felt that Linewray was the only possible choice.

In addition, the establishment of special yearly allowances for each of the ordnance officers was criticised as was the general tendency towards financial carelessness and laxity within the office. This unusually detailed attack on various individuals and practices within the ordnance office points out many areas in need of reform. Although few of the substantive proposals were adopted, changes did occur within the office, possibly as a result of this project. Lee remained as keeper of the stores, but Paulfreyman was granted his patent as keeper of the small guns. Hogge and Linewray held the joint office of clerk of deliveries for three more years, until it was finally granted solely to Linewray. The powder store was eventually moved to a new storehouse in the White Tower, although this was not until much later. Payment for gunpowder continued to be made out of the exchequer rather than by the lieutenant. Artificers were still lucky to be paid quarterly and ordnance officers continued to fight for their 'turf' and to expand their personal status in the office with no effective attempt to establish a truly functional basis for organisation.

The impact of attempt at reform was limited, yet it was clearly an interesting initiative in office reorganisation drawn up by someone who seemed to have an in-depth knowledge of office problems. If one had to speculate on authorship, one would have to say that the reformer was someone inside the office, with an interest in more efficient and honest management, although self-interest cannot be excluded. One of the few individuals who might fit this description is John Linewray. Although evidence is lacking, it is probable that Linewray was the author of this proposal. If this was the case, the 1598 proposal was therefore a preliminary to the more comprehensive, yet more political, report on abuses made by him in 1601.

The 1601 report

The report to the commissioners for the ordnance office in 1601 by John Linewray adds a great deal to our knowledge of corruption within the ordnance office.[41] Linewray exposed a wide range of corrupt practices uncovered

---

[41] BL, MS Sloane 871, fos 127–51b, copy of Linewray's book. This report, alleging that over the years £60,000 had been embezzled, was, according to an unknown correspondent of Sir Robert Cecil in 1601, probably exaggerated: HMC, *Salisbury*, xi. 551.

in the course of his investigations while acting for the commissioners for abuses Sir Drew Drury, Sir John Peyton and others.[42]

According to Linewray, and echoing the 1598 report, the most common form of corruption in the ordnance office was the forging of false indentures for receipt and delivery. Both William Paynter and Sir William Pelham (clerk of the ordnance and lieutenant of the ordnance, respectively) had been previously convicted of siphoning-off over £11,000 using that method. These false records allowed officers to embezzle munitions without fear of discovery and to then sell them for their own profit. Richard Bowland (keeper of the stores 1572–89) was charged with embezzling almost £60,000 in this way although this was probably an exaggeration. More realistically, in 1593 surveyor John Powell was convicted of embezzling £1,200 by the use of false indentures.

In addition, Linewray accused some of the officers of collusion in fixing higher prices with suppliers, presumably with some of the excess being returned to the officers from the merchants. Some examples of the resultant price increases included an almost 40 per cent rise over recent years in prices for cases of plate, pullies and camphor (used for 'fireworks', or fire-bombs against ships). Linewray also protested against the practice of having the officers who were authorised to receive goods into the stores being the same as those who were to be held financially accountable for those stores. In this unique attack on conflict of interest, Linewray was attempting to ensure that other officers who were not directly involved in a transaction should be present to supervise or at least to verify the supply action. This would have helped restrict potential abuses by officers who discharged financial responsibility on their own authority.

Linewray proposed a series of administrative reforms to correct the worst of these abuses. These included changes in procedures to insure that warrants were on hand before issuing supplies, closer supervision of the proofing process to prevent the stealing of powder and shot before it had been proved and thus before the office became accountable for it, and ensuring that no faulty remains of supplies coming off ships were taken. Officers had apparently been keeping the excess, unlisted remains, and selling them. In addition, Linewray recommended that other 'neutral' officers be involved in the receipt and issue process to double-check warrants, indentures and quantities of supplies processed. In part this was probably a self-interested attempt to involve the clerk of the deliveries in the procedures for the receipt of goods. The inclusion of that officer in a receiving process which already included the lieutenant, the keeper of the stores, the clerk of the ordnance and the surveyor, would have added complexity to the system without adding

---

[42] Commission of inquiry established 10 Dec.1600 by the privy council: *APC 1599–1600*, 817–18. Other members included, 'Mr. Dr.' Caesar, Mr Wilbraham, William Waad and Henry Maynard.

perceptibly to the security of the transaction unless the individual holding that office was to be trusted.[43]

Here again we see that even reformers in the office were failing to see the true reason for the problem. Administrative organisation or reorganisation alone was not sufficient to ensure official probity since checks and balances do not function without a well-paid, highly trained civil service. As long as offices were held by underpaid individuals whose sense of loyalty was less to the administrative system than to their personal power and office, no amount of administrative tinkering or interlocking office ledgers could solve the problem.

Not content with merely reorganising the ordnance office, Linewray took the unusual and important step of recommending that other branches of the government should bear a share of responsibility for abuses in the sale and transportation of munitions. In particular he condemned the sloth and corruptibility of the court of the exchequer in trying cases of illegal shipment of goods which had been sold to merchants through the corrupt ordnance office. His accusation that for £10 the court would discharge an offender of a £100 fine rings true, especially to modern ears accustomed to the abuse of plea-bargaining, although specific examples of this practice are lacking.

Nor was the exchequer alone in these abuses. The officers of the custom houses were accused of winking at concealed goods (especially the searcher 'to whom no certeyne fee belongeth') and allowing goods under restraint such as iron ordnance and gunpowder to pass unchallenged. These goods could only have been obtained by merchants with the connivance of the ordnance officers, but the customs officials also had some responsibility for helping to create a market for these goods. The solution, according to Linewray, was for the queen to take the customs into her own hands rather than allowing it to be run by the customs farmers. The queen should also fire all the customs officers including the common measurers, packers, 'wayers' and 'gagers', and reappoint only honest subjects 'of good religion and creditt for a yearly rent' who were capable of taking out large performance bonds. Customs reorganisation on Linewray's model was not forthcoming nor did his recommendations for preventing further abuse in the ordnance office or the exchequer have their desired effect.

Complaints about corruption and abuses in the ordnance office seemed to slacken after Linewray's attack in 1601. However, this was probably due as much to the deceleration of the war with Spain and the defeat of the Irish rebels in the last years of Elizabeth as to any improvement within the office. The level of expenditure deceased rapidly from £16,300 in 1602 to £10,300 in 1603 and £6,400 in the following year. With less money, the scope for the potentially corrupt officer narrowed. Linewray took over the job of watchdog

---

[43] This attempt failed. The office remained outside that process and stayed a decidedly junior partner in office management.

within the office as surveyor of the ordnance and Carew returned from Ireland to take over daily responsibility for the office as lieutenant. While his deputy, Harvey, had not been accused of corruption, lack of strong management by the principal office-holder and the resulting feuds within the office had doubtless improved the climate for abuses.

The Dallison scandal

Carew's presence and less activity in the office, resulted in a period of fiscal and administrative retrenchment. This was to last until Carew left office as lieutenant in 1608 and became master of the ordnance. However Carew's direct involvement in the management of the office then seems to have diminished to such an extent that he virtually abdicated the running of the office to his successor as lieutenant, Sir Roger Dallison. In Dallison we see the extent to which one individual's ruthless and corrupt pursuit of personal gain could negate all the supposed checks on the abuse of power recommended or implemented in the preceding years. The Dallison case encapsulates all the weaknesses of the Tudor and Stuart administrative system; it was so destructive to good management in the ordnance office that the effects were to last at least until the end of the reign of James I while others – up to the highest levels of the privy council – were implicated in the scandal.

The exact extent of the depredations of Sir Roger Dallison upon the ordnance office and the exchequer is still unclear. Apparently from almost the first day in office, he began to embezzle, cheat and cover-up his activities on a shameless scale. He brought in supplies to the office from the usual contractors, but instead of paying them, he apparently took the money from the exchequer and put it to his own uses. He failed to pay the merchants and craftsman what was owed to them, either by payments from the ordinary allowance or from the money he received from various privy seals. Even his fellow officers were not paid from 1614 to 1616, although the ordinary of £6,000 per year was paid to him for all the years he was in office.[44] As if this were not enough, Dallison systematically used his position as lieutenant of the ordnance to obtain 60-year leases on large amounts of crown property in the Minories and proceeded to evict artificers from their various workshops in order to turn them into private residences which he could rent out to his own benefit. Commissioners investigating Dallison in 1620 ordered the return of these properties to their original owners, and thus to His Majesty's

---

[44] *CSPD James I, 1611–18*, 346, book of debts owed by Dallison through Jan. 1616 in part of £9,900 'in which he is indebted to the king and for which his lands are extended', [Jan? 1616]; PRO, SP 14/87/82, account of debts owed by his Majesty in the ordnance office [due to Dallison] for stores from 1 Apr. 1614 to 30 June 1616.

service, but another survey in 1623 reported that nothing had been done about actually returning the land.[45]

That these gross abuses were not exposed until 1616, almost eight years after Dallison began his career in fraud, tells us a great deal about the lack of any effective supervisory mechanisms. The quarter books of the office, supposedly reviewed every three months by the master of the ordnance, almost immediately showed that there was at least £3,000 which was not paid out of the ordinary to the suppliers. Much of what was owed to suppliers was kept on the books for years as a floating debt.[46] However, the first official audits of Dallison's accounts, taken in 1611 and 1612, do not give even a hint at a problem with the account for 1608 for they show Dallison with a surplus of £376 and in debt in 1609 for only £291. There was obviously something seriously wrong with the auditing procedures in the exchequer if the growing debt of the office did not show up in any official record outside of the ordnance office itself.[47] The fact that Dallison's accounts also do not agree with the indentures made out by the office itself in those years would also be significant if it were not for the fact that this was also the case for virtually all the years between 1590 and 1625. It does serve to point out that the lack of administrative consistency and insufficient exchequer oversight, along with that office's own administrative complexities, made it virtually impossible to discover fraud even after it had occurred. The situation was not helped at all by the gap between the year of account and the year in which the audit was taken for the years following 1609. The account for 1610 was not taken until 1619, long after the discrepancies had already been discovered by other, presumably less institutionalised and ossified, means while the accounts for 1611–15 had been taken, inexplicably, in the previous year, 1618.[48] It was not until the account had been taken for the years 1613–15 that the exchequer reported that Dallison was suddenly in debt to them for £9,887 4s. 10d. By this time Dallison had already been imprisoned and his lands seized to repay the debt. Such cumbersome auditing procedures, when coupled with obvious inconsistencies in the office's internal administrative procedures (for which Carew as Dallison's superior must share the blame), were of little value in discovering and remedying fraud.

---

[45] Ibid. SP 14/176/8, order in council for lands to be restored, 2 Dec. 1623; SP 14/156/13, fo. 38, survey of the Tower and certificate of what had been done in response to the report of 4 July, 1620, 31 Dec. 1623. For a copy of the report of 4 July see BL, MS Harl. 1326, fos 94–5b, survey of forts 1623, 30 July 1623. This also includes a copy of the Tower survey of 31 Dec. 1623. See also SP 14/116/5, order in council, on report of Sir Edw. Cecil, of abuses in Tower, Minories, etc., 4 July 1620.
[46] Ibid. WO 54/5, 6.
[47] Ibid. SP 14/39, account of Sir Roger Dallison, 1608; E 351/2644, 2645; AO 1/1839/45, declared accounts of Sir Roger Dallison.
[48] Ibid. AO 1/1839/45, 1840/47, 48, 49, declared accounts of Dallison.

The Cranfield commission, 1618-19

The other, non-institutionalised, method for uncovering bureaucratic abuses was the special commission, which, as we have seen in the 1601 court of inquiry, could assist in uncovering fraud after the fact but which was apparently unable to stop illegal practices for any great length of time. The 1601 commission had discovered many frauds and slipshod procedures despite the host of special instructions given to the office in 1584, 1589, 1596 and 1597. The 1618 commission, led by Sir Lionel Cranfield and including the new lieutenant, Sir Richard Morison, the clerk of the ordnance, Francis Morice, and the surveyor of the ordnance, Sir John Kaye, has been shown by Michael Young to have been little more than an *ad hoc* committee to examine a new proposal for munitions, and not a far-ranging commission for reform as had previously been believed.[49] According to Young, the real work of reforming the ordnance was done by the commissioners of the navy, who had started their work in June 1618 under Sir John Coke, that 'guiding spirit of naval reform'.[50] One copy of the report of the commission listed the key officers and their traditional duties along with the statement that abuses in the office did not all result from a poorly organised office, but rather from neglect by the officers. The commissioners claimed, with some justification, that disorders arose

> onely from the neglect and bretch of his Ma[jesty's] direcions in his warante under the privye seale which may be prevented by the regular form of Interessing the whole office in the knowledge of all demand and receipte and by not suffering the Lieuten[a]nte alone to have power to keepe the moneyes concealed in his hande and to pay but whome he list.[51]

In essence, they saw that the rules were already in place for effective management of the office, but that a determined lieutenant such as Dallison could usurp all the financial functions into his own hands with few checks upon his behaviour. Other violations of traditional procedures included the failure to pay all suppliers promptly, in Dallison's case often only after a delay of two years, and the neglect of the yearly audit by the exchequer. Sloppiness and neglect, springing directly from Dallison's behaviour in office, were the concern of the commissioners rather than the remedying of any institutional weakness. The reform impulse in 1618–20 was to have as little lasting significance in most areas as had previous initiatives.

---

[49] Young, 'Illusions of grandeur'. Young's persuasive re-examination of Cranfield's role in the reform of the ordnance office gives us a much clearer picture of administrative reform in the early seventeenth century than that of Menna Prestwich, although her work on Cranfield remains the best overall assessment of Cranfield's wider role in government.
[50] Ibid. 57
[51] PRO, SP 12/237/114, partial copy, with the answers of the ordnance officers, of Cranfield's report on the ordnance, [1618].

The ordnance survey itself was mostly finished by early 1619, but implementing the reforms probably took second place in Cranfield's mind to his own need to arrange a profitable financial deal with the ordnance officers. Cranfield used his influence with the ordnance office to exchange his small income from the petty customs for the much more valuable land which had been seized from Sir Roger Dallison and then given to the ordnance officers to help pay the debts which Dallison had accrued. In return for this deal, it seems clear that Cranfield ensured that any major reform within the office would be left up to the ordnance officers themselves and thus the shady profits of the minor officers and clerks could continue without interference from the government. Despite Prestwich's declaration that Cranfield's role in reform of the ordnance and other governmental agencies (i.e. the wardrobe, the household, and the navy) was 'crucial', this now seems doubtful.[52] Likewise the claims made by the king in 1621, and echoed since by historians, that Cranfield's 'reform movement' of 1617–19 saved the government huge sums of money. In particular, in a speech to parliament on 30 June 1621, James I stated that he had saved £18,000 per year on the navy 'and for the ordnance, that is brought from 34,000l. [to 14,000l.] and yet better served then before'.[53] Since the ordnance office, according to my calculations, spent, on average less than £8,000 per year from 1608 to 1621, it is difficult to see where the king obtained his figures. Even at the height of the Irish rebellion in 1599, when expenses were at a post-Armada peak, the ordnance office spent but £21,600 for the year.[54] Only in 1624, when one finds the massive amount of the subsidy being spent on arms (in excess of £40,000) does one find such huge expenses as James used for comparison. Perhaps James was referring to the decreases in the size of the ordnance office debt, but even that does not account for a savings of £20,000. His figures remain puzzling.

Sir Roger Dallison could not have been so successful in his rapacious dealings in the ordnance if he had not been aided and abetted by other individuals within the Stuart government. This does not necessarily mean other officers of the ordnance, since the powers of the lieutenant, especially those involved with the paying of suppliers and the handling of the office

---

[52] Prestwich, *Cranfield*, 248. For her clear exposition of the extreme complexities of the Dallison land issue see pp. 393–9. Her comments that 'The ordnance had been scandalously mismanaged' and that Dallison (miscalled by her the master of the ordnance) was, as a client of the Howards, 'as fraudulent and rapacious as his patrons' seem fully borne out by the evidence. See also pp. 218–19.

[53] *Commons debates 1621*, ii. 8–9. Notestein's statement that 'there seems no doubt that the latter was reduced from £34,000 to £14,000' was echoed by Prestwich and other writers on the period have repeated these inflated figures. See for example Conrad Russell, *The crisis of parliaments*, London – New York 1971, 290. All seem to have believed this claim and seem to have been mistaken.

[54] PRO, AO 1; E 351, declared accounts for the years. See also Young, 'Illusions of grandeur', 60–1.

funds, were such that no subordinate officer could have effectively restrained him. However, their silence for so many years certainly allows us to charge them with the sin of omission in failing to report their superior's dealings. Even when their superior was not paying them their salaries they do not seem to have complained, except for one hint in the Suffolk case which indicates they may have said something to the Lord Treasurer which he ignored.

The Dallison scandal also leaves us unable to explain the behaviour of the experienced and capable master of the ordnance at the time: Lord Carew. Certainly Carew must be blamed for failing to adequately supervise the activities of his lieutenant. It seems, however, that no investigation even hinted at implicating or blaming Carew for any of Dallison's shortcomings. Either he was being protected by his numerous friends at court, or else the commissioners felt that it was not the function of the master to supervise the ordnance in any meaningful way. Carew's role remains unclear.

The major responsibility for failing to detect Dallison's corruption seems to lie with the offices of the exchequer and of the lord treasurer since their financial procedures were specifically designed to prevent such flagrant corruption. Yet, as we have seen, no accounts were taken of Dallison from 1612 to 1618 and even those taken in 1618 and 1619, after proof of corruption was available, failed to detect exactly how or when Dallison's embezzlements occurred. Such blindness implies high level corruption and complicity in Dallison's actions. It is thus no surprise that the commission of inquiry moved on to examine the exchequer in 1619 and caught a very large fish indeed in its nets: Thomas Howard, first earl of Suffolk, a former lord chamberlain and by then lord treasurer of England.

Lord Treasurer Suffolk was deeply implicated in the Dallison affair, and his case shows how limited were the built-in checks on corruption within Stuart administrative procedures.[55] In a long and informal report on the investigation into Suffolk's activities, Sir John Finet reported to the earl of Salisbury (Sir Robert Cecil's son and Suffolk's son-in-law) that after only a few witnesses had been called, it quickly became apparent to the investigators that there was 'a double hand in the disposition of the 6,000l. allotted yearly by his Majesty for the payment of officers and other charges belonging to the ordnance'.[56] The ordnance books had not been brought into the exchequer on a regular basis as required by both ordnance office and exchequer administrative procedures. Thus, through Suffolk's negligence, Dallison's failure to pay the suppliers and the officers' wages was not detected. The Court of Star Chamber, which investigated the charges, was told that 'in the precedent

---

[55] The many charges against Suffolk show just how deeply he was involved in a wide range of shady practices including mishandling of the alum mines, embezzling money sent from the United Provinces in payment for the cautionary towns before their return to Dutch control, and other charges of malfeasance in office: HMC, *Salisbury*, xxii. 96–7. 27–9, Sir John Finet to earl of Salisbury, Oct. 1619.
[56] Ibid. 94–5, 100–1 (22, 27, 29 Oct. 1619).

Treasurer's time Dallison was not to be found in arrearages, but while my Lord of Suffolk was Treasurer he grew in arrears in the space of 2 years and a half above 9,000l'.[57] This was made worse by the accusation that not only had Suffolk continued to pay the ordinary allowance to Dallison, he even paid him an additional £2,500 after he had left office.[58] Serjeant Richardson, testifying in Suffolk's defence, answered that Suffolk should not be held accountable for the use to which the ordinary allowances had been put, for that was solely the responsibility of the lieutenant. As for not bringing in the books on a regular basis, Richardson used the weak defence of ignorance. The errors, according to Richardson:

> were affirmed to grow from Dallison's protestations to my Lord that they were subscribed, [verified by the other officers] who then of that state and reputation of honesty might easily beget belief in his Lordship; so as it the earl, he said, had erred it is not of wilfulness but of too much credulity, much less of corruption, as by the bill he stood accused.[59]

In other words, Suffolk had believed Dallison for over two years without asking for any proof. Such credulity in a lord treasurer is in itself almost a crime, even if one gives Suffolk the benefit of the doubt on the charges of active compliance. Acting upon Suffolk's order, which they had no reason to doubt, the appropriate tellers of the exchequer had issued the sums mentioned to Dallison. Suffolk had not even examined the books on an annual basis as he was supposed to do. It was quite clear that Suffolk was much to blame for this failure:

> he should with his own [eyes] have seen their books brought in due time and order, wherein failing his fault was wilful and punishable, and though he found no corruption of gain proved about the ordnance, he found in him corruption of affection in yielding more to his friend [Dallison] than to his duty.[60]

Although many of Dallison's abuses dated from before he took office in 1614, Suffolk was fined and imprisoned.

The Suffolk case, which ended with his disgrace and discharge from office, a £30,000 fine, and a spell in the Tower, was just one instance of the attack on corruption in the ordnance office and the rest of the government in the last few years of the reign of James I. However, the results were limited in nature and short-term in effect. Dallison was sacked, as was Suffolk, Lord Admiral Nottingham and others, and yet the ordnance office successfully resisted true administrative reform. The system continued to depend on

---

[57] Ibid. 95.
[58] A. P. P. Keep, 'Star Chamber proceedings against the earl of Suffolk and others', *EHR* xiii (1898), 716.
[59] Ibid.
[60] Ibid. 110. Finet's request that Salisbury 'burn this hasty and ill-digested relation intended to no man's reading but your Lordship's' was obviously ignored.

individual honesty, especially in the office of lieutenant, despite attempts to involve more officers in the lieutenant's role as office paymaster. Even Cranfield, the supposed great reformer, got caught up in the ordnance web, both in his shady land deals and in his failure to ensure that the gunpowder contracts remained in force. All these charges were thrown up against him in May 1624 at his trial in the House of Lords.[61]

While one may argue about the political motivation behind the attack on Cranfield, there is little question that his dealings with the ordnance office had not improved office efficiency. Cranfield's plea during his trial that his policies had not denuded the stores of their supplies but that 'if they have less Proportions of some Sorts of Provisions than were set down in the Commissioners Books, yet they have more of other Sorts of Provisions which have since been thought more useful and more necessary' was ingenious, but a look at the state of the office in 1624 indicates otherwise. The quarterly allowance had not been paid since 1617 except for a few hundred pounds per quarter for officers' salaries. What supplies had been provided in the intervening years had been paid for by privy seals. This method of managing the office virtually ensured that there would be a glut of supplies for one short period of the year and a dearth during the rest of the time. This prevented the ordnance officers from arranging for a regular, systematic supply for the office to insure that a 'staple' of crucial items was on hand. Without a regular allowance, old supplies could not be maintained, new supplies could not be purchased, and craftsmen could not be satisfied. The suppliers, faced with wildly fluctuating periods of great demand followed by none, probably grew wary of supplying the office at all. Management by privy seal, the result, doubtless, of an understandably deep distrust of the lieutenant's ability to cope honestly with a regular allowance, created more problems than it solved. There was less scope for corruption within the office since the officers handled less money, but direct management by Cranfield's office ensured that the office was less capable of performing its primary duty of procuring and maintaining the arms of the kingdom.

The evils of Cranfield's mismanagement of the ordnance were amply exposed in his trial before the House of Lords. The most damaging charges stemmed from an examination of the poor state of ordnance supplies in 1624. This was especially true in the case of gunpowder supply where a clause in the contract with John Evelyn, the powdermaker, allowed him to stop bringing powder into the office if he had not been paid for over three months. Although the contract had been made, and broken by failure to pay Evelyn after the first five months in the previous lord treasurer's time (Lord Mandeville), it is apparent that Cranfield did very little to solve the problem and improve the flow of gunpowder into the stores. In 1617 the powder store contained 300 lasts of gunpowder; by 1624 it was down to only 133. The

---

[61] LJ iii. 329–34, 367–8. By then he was the earl of Middlesex and lord treasurer.

commissioners who ran the survey estimated that this left the stores short by at least 188 lasts which would take a cash infusion of almost £16,000 to remedy.[62] In all, the surveyors estimated that the stores under the strict financial policy of Cranfield had shrunk to a point where over £50,000 was necessary to return them to the status of 1617. While Cranfield was faced with a series of financial crises which left him with little room to manoeuvre, the sorry state of the chief storehouse in the realm suggests that he had engaged in false economy. The kingdom was not prepared for war in 1625 and Cranfield must share at least some of the blame.

It is possible to say that while charges of corruption in the ordnance office throughout this period were perhaps exaggerated and often self-interested tirades, there were still enough genuine instances of corruption to hamper the efficient running of the office. To some extent this was an inherent problem in the office since the nature of Tudor and Stuart administrative organisation left many loopholes for private gain and provided little in the way of an official salary to allow the officers to resist temptation. However, as the commission of 1618–20 indicated, the organisation of the office was such that if all established procedures had been followed, the opportunities for corrupt behaviour would probably have been reduced. This judgment is reinforced by the relatively petty abuses of the period of Carew's lieutenancy when compared with those of Morrison and Dallison. At least in the cases of Carew and Dallison, we know that the same administrative checks and balances existed for each lieutenant, yet the personal honesty and ability of Carew ensured a very different result from that obtained under Dallison's administration. Thus we can see that office procedures are not as important to the study of corruption in the ordnance office as the personalities of the office-holders. The key to stopping corruption lay in the appointment of high quality officers and in the careful supervision of those officers rather than in adding new layers of complexity to office management procedures.

The importance of personality comes through clearly when we note the very different measures of success of the tenure in office of the earl of Salisbury as lord treasurer when compared with the earl of Suffolk. Both men had the same responsibilities, yet supervised the ordnance office accounts in very different ways. Salisbury, despite the resounding failure of the Great Contract, was a model of efficiency and honesty when compared with Suffolk. Suffolk used his office for personal gain on a grand scale and neglected his duties to such an extent that the ordnance office was allowed to be sacked by Dallison.

---

[62] See the survey comparing 1617 with 1624 in PRO, WO 55/1680. While the gunpowder and smaller, more perishable, supplies were in a sad state, the brass ordnance was in good condition and quite plentiful. However, the iron ordnance, much of which had doubtless been sold off during the years of peace, was more that 400 pieces short with a value of over £2,538. The surveyors estimated that it would take £15,500 to purchase cannon shot in the quantity needed for the 'staple' or fixed minimum supply.

Other reform efforts

The ordnance office was not the first office to receive the attention of Cranfield and the other reformers. In fact it was the household, one of the largest of the court departments, that Cranfield first attempted to reform. Relative success in reforming that carried him into the navy, then into the treasury, the exchequer, the court of wards and the wardrobe. It seemed that each investigation uncovered new abuses and new potential for saving the crown some of its hard earned revenue. While this is not the place for an exhaustive examination of these reform efforts, it might be instructive to take a general overview to identify points of comparison with the ordnance.[63]

The household, Cranfield's first target, was a particularly lucrative one. It was a notoriously expensive department with a reputation for over-staffing, peculation and for 'being a tangled nexus of enmeshed interests'.[64] Other attempts to save money and reform the household in the reign of Elizabeth had failed under the pressures of court connections, the self-interest of suppliers to the household, and the corruption of the key officers. While some of the increased cost of the office during the reign of Elizabeth can be blamed on the inflation of the later sixteenth century, much of it resulted from the increased numbers, the inefficiency, and the corruption of household officials.

Cranfield and his specially appointed sub-commission of reformers took the bit between their teeth and launched an in-depth investigation of household expenditures. Cranfield himself, in a practice he was to use in many later reform attempts, conducted detailed inventories of household purchases, concluding at one point that at least 132 1/2 oxen and 1,248 sheep were not accounted for in the household figures.[65] Such attention to detail undercut the attempts of the household officers to justify their expenses.

To cut back on expenses, the reformers deleted courses from courtiers' meals, sold leftovers, required the using of an entire candle rather than discarding it after the first part burned down, and a host of other seeming retrenchments. However, as a result of such detailed investigations and resultant reforms, the household was saving £18,000 a year by 1621.[66] So successful was Cranfield, that he managed to prove to the king and the court what could be achieved through zealous reform. The way was clear for more wide-ranging investigations into the way the crown did business.

This first attempt at reform set the standard for the others in the later years of James I. The special commissions, chaired by Cranfield and working

---

[63] For a new discussion of the various attempts to reform the navy see Linda Levy Peck, *Court patronage and corruption in early Stuart England*, Boston, Mass. 1990, 106–33.
[64] Prestwich, *Cranfield*, 206–7.
[65] Ibid. 208.
[66] James gave this figure to the House of Commons in 1621: *Commons' debates, 1621*, ii. 8–9.

outside the normal court structure and thus outside the normal patron–client relationships, delved deeply into the office in question, forced it to account for each and every expenditure, and made the officers justify their procedures. Reforms were then proposed and enacted, often after painful negotiations with the officers of that department, whatever officers were left after the investigation. The reform commissions would obtain real, if often short-term benefits, in part by its ability to cow the regular department officers into compliance.

There was a price to be paid for household reform, a price duplicated in each future reform effort. This included the permanent alienation of numerous courtiers and small court officials whose income, power or perquisites were diminished by the reforms. Such alienation was exacerbated by each reform effort, thus insuring the eventual accretion of enemies with grudges against the head of the commissions – Cranfield – just waiting for a mis-step on his part. In addition, the various suppliers of foodstuffs to the household were doubtless discommoded by the cutbacks in purchases and by increased scrutiny of the accounts. Cranfield recognised the extent of this problem and during his later reform efforts in the wardrobe, attempted to cope with it by meeting merchants and suppliers. In this instance, he lectured the suppliers on the new regime and on how much value he wanted to get in the future for His Majesty's money. However, he also held out the promise of paying accounts promptly, which much have impressed the suppliers.[67] Cranfield was astute enough to see the need to bring all the elements of the department – suppliers as well as officers – into line with the new reforms if he was to be successful in long-term retrenchment.

In each later attempt at reform, in the navy, the treasury, the exchequer, the ordnance and the wardrobe, Cranfield and the other reformers followed a similar course. The reformers audited the accounts, fought the entrenched interests of the office, attempted to cut back expenses, located and replaced corrupt officials, co-opted the other officers, worked with the office suppliers and managed to obtain some savings for the crown. That these savings were often transitory, and equally often consumed by the avarice of Cranfield, should not detract from the attempt of the reformers to clean the house. To match the savings of £18,000 in the household, we find a savings of almost £22,000 in the wardrobe, almost as much in the navy and increased revenue from the customs, the wards, crown lands and old debts. In the Court of Wards alone, revenue rose from £29,000 to £37,000 under Cranfield's hand. The reformers' diligence may have gored many a courtier's ox, but the kingdom, with the exception of the ordnance, seemed to benefit from their work.[68]

The ordnance office reforms of 1618 must therefore be seen, not just as another in a long line of attempts to make the office more efficient, but also

[67] Ibid. 230.
[68] Ibid. 199–252.

as part of a broad based attempt to investigate and realign the entire system of crown offices. The reforms of 1618 were closely inter-related. Each reform attempt picked up clues during investigations in one office that tied into yet another. For example, the Suffolk case, which was the highlight of the reform of the treasury, depended heavily on information gleaned from the Dallison scandal enquiry. The navy investigations doubtless led the commissioners to the ordnance office since that office dealt so closely with the navy. The need for financial retrenchment, so apparent after investigations in the treasury and exchequer, led Cranfield into taking over the Court of Wards, one of the biggest sources of crown revenue. All the reforms were interconnected both in the person of Cranfield and the flow of information that led from one office of the crown to another.

It was like the proverbial run in a sock. When one pulled on one loose string, it connected to another and caused the entire sock to unravel. The reforms of the later period of James's reign, of which the ordnance was just a part, attempted to trace each thread to its logical conclusion. The Jacobean sock unravelled all too well. The reformers, however, were unable to knit a new sock which would stand the test of time. Savings were transitory and some of the reforms caused almost as many problems as they solved.

Conclusions

It would be safe to conclude that comparative judgements which state that Stuart administrative procedures were better or worse than those used by Tudor office-holders are of little value. There was no 'decline' in administrative or bureaucratic organisational ability from the Tudor to the Stuart periods. Instead, it appears that the relative inefficiency and corruption of the later period was due in large part to the individuals who were appointed to office. This judgment relies to a certain extent upon hindsight, but it is necessary in some way to explain why the same administrative network created such dissimilar results over the period from 1585 to 1625. From our perspective it is possible to see that only through the creation of a civil service based on ability along with better accounting and inventory procedures, could the office of the ordnance have silenced its critics and performed its duty of being prepared for war. Corruption, real or imagined, was a symptom of this administrative deficiency and served to hinder the performance of the office's mission without crippling it completely.

The various attempts at reform were able to accomplish some small savings, although often at an enormous cost. Corruption and inefficiency in the ordnance, while beaten back, would nevertheless remain a problem within the office. The 'unsavoury reputation' was easy to gain and hard to lose. That reputation would also complicate the always uneasy relationship between the ordnance office and those craftsmen, artificers and merchants upon whom it relied for the production of most of the supplies brought into the stores.

4

Ordnance Supplies and Suppliers: The Great Ordnance

> And, O you mortal engines, whose rude throats
> The immortal Jove's dread clamors counterfeit
>
> – Shakespeare, *Othello*, act III, scene iii

The ordnance office had to deal with a wide variety of merchants, craftsmen and entrepreneurs in order to accomplish the task of procuring arms for the main stores of the kingdom. Despite a small internal arms and equipment production capability, the ordnance office relied heavily upon independent and semi-independent craftsmen and contractors for the majority of the items required for the stores. The office maintained its own carpenters, wheelers, blacksmiths, plumbers, bowyers and fletchers. However, for speciality items requiring a substantial capital investment, such as heavy ordnance, small arms, or gunpowder, the office contracted directly with the manufacturers. Even in these instances some craftsmen were kept on a form of retainer with many of them having special titles and salaries such as 'Her Majesties Gunfounder of Copper Ordnance' who was paid a salary out of the household accounts of £12 3s. 4d. per year.[1] In addition, there were a host of smaller craftsmen and merchants who provided all the other miscellaneous supplies needed to support an army in the field or a fleet of ships at sea.

In order to analyse the overall effectiveness of the ordnance office it will be necessary to look at some of these craftsmen and merchants and the products they supplied. What items did they supply and what was the state of the basic arms industry in England in war and peace in this period? To what extent did the government and the ordnance officers supervise each industry in an attempt to control the quantity and quality of arms and other military supplies? How much did each item cost and did these prices rise during the period in question? Any answers to these questions, however tentative, should tell us a great deal about the relationship between the central government, its military bureaucracy, and the basic armaments industries which

---

[1] Other examples include 'Her Majesty's Founder of Iron Shot and Gunstone Maker', paid 6d. per day or £9 2s. 6d. per year; 'His Majesty's Gunsmith of Small Arms'; a saltpetre maker; and a 'Gonnestonemaker', all of whom were paid the same as the founder of shot: PRO, SP 12/221, book of crown offices, [1588?].

inevitably grew up during the years of Elizabeth's wars. The extent of the collapse of the network of suppliers in the years of peace from 1604 until the late 1620s when war again appeared likely should also prove of interest. How then did the government cope with the need to resuscitate these industries and were they successful? The war effort of the late 1620s must be seen in the context of the late sixteenth-century conflict with Spain. Central to this study of the war industries is an examination of the manufacture and sale of the heavy, or great ordnance, from which the office took its name.

The great ordnance

Few other aspects of early English industrial development have attracted so much interest as the rise of the iron gunfounding industry.[2] While the role of armaments in the overall story of the rise of English industry was relatively small, the centrality of its production to the security of the state and the nationalistic overtones of the necessity of domestic manufacture make it a key part of pre-Industrial Revolution studies of manufacturing techniques and government involvement in industry.

The history of artillery production in England can truly be said to have begun with Henry VIII, who imported gunfounders into England to start a domestic industry rather than rely upon foreign sources.[3] Initially, production was almost entirely of brass ordnance, since brass was easier to work with, lighter and easier to recast if cracked. However, it was much more expensive and while it remained an important element in the artillery parks of Elizabeth and James, iron pieces gradually replaced brass as new techniques were developed to allow for their rapid and cheap production.

Early production of iron guns, first forged then cast iron, centred on the Weald area of Kent and Sussex.[4] At least nine furnaces in that area were

---

[2] Works on the increase in production and use of artillery include Charles J. Ffoulkes, *The gun-founders of England*, 2nd edn, York, Penn. 1969, and Hogg, *English artillery*. In addition, the massive works by Shubert and Nef on the rise of the iron and coal industries necessarily included sections on gunfounding and armaments production: H. R. Schubert, *History of the British iron and steel industry*, London 1957; J. U. Nef, *The rise of the British coal industry*, 2 vols, London 1932. The critical area of the Sussex Weald has also had its historian in Ernest Straker, whose *Wealden iron*, London 1931, remains the starting point for anyone examining the origins of iron production in England.

[3] Hogg, *English artillery*, 209.

[4] Schubert, *British iron*, 246–7; Ffoulkes, *The gun-founders*, 121. Forged iron (also called wrought-iron) guns were popular before the development of better ways to cast stronger iron pieces. The process involved welding iron bars together and wrapping bands of iron around them to strengthen the piece. It was a very time-consuming and crude procedure, and the piece was very heavy. However, the result was considerably stronger than the more brittle early cast-iron pieces: ibid. 8–12.

capable of producing iron ordnance and shot by 1573.[5] Overall iron ordnance production by this time has been estimated at from 500 to 600 tons of iron ordnance per year.[6] This level increased slowly over the years as more furnaces in Sussex and other regions began producing iron. By around 1585, output had probably risen to 600–700 tons of ordnance per year, and went up almost to 1,000 tons by 1600.[7] It is likely that iron ordnance production decreased from this high point with the decline of the domestic market. As Straker has put it, 'The period from the death of Elizabeth till the outbreak of the Civil War was almost free from foreign wars, so the demand for guns and shot was small.'[8] By 1609 there were only five furnaces left in production which were capable of making iron ordnance: three in Sussex, one in Kent and one in Glamorgan, Wales.[9] In 1613 there were still only five furnaces remaining, and by 1620 only John Brown's furnace at Brenchley, Kent, was allowed to manufacture and sell iron ordnance. According to Brown, even this one furnace could produce more ordnance than the peacetime domestic market could absorb.[10]

The ordnance industry had more to deal with than just market forces, since the production of iron ordnance was a political problem as well as an economic one. The needs of the state were generally more crucial than the welfare of the gunfounders. As such, the control of those furnaces which were capable of producing iron ordnance was a matter of some interest to the government throughout the Tudor and Stuart periods. Domestic production had to be kept high enough to furnish the state and the merchants with a regular supply of ordnance without producing so much that the gunfounders would be tempted to sell the excess overseas to potential or actual enemies. Complaints of illegal trade often came from gunfounders on retainer from the ordnance office. In 1574, for example, Ralph Hogge, master gunstonemaker to the queen, complained to the privy council that his rivals were selling so much of their production overseas that 'yor enimie is better fourneshed with them than or owne country ships ar'.[11] He further requested that the privy council do something about limiting the number of the furnaces since he

---

[5] *CSPD Eliz. I, 1547–80*, 474–5, bonds of at least 40 owners of iron furnaces capable of producing ordnance in Kent, Surrey and Sussex, 15 Feb.– 16 Mar. 1573.
[6] Schubert, *British iron*, 250. Ralph Hogge's estimate in 1574 that some 4,000 tons were being produced per year must have been an exaggeration calculated to buttress his claim of dangerous over-production of ordnance leading to illegal sales overseas. Hogge held the monopoly in the export of iron ordnance at the time and was probably jealous of his profits.
[7] *CSPD Eliz. I, 1581–90*, 165–6, Wm. Pistor to Sec. Walsingham, [1585?]. Pistor was justifying his job as a searcher for illegally exported ordnance and may have exaggerated the amount produced and sold overseas.
[8] Straker, *Wealden iron*, 60.
[9] Schubert, *British iron*, 250.
[10] PRO, SP 15/42/28, 29, his Majesty's gunfounder to privy council, Dec. [?] 1620.
[11] Ffoulkes, *The gun-founders*, 74

estimated that the annual production of ordnance exceeded 4,000 tons (a wild exaggeration) and much of it would have to be sold overseas, 'either by lawfull meanes or by stelth'.[12] In that same year, probably in response to that complaint, the council ordered that all furnaces which were capable of casting iron were to take out bonds for £2,000 that they were not to cast ordnance without a license from the council and were not to sell any of it overseas without specific permission. The orders further specified that all founders were to bring their pieces to Tower Wharf to be sold and were to send in yearly returns to the master of the ordnance listing the number of guns produced and to whom they were sold.[13] Orders in 1619 further restricted all gunfounding activity to Kent and Sussex, again required that the guns be landed only at Tower Wharf in London and specified that the gun market in East Smithfield was to be the only place in the kingdom where they could be bought and sold.[14] The need to keep an eye on the production of this strategic resource demanded such drastic, direct control of the industry.

Despite increasing governmental interference with iron ordnance production, the quantity of ordnance remained adequate, perhaps even excessive, for national defence needs throughout the period of the war with Spain. This was true despite the decrease in the number of furnaces resulting from the political necessity of restricting the overseas sales of ordnance. The profit-margin for those allowed to participate in the legal manufacturing of ordnance was apparently enough by itself to sustain the industry. Iron ordnance generally sold for about £10 per ton up to 1598, declining to £8 and £9 per ton by 1600. This, when compared with the price for regular bar iron which averaged £2 less per ton, made iron ordnance a profitable item since the production costs were not too different.[15]

The decline in ordnance prices by 1600 was probably due to a slackening of demand since expenditure on the navy was temporarily frozen because of the escalating expense of the land forces in the Irish war. The navy was usually the major market for iron pieces, since brass ordnance cost from £40 to £60 per ton. The merchant fleet probably also bought a large number of iron pieces, but no firm figures exist.[16] The fact that it was reported that some

---

[12] Straker, *Wealden iron*, 55. Hogge also mentioned that more furnaces were being set up in Wales, thus adding to the problem of over-production and making control over where the guns were being sold extremely difficult.

[13] Oppenheim, *Royal navy*, 159. See also APC 1571-5, 254-5 (19 June 1574). Since the orders were repeated in 1588, 1601 and 1619 at least, and as there is no evidence of annual reports being filed in the lieutenant's office, it is likely that this initiative was in the long run unsuccessful. However, 32 bonds do exist for the first year: *CSPD Eliz. I, 1547-80*, 474.

[14] Oppenheim, *Royal navy*, 212. See also BL, MS Cotton Otho E, VIII, fo. 78.

[15] Schubert, *British iron*, 253; Oppenheim, *Royal navy*, 159.

[16] For collections of these bonds see PRO, E 101/64/23; SP 12/183/77; E 101/690/29, 30; E 122/91/13.

Spanish agents were willing to pay £22 per ton for iron ordnance in 1594 doubtless encouraged the over-production of some of the furnaces during the war years.[17]

Most iron ordnance was manufactured at the foundries in Brenchley, Horsemonden, Ashurst, Maresfield and Riverhall. The Weald area had several advantages over other foundries in Wales or Lancashire. Chief of these was proximity to the only official market for ordnance on Tower Wharf. Other advantages included ready access to water transport (the Medway was not far), the availability of shallow deposits of iron ore and a well-established charcoal industry.[18] In addition, the Weald had a long history of iron founding, and this helped to ensure that there were skilled, experienced iron workers on hand.

The guns were cast using loam moulds with a core inside so that the pieces came out of the mold with extremely rough and non-standard bores. The rough edges in the bores of the guns were cleaned using a radial drill. This method was different from that of the eighteenth century when solid pieces were cast which were then horizontally bored out to a very fine tolerance. The result of this early and crude method of casting was that each piece was different from any other so that there was no standard weight nor bore. Even Sir George Carew, a noted expert on artillery, was forced to admit in 1594 when asked about the weights of some demi-culverins,

> I cannot unlesse I did see the peaces . . . [since] The founders at no tyme do Cast these peeces so exactly but they dyffer many times : 2 : or : 300 wt in a peece so that without seeinge the peeces no man can precyslye tell what they wyll wayghe.[19]

After the pieces had been reamed out and weighed, they were dragged on sleds from the foundries to the nearest stream and then floated downstream to Milhall, in Kent. At Milhall they were loaded onto lighters or hoys for the short journey to London.

Once in London, each iron piece not already proofed would be tested for quality at the ordnance office by having two rounds fired through each by the

---

[17] The profit to be made through illegal sales was apparently worth the risk. The high bids made for their goods by the Spaniards also encouraged the English, and most historians, to believe that their ordnance was far superior to any in the world: Oppenheim, *Royal navy*, 159; Schubert, *British iron*, 253.

[18] Large quantities of timber were needed to make the charcoal required for the production of high quality, impurity-free, ordnance. So great was their use of timber, that the ironmasters found themselves in direct competition for this scarce resource with other industries. In one instance, sometime during the reign of James I, some petitioners at Cranbrook in Kent complained that nearby iron mills were disrupting the cloth trade through their excessive wood consumption: HMC, *Salisbury*, xxiv. 255, petition of James Cotford to the king [temp. James I].

[19] PRO, SP 12/249/43, Carew to Cecil, 31 July 1594.

master gunner of England and the other proofmaster.[20] This was the common practice during Elizabeth's reign. However, by 1618 there are regular entries in the ordnance office indenture books for sending powder, shot and proofmasters to Milhall to proof the ordnance before it was shipped.[21] This was a way of saving the cost of shipping inferior pieces to London only to have them fail proof there. However, when the travel costs of the proofmasters are added, the savings were probably minimal. In July 1625 Thomas Powell was indented £17 10s. for taking fourteen days to travel to Milhall to proof ordnance for 'the Newcastle ships' accompanying the expedition to Cadiz. With the cost of shipping the powder and shot to Milhall (in 1626 it cost £3 to ship 1,200 pounds of gunpowder, shot, ladles and sponges to Milhall for that purpose) the expense was clearly sizeable. On the other hand, if the piece failed proof at or near the foundry, the ordnance officers were in a much better position to demand an instant replacement. This fact alone probably made it worthwhile, in non-economic terms, to proof as near to the foundries as possible.

After the ordnance had passed proof, it was either brought into the ordnance office and an indenture made for each piece by weight, or else set out on Tower Wharf for merchants to buy. Since the pieces were far from being standardised, each piece was accounted for by its weight. This was listed on the indenture for each piece brought in and often engraved on the side. Any other engravings – coats of arms or gunfounders marks – were sometimes added to the indenture as an additional means of identifying the piece. Despite the variance in the bore size and weight of each piece, by the late sixteenth century the most common types could be relied upon to be close to the size of the pieces listed in table 2.[22]

While the Weald dominated iron ordnance production, there were attempts to establish smaller iron forges in various other parts of the country near supplies of iron, timber and water. In 1592, one Chrystofer Croftes, gent., was granted a warrant from the chancellor of the duchy of Lancaster to establish some iron mills there.[23] There is no evidence of any great success. There were also attempts to set up forges in Shropshire, but mainly for producing armour and small arms. Secretary Walsingham had apparently been very interested in dispersing the arms industry over a wide area of the country and between numerous craftsmen. However, when Sir Henry Lee tested some of the iron produced in these new forges, he found it 'greatly

---

[20] Ibid. WO 49/17.
[21] Ibid. For instances in the 1620s see WO 49/50, 54, 55.
[22] James Sheriffe's table of ordnance, taken from Hogg, *English artillery*, 26. For another table, which includes the number of horses required to pull each piece in a field environment see BL, MS Add. 6177, fo. 56b.
[23] *APC 1592–3*, 379–80, privy council to Sir Geo. Hastings, Sir Thomas Stanhope and Sir Humfry Ferryes, 9 July 1593.

Table 2
English ordnance, 1592

Piece	Calibre	Weight	Shot	Powder	Range
Cannon	8 in.	6,000lbs.	60lbs.	27lbs.	2,000
Demi-cannon	7	4,000	25–30	18	1,700
Culverin	5.5	4,500	$17^{1}/_{3}$	12	2,500
Demi-cul.	4.5	3,400	$9^{1}/_{3}$	8	2,500
Saker	3.5	1,400	$5^{1}/_{3}$	$5^{1}/_{3}$	1,700
Minion	3.25	1,000	4	4	1,600
Falcon	$2^{1}/_{3}$	800	3	3	1,500

(Range is in paces)

inferior to Hungarian iron' and, although in sympathy with the idea, rejected this specific project.[24]

The only other major production site for great ordnance was in Wales, probably in Glamorgan. However, this location often made the privy council uneasy with reports as early as 1591 that 'Hamburg men' in Bristol had been secretly buying the ordnance to resell overseas to the highest bidder.[25] There was also another forge, in the Taff valley near Cardiff, which was suppressed by the privy council in 1602 for allegedly 'losing' too much of the ordnance produced to Spanish merchants.[26] The difficulties of policing distant forges must have convinced the government of the wisdom of restricting the industry to the nearby Weald. As late as 1616, a forge owner was arrested in Glamorgan for illegally shipping ordnance from his furnace to Cardiff and then overseas. The ironmaster, Peter 'Seymaine', was arrested but escaped, which prompted the privy council to order some local justices of the peace to 'give presente order both that his forge and furnace may bee presently suppressed, and his fyer quit put out'.[27] Putting out such 'fyers' when there was a demand for the product was not easy and the control of illegal production and sale of iron ordnance was a continual problem for the council and for parliament.

It has proved very difficult to discover much about the individual gunfounders. In the ordnance office accounts one finds little more than the supplier's name, the item, its cost and the date supplied. For iron ordnance, the only two major suppliers throughout this period seem to have been

---

[24] *CSPD Eliz. I, 1581–90*, 692 (12 Oct. 1590).
[25] *CSPD Eliz. I, 1591–4*, 72–3, report of Thomas Cely to [Lord Treasurer and Lord Admiral], 17 July 1591.
[26] Rhys Jenkins, 'Early gunfounding in England and Wales', *Transactions of the Newcomen Society* xlix (1971–2), 145–52. The forge was owned by Samuel Mathews and leased to Peter Samuell. I am grateful to Dr Ian Roy for this reference.
[27] *APC 1616–17*, 47, letter from privy council to Sir Thomas Mansell and Sir John Stradlinge, JPs, 18 Oct. 1616.

Thomas Johnson and the various members of the Brown (or Browne) family. Thomas Johnson ran a foundry in Combe, Kent and was possibly a descendant of Harry Johnson, an alien who became a master gunner under Henry VIII.[28] Little is known about Johnson except that by the time of his death in 1596, he had obtained the title of 'Her Majesty's founder of Cast Iyron ordnance' and received a small stipend for the post.[29] Johnson supplied the ordnance office with at least 345 pieces of iron ordnance over the years 1584–93 according to a note in the state papers attested to by Sir George Carew and two under-officers.[30] In addition, he supplied many tons of round and 'cross barred' shot every year. In one delivery alone early in 1593 he supplied more than 26 tons of shot which, at £8 a ton for round shot and more for the bars which were thrust through them to make cross barred shot, cost over £256.[31]

Substantially more is known about the Browns, whose connection with iron ordnance and shot production dates back at least to 1512. By 1589 Thomas Brown had been granted a licence to cast iron ordnance at Ashurst in Sussex. By 1609, he stated he had produced over 463 tons of ordnance since 1591, averaging over 24 tons per year.[32] He was even granted a pension of 18d. per day for life in 1612 'in consideration of his extraordinary skill and experience' which was passed on to his son, John, in 1618.[33] John Brown was soon the master of his own furnace in Brenchly, Kent, which, if his figures are to be trusted, employed around two hundred men. With domestic demand so low in the peaceful years of James, there were only four furnaces in Sussex by 1618 still casting guns, with Brown holding the monopoly for selling guns to the Royal Navy. A courtier, Sackville Crowe, also worked a furnace at Maresfield and had obtained a similar monopoly for merchant vessels. Brown complained bitterly of this situation since, in order to keep his men gainfully employed, he felt he should have the monopoly or at least the access to both markets.

In 1621, Brown complained to Solicitor General Heath that he and his

---

[28] Thomas's father was John Johnson, a servant of Peter Baude from whom he learned how to cast iron ordnance: Ffoulkes, *The gun-founders*, 47, 121.

[29] PRO, WO 54/1.

[30] *CSPD Eliz. I, 1591–4*, 336, note by Carew, Powell and Bedwell on Johnson's ordnance, 1584–93, Mar. 1593.

[31] PRO, WO 49/17, 2 Jan. 1593. The shot provided was for culverins, demi-culverins, sakers, minions and falcons. The larger cannon and the smaller port pieces and murderers commonly used stone shot in order to create a shrapnel effect.

[32] Ffoulkes, *The gun-founders*, 75. Ordnance office records for the period 1593–1605, however, show him providing only iron shot to the office. He was paid over £1,290 for shot during the peak years of 1598–1601: PRO, WO 49. This would have been the equivalent of producing 12 major pieces of ordnance per year of the culverin or demi-culverin size or 40 of the smaller saker or minion pieces.

[33] Straker, *Wealden Iron*, 162. This despite the grant, in Feb. 1613, to one John Bucke of the office of making all brass and iron ordnance and guns for life: PRO, SP 14/141/102.

father had been making guns for the king for over thirty years and yet the king's yearly demands for ordnance could be filled in only ten days production time. He felt that he had to have access to other markets. Crow's patent was interfering with the merchant market which, according to Brown, threatened to put him out of business. Pleading the equivalent of national security, Brown stated that if he was forced to shut down and the king needed 'any sudden service', it would take a long time to gather the workmen, cut the wood, dig the ore and cast the pieces. As it was, he claimed that he could, if required, produce 200 pieces of ordnance in 200 days.[34]

Under the slow market conditions of the time, Brown tried to sell most of his ordnance in the Low Countries.[35] In 1619 he had arranged to sell the ordnance to an agent of Noel de Caron, the ambassador of the States General in the Low Countries, in the belief that licences to export would be virtually automatic during time of peace. He claimed that since there was no demand by the government or by the East India Company for his wares, he had every right to produce and ship the cannons to whoever would buy them. Otherwise, he asserted, he could not have kept his men at work, 'who beeinge once dismissed, are hard to bee gotten againe, what occasion of service for his Ma[jesty] or otherwise soever hadd required'.[36] The pieces had been cast and sent to Milhall, where they remained for several years until grudging permission to export was given. The export of such huge quantities of ordnance was a major political issue, but it is difficult to see what other choices Brown had if he was to maintain his furnaces and work force despite the lack of a sufficient domestic market.

The Brown family was also involved in the production of 'brass' or bronze ordnance, often called copper ordnance. Although bronze ordnance was slowly being replaced by cast iron pieces, as late as 1636 John Brown was given the task of casting 30 tons of brass into ordnance to include 13 sakers, 4 demi-cannons, 8 culverins and 10 demi-culverins.[37] This was in addition to his iron ordnance production. 'Brass' ordnance was a mixture of copper and tin at a proportion ('admixture') of 12 pounds of tin for every 100 pounds of copper as opposed to 20–3 pounds of tin for every 100 pounds of copper as was common with making bronze bells.[38]

The production of bronze guns was a very different industry from that of iron ordnance. Bronze was much more popular than the early forged iron

---

34 Ibid. SP 15/42/66, Dec.[?] 1621.
35 *CSPD James I, 1619–23*, 12, examination of John Brown, 11 Feb. 1619. See also Ffoulkes, *The gun-founders*, 75; Straker, *Wealden iron*, 162–3.
36 PRO, SP 15/42/29, petition to privy council from John Brown, his Majesty's gunfounder, [1620?].
37 BL, MS Harl. 429, fos 150, 157–60, 165.
38 Ffoulkes, *The gun-founders*, 25; Robert Norton, *The gunner*, London 1628. Brass is really a mixture of copper and zinc, so the term 'brass' is not here technically correct. However most inventories of the time referred to bronze guns as 'brass' or simply 'copper', with no regard for technical accuracy.

pieces. It was lighter to haul which made it infinitely better suited for army field operations and for use on shipboard, with the added benefit of being resistant to corrosion and rust. If cast correctly, it was somewhat stronger than forged or cast iron since it was more flexible. This allowed it to expand with the heat and pressure of firing without cracking as did the brittle iron pieces upon occasion. It had the additional advantage of retaining its value even if it did crack, since it could easily be recast into a new piece with very little wastage of metal and with much less fuel consumption than in the iron casting process. Captured pieces, or even bells taken from towns seized in a raid, could be and were recast as well.[39] Bronze was so valuable that a law of Henry VIII prohibited the export of bell metal or gun metal as a strategic resource of the kingdom, thus effectively reserving the use of bronze ordnance to the king's forces.[40] It was a resource jealously guarded.

Bronze ordnance was so important to the security of the kingdom, that measures were taken by direct government subsidy to locate and develop new sources for copper. By at least as early as 1597, the government had spent huge sums of money upon developing the royal copper mines at Keswick for the express purpose 'that Her Majesty and the realm might be served with that commodity to make ordnance, & c., rather than stand to the courtesy of strangers who served the realm as they pleased'.[41] The search for new sources of copper continued under the sponsorship of Sir Robert Cecil. In 1605, Cecil, by then Viscount Cranbourne, and Sir John Popham were able to report to Sir John Fortescue, chancellor of the duchy of Lancaster, that the directors of His Majesty's Mines Royal had discovered a copper mine in the mountains of Lancashire. This mine, Furnes Fels at Coniston, was to be the means of furnishing of the kingdom with its own supplies of copper which would free it from dependence on foreign supplies and suppliers.[42]

When not in active use, bronze ordnance was removed to the Tower

---

[39] Ffoulkes, *The gun-founders*, 25–6. When Cadiz was captured by Essex and Howard in 1596, part of the loot which was successfully returned to England was 74 pieces of bronze ordnance worth in excess of £2,500: PRO, WO 49/20.

[40] *Statutes of the Realm*, 33 Henry VIII, c. 26. That this was no dead letter is shown by the fact that 1,400lbs. of bell metal was seized in 1582 on information alleging attempted violation: PRO, SP 12/152/90, abstract of information by Holmes and Thwaite against one Corsini for illegal export of bell-metal, March 1582.

[41] *CSPD Eliz. I, 1598–1601*, 229, privy council to Lord Scrope, warden of the West Marches, June 1599. See also *CSPD Eliz. I, 1595–7*, 461–2, Marcus Stainbergerus, Emanuel Hechstetter and Richard Ledes to Secretary Cecil, governor of the Mines Royal, July 1597.

[42] It is likely that Cranbourne had in mind a major source of royal revenue, perhaps like the royal monopoly held by the king of Sweden who had discovered and exploited a huge source of copper. Such a windfall would have been doubly desirable since the problem of the king's finances was seldom far from Cranbourne's mind: *CSPD Add. Eliz. I and James I, 1580–1625*, 457, Viscount Cranbourne and Sir John Popham to Sir John Fortescue, 12 Feb. 1605. I am indebted to Professor Conrad Russell for this analysis of the probable financial benefit of a royal mines scheme.

where, because of its value, it was more regularly inventoried than the other supplies. In 1588, for example, there were bronze pieces worth over £27,000 in the Tower.[43] By 1609 the overall number of pieces had increased, especially in the increasingly popular culverin and demi-culverin size (eighteen and nine pounders) so that the bronze ordnance in the Tower must have exceeded £30,000 in value.[44] However, with the increasing use of the much cheaper iron pieces, fewer and fewer pieces of bronze ordnance were being cast in the 1620s, so that the store had decreased by almost 85 per cent, from 776 pieces in 1588 down to 114 bronze pieces in 1624. Iron was simply cheaper than bronze, costing at most only £13 per ton, with bronze costing approximately £62 per ton – almost five times more expensive. While bronze did not pass out of use until the advent of steel in the nineteenth century, it was becoming decidedly less popular to a cost-conscious government. In 1628 the privy council ordered that a view be taken of all bronze ordnance in the kingdom with the aim of replacing all the bronze pieces in forts and bulwarks with iron. This would free the bronze ones for use on ships.[45]

Even more telling was the section in the inventory of 1624 which listed the 'defect' or the number of pieces which the commissioners determined should be purchased to make up for shortages in the store. They listed the need for over 400 pieces of iron ordnance at a cost of some £2,538. However, they only mentioned the need for 26 additional bronze pieces, costing less than £700. This strongly indicates that bronze ordnance was considered a resource which was to be used as long as possible, but not to be replaced when lost or cracked.[46] While some repairs were made to bronze ordnance and even a few small pieces were bought, on the whole the use of bronze ordnance was declining and the use of iron increasing.

The physical plant for the manufacture of bronze ordnance was much smaller than that required for iron. Since there was no requirement to be near abundant sources of timber or ore, foundries were often located near to London: in Houndsditch, Vauxhall and Southwark. The Houndsditch foundry is of some interest since foreign craftsmen began making cannon there in 1511 in a tenement called the Bell House. This serves to point out the close connection of the craft of bronze ordnance casting and that of bell making. Craftsmen who made bronze cannon were able to employ their workmen in the allied trade during periods of low demand for ordnance. To a certain

---

[43] PRO, E 101/64/19.
[44] Ibid. WO 55/1676. In crude terms the number of actual pieces remained much the same – 776 major pieces compared with 763 in 1588. However, the number of heavier culverins and demi-culverins had increased and of lighter minions and falcons decreased so that the weight of bronze was considerably more. Culverins increased in number from 108 in 1588 to 177 in 1609 and demi-culverins from 168 to 227.
[45] BL, MS Harl. 429, fo. 47. By 1628, as a result of the cost of iron ore and 'seacoals', iron was selling for £18 per ton but even this was cheaper than bronze.
[46] PRO, WO 55/1680, survey 1617–24.

extent this was also true of iron gunfounders or, as we shall see, of small gunmakers whose skills could be used in the blacksmith trade, but the financial overhead for bronze casters was considerably less than that of the ironmasters.

Probably because smaller physical plant was needed and overheads were lower, more craftsmen were involved in supplying the ordnance office with bronze guns than with iron, although each individual produced fewer pieces. One of the oldest families of founders of bronze guns was the Owens, John and Robert, who began casting at least as early as 1531 and by 1546 had been appointed king's gunfounders.[47] The family tradition was continued by Samuel Owen who produced cannon of all sizes for the ordnance office between 1593 and his death in 1603. He delivered over £230-worth of ordnance to the office of the ordnance in those years.

Like most of the gunfounders under government contract, Owen was generally issued with shivers of brass and tin out of the 'strategic stockpile' of the metal in the Tower from which he was expected to provide a certain weight of ordnance, less a small proportion for wastage in casting.[48] This practice led to trouble in 1592 when another gunfounder, Peter Gill, was accused of embezzling over £1,110-worth of bronze between 1587 and 1592 by exaggerating his reports of wastage and saving the excess metal to cast extra pieces for his own profit.[49] While this dispute seems to have been settled by 1595, Gill was again in trouble by 1600. In a warrant sent to George Harvey by the privy council in May 1600, the accusation was made that 'there are certaine peeces of brass ordonance now in the possession of one Peter Gill, a gunfounder, which do belonge of right unto her Majestie'. Harvey was authorised to seize the guns, two culverins and one saker, and take them to the Tower.[50]

Gill continued to provide ordnance for the office until his death in 1605, so these incidents do not seem to have been held against him. Between 1590 and 1605, he provided 19 major pieces of ordnance, worth some £550. He does not seem to have done badly in his trade, since his will is extant and it lists substantial assets in land, tenements, and debts owed to him.[51]

Perhaps the most famous, and certainly the most prolific, producer of bronze ordnance was the Pitt family which had been associated with the Owens in the Houndsditch foundry. Early evidence of their activities is

---

[47] Ffoulkes, *The gun-founders*, 47.
[48] In 1604 Henry Pitt was granted a deduction of 8lbs. per cwt for 'wastage', which seems to have been the usual proportion: PRO, WO 49/30, 34.
[49] Ibid. E 101/67/24.
[50] APC 1599–1600, 293, warrant to Sir George Harvey and to Sir George Carew, 9 May 1600.
[51] One of those debts was for 8,400lbs. of Spanish iron sold to the ordnance officers: PROB 11/106, 59 Hayes. Gill is listed as citizen and armourer of London. He is not listed in Ffoulkes's list of gunfounders which is certainly a curious omission given the number of records in which he appears.

lacking, but by the 1590s Henry Pitt was established as the major producer of bronze ordnance for the queen. He was most active in delivering ordnance between the years 1593 and 1605, providing some 41 pieces of ordnance worth £1,080 in that period. He shared his business with his eldest son, Thomas, beginning in 1603, and then with his other son Richard in 1613 until his own death in 1615.[52] Richard Pitt was granted the office of gunfounder for life in October 1613, but he had little in the way of business until the war with Spain began again in 1625.[53]

The Pitts seem to have been the most skilful of the bronze ordnance founders of the time. In 1610, then master of the ordnance, Lord Carew, chose them to make the working model of his new invention. This was a demi-culverin which could break down into several pieces, each weighing less than 200 pounds, for ease of shipment and deployment. It had the additional advantage of economy since if one piece was broken, theoretically only that section would have to be replaced. An early attempt at making interchangeable parts would only have worked if the craftsmen were trained in creating parts of uniform size and tolerance. The experience of Carew in the difficult terrain of Ireland, when coupled with the technical skill of Henry and Thomas Pitt, came up with a technological innovation of potentially revolutionary impact. Fast moving field artillery, composed of interchangeable parts, might have immortalised both the Pitts and Carew if they had not suffered under the disadvantage of inventing a new weapon during peacetime in the least warlike nation in Europe.[54]

There were numerous smaller scale bronze gunfounders. John and Richard Phillips, for example, cast pieces at least from 1588 until 1624, although the bulk of their business fell in the years up to 1605.[55] Ordnance indenture records for 1593-1605, complete except for 1597, show them providing 24 major pieces of ordnance worth £725 during this period.

On the same scale as the Phillips' was the production of George Elkin, an obscure gunfounder, who delivered 10 culverins and 5 demi-culverins to the

---

[52] PRO, WO 49. His son Richard died in 1638, Thomas in 1645 and grandson Richard in 1658.
[53] Ibid. SP 14/141/96, grant of office of gunfounder for life, 31 Oct. 1613. Richard and Thomas Pitt probably worked together in the business at least through 1629: BL, MS Harl. 429, fo. 61, 10 June 1629.
[54] BL, MS Royal 17A, LIII, IV. Carew referred to Ireland in his elaborate justification of the uses of an artillery piece of this type, saying that the siege pieces taken to Ireland by Essex were so cumbersome that they had to be left in castles in Ireland since it was too expensive to haul them home again. See also H. L. Blackmore, *The armouries of the Tower of London*, I: *The ordnance*, London 1976, 10.
[55] *CSPD Add. Eliz. I and James I, 1580–1625*, 254, warrant to cast 12 bastard (shortened) demi-culverins, for the defence of Middleburg in Zealand, 16 Aug. 1588; PRO, WO 49/17, 19.

ordnance office, worth some £620, between 1594 and 1600 although he had been producing ordnance at least since 1590.[56]

There were other suppliers of ordnance to the government, but they were mainly middle-men who had picked up isolated pieces in their various transactions. These 'merchants of opportunity' included some of the ordnance officers who would provide various pieces of ordnance for cash. Examples included clerk Richard Haynes, who provided £439-worth of ordnance in 1603–4, and Stephen Ridlesden who brought in £526-worth of ordnance in 1601.[57] These men, and other small scale 'providers' of ordnance who were not gunfounders themselves, were responsible for bringing in over £3,700-worth of ordnance or gunmetal in the years 1590–1604. There were also some 31 pieces of Spanish ordnance received into the store from George Clifford, earl of Cumberland in December 1599, worth £2,691 4s. 3d.[58] It is possible that many of these pieces were obtained by capture and seizure as enemy prizes, since after the end of the war supply of this sort by non-gunfounders seems to have stopped. This would help explain why private sales were almost exclusively an Elizabethan phenomenon.

Ordnance from Spanish wrecks, however, especially from the 1588 Armada, were brought into the office at various intervals throughout the early Jacobean period as enterprising individuals recovered them. In February 1611 Sir Roger Dallison was ordered to pay £635 19s. 3d. to James Steward and Maximilian VanderLew for several pieces of Spanish bronze ordnance 'by them recovered out of the Seas upon the coast of Ireland and by them brought over into England'.[59]

The occasional provision of isolated pieces of ordnance was a very different matter from the regular industrial production of a vital commodity. The bronze cannon industry, although small and spread out over a number of craftsmen, maintained a constant supply of artillery pieces which were the equal of any cannons cast on the continent. Production levels remained low, however, and between the end of the war with Spain in 1604 and the renewal of the war in 1625, the industry virtually collapsed. The pressures of peace and the improved quality of iron ordnance reduced the number of bronze gunfounders supplying the government by 1625 to three: the youngest Pitt, Richard Philips and John Brown.

In sum, the production of iron and bronze ordnance was a major concern

---

[56] Ibid. WO 49/17–25.
[57] Ibid. WO 49/30, 127.
[58] Ibid. WO 49/24. This document does not explain why Cumberland sent this ordnance to the Tower or where he got it from. It stated only that there was an agreement between the earl and the privy council. However, according to the DNB, Cumberland had outfitted several failed privateering expeditions between 1586 and 1598, and perhaps these were his only spoils. Alternatively they may have been guns left over from his privateering vessels after they had returned home.
[59] Ibid. WO 54/7.

Table 3
Ordnance office expenditure on great ordnance and shot, 1594–1625 (in pounds sterling) compared with total ordnance office expenditure in selected years

Year	Ordnance expense	Shot expense	Total office expenditure
1594	1,065	0	9,980
1595	1,110	0	14,820
1596	2,500	290	25,900
1597	–	–	17,130
1598	100	640	12,500
1599	4,510	950	19,430
1600	390	520	14,520
1601	880	175	15,720
1602	230	0	17,320
1603	810	103	7,760
1604	1,350	55	5,050
1605	135	650	5,100
*1610	0	110	6,800
1619	170	0	4,560
1620	0	1,480	4,680
1621	0	0	14,250
1622	0	0	4,500
1623	0	0	8,500
1624	30	3,035	16,880
1625	5,610	2,930	49,360
Total	£18,890	£10,938	£274,760

* The years 1610–19 were years of virtually no ordnance or shot production. It is probably no coincidence that they were the years when the lieutenant of the ordnance was the corrupt Sir Roger Dallison.

of the government and the ordnance office throughout the period. The needs of the government fluctuated over the years depending on the military and political constraints of the time, as can be seen in table 3.[60]

As table 3 indicates, the busiest years for buying ordnance seem to have been the period from 1594 to 1603 with the peak of ordnance purchases coming in 1599. Ordnance seems to have taken up a small proportion of office expenditure, from 11 per cent in 1594 down to 1 per cent in 1598 and up to 23 per cent in 1599. The heavy expenditure on small arms and

[60] These figures are estimates based on the indentures for supplies actually brought into the office in the years listed using the WO 49 indenture book series.

gunpowder in 1625 gave even the large ordnance purchases of that year only 11 per cent of the total expenditure for that year. Overall, the level of purchases, not surprisingly, slackened dramatically in the inter-war years until 1624 when the sudden demand for ordnance brought massive orders. The lack of ordnance purchases may have been due to the wide scale buying of ordnance in the years before 1594 for which years the records in the ordnance office do not exist. However, it seems that the office kept up a fairly steady purchase of ordnance during the later war years of the reign of Elizabeth. In addition, a surprising amount of money was spent on ordnance in 1604 which indicates that it took a while for the bureaucracy to accommodate itself to the peaceful intents of their new monarch. Doubtless orders had been placed at some time in the past and the delivery of and payment for the weapons happened to coincide with the outbreak of peace. At that point a general neglect set in until the need for new pieces of ordnance in 1624–5. The increase in ordnance office expenditure in 1621, due to preparations for the expedition to recover the Palatinate, does not seem to have been used for heavy ordnance. The character of this planned expedition determined that small arms would be needed, but not any great quantity of new, heavy ordnance.

The need to maintain at least some production capacity for iron ordnance became readily apparent in 1624 when war was again on the horizon. The ordnance office purchased no major pieces of ordnance from 1620 until the end of 1624, although the government need for shot ensured that at least John Brown had some work for his men. However, the political climate in 1624 unexpectedly changed upon Prince Charles's return from Spain without his promised bride and the kingdom soon required massive armaments purchases as war seemed more and more likely. Over £41,200 worth of munitions was contracted for between May 1624 and July 1625 out of the parliamentary subsidy of 1624.[61]

Of this, no less than £9,600 was spent on ordnance, chiefly iron ordnance, with an additional £6,500 spent on iron shot to replenish the depleted stores of the ordnance office.

The massive infusion of money in 1624 found John Brown surprisingly well prepared to back up his earlier claim that he could produce 200 pieces in 200 days. He was given a warrant on 11 December 1624 to produce 300 demi-culverins and 200 sakers. Living up to his boast, he was able to produce 300 demi-culverins and 180 sakers by 1 June of the following year. He also brought into the stores nine culverins and twenty-one minions along with several thousand rounds of iron shot.[62] By dint of what can only be called extraordinary exertion, Brown did his best to make up for years of neglect of

---

[61] Ibid. WO 49/54, first section of the indenture book of the ordnance office for 1624.
[62] Ibid. WO 49/54, 55. The shot alone was worth £5,300, while his ordnance cost the government over £9,000.

the ordnance stores of the kingdom. The government of England, however, was somewhat less than grateful since the finances of the kingdom were not prepared for such an outlay. By June 1628 Brown was owed over £11,000 for ordnance which he had delivered but for which he had not been paid.[63] In fact, his finances were certainly more troublesome to the king than the lack of ordnance. In 1628, Philip Burlamachi, financier and arms merchant, was directed to sell some 4,000 tons of iron ordnance overseas in order to redeem the crown jewels from the Dutch. Charles may have needed ordnance to fight his wars, but the true 'sinews of war', as had been remarked by Alberto Struzzi in the Netherlands, was money.[64]

The need for field pieces, and all kinds of ordnance for ships and castles, became painfully apparent in 1624. England, however, was fortunate in that the lightly supervised ordnance industry was capable of fulfilling such demands at short notice. Certainly neither the ordnance officers nor the privy council can be credited with unusual foresight or care in supporting the industry. In no other industry was it so essential for the government to maintain a rational procurement system which would insure that a minimum, if not an expandable, production capacity was maintained. This could only have been achieved by systematic planning and a regular, long-term programme of purchasing iron ordnance. Such a system did not exist and it was only by good fortune that the industry was as prepared for the renewal of war as it was. Even so, ordnance was just one of the items which were needed to replenish the neglected stores. A significant proportion of the money spent on preparing for any expedition or army went on gunpowder which presented the ordnance officers with a host of new and expensive challenges.

---

[63] Oppenheim, *Royal navy*, 288.
[64] For this quotation and a classic account of the value of finances and logistics in warfare see Parker, *Army of Flanders*, 3.

5

Gunpowder and Saltpetre

> 'The three great elements of modern civilization, gunpowder, printing, and the Protestant religion.' – Thomas Carlyle, *Critical and miscellaneous essays: the state of German literature*, 1827

Throughout the sixteenth century, gunpowder was increasingly seen as an essential commodity in the supply train of any modern army. The development of the mobile cannon and refinements in individual firearms changed the face of war in Europe. Gunpowder became a vital, strategic resource, and its manufacture, refining and sale quickly became a government monopoly in England as it had earlier in France.[1] In their drives towards military self-sufficiency, both Henry VIII and Elizabeth I placed a high priority on developing and controlling the gunpowder industry and especially on preserving the domestic supplies of saltpetre, the most necessary component of gunpowder. England's dependence upon domestic saltpetre stocks was, however, to have unfortunate social, political and military consequences. This humble by-product of human and animal wastes was to be the source of complaints and problems which reached from the smallest landowner in the county to the halls of Westminster.

The petremen

The procedures for extracting saltpetre, or potassium nitrate, out of waste-soaked earth – the earth under outhouses, dovecotes, pigeon coops, stables and barns was ideal for this – were complicated and messy.[2] However, there was no viable alternative at the time. Numerous entrepreneurs offered to the privy council cheap and easy methods of producing saltpetre over the years, but there was not yet any effective substitute for digging the vital product out of earth which had been saturated with animal and human waste products. It was not until the 1620s that stocks of saltpetre began to be imported from the

---

[1] J. U. Nef, *Industry and government in France and England 1540–1640*, Ithaca, NY – London 1969, 59–68, 88–98. Spain was apparently an exception. According to Thompson in his *War and government in Habsburg Spain*, 234–5, 'The Spanish kings in contrast to the practice in England and France, also manufactured their own gunpowder in their own gunpowder mills.'
[2] PRO, SP 9/7/101–12.

east, mostly from India, by the East India Company. Even then it was several years before the supply was large or reliable enough for the government's needs.[3]

By the late sixteenth century, the ratio of saltpetre to the other ingredients of gunpowder (sulphur and charcoal or coal dust) had risen from 1:1:1 to 6:1:1. In addition, if the saltpetre was not pure enough, the resulting mixture would not burn or explode properly.[4] Early gunpowder had been composed of ingredients at a ratio of 1:1:1 or 2:1:1, so the increasing amount of saltpetre required for better powder produced greater demand for the commodity. This increasing demand led to greater numbers of saltpetremen in the counties and more complaints about their behaviour.

In the sixteenth and early seventeenth centuries, the nation's stock of saltpetre relied upon individuals called petremen or saltpetremen who toured the countryside looking for likely caches of saltpetre-producing earth. The petreman, who generally worked for the gunpowder patentee, would move into a county, establish a central processing point near a handy source of water and firewood (for the boilers) and then send out teams of men to scour the surrounding countryside for saltpetre deposits. The workmen would find earth which was rich in nitrates by using a rough and ready method of assaying the ground by putting some earth on the tip of the tongue to test for bitterness: the more bitter, the better the ground. The crew would then dig up all the earth in the immediate area down to a six or eight foot depth and load it all into barrels or tubs for transfer to the central processing point.

After digging up the 'rich' earth, the petremen were supposed to fill in the hole with dirt mixed with dung and liquid waste so that it could produce another 'crop' of petre within five or six years. The fact that workmen were seldom so courteous or long-sighted as to do this helps explain, in part, why they were so unpopular. Often they left gaping holes in the ground, disturbed animals and disordered dovecotes in their wake.

Once the earth was packed into barrels or tubs, it was loaded onto carts (purveyed from local farmers at the rate of 4d. the mile in 1589, increased to 8d. a mile by 1618) and taken to the central point where boilers had been set up. The earth would be mixed with water and undergo numerous boilings and strainings to obtain the necessary degree of purity. The resulting petre

---

[3] K. N. Chaudhuri, *The English East India Company: the study of an early joint stock company 1600–1640*, New York 1965, 189. Saltpetre was a 'growth' industry which contemporary traders compared favourably with the sugar trade. By the 1630s the English were bringing some 200 tons of it into England annually. This would have made around 485,000lbs. of gunpowder.

[4] For the methods of making saltpetre see Thomas Henshaw's pamphlet in PRO, SP 9/7/101–12. See also J. Ferris, 'The saltpetremen in Dorset 1638', *Proceedings of the Dorset Natural History and Archaeological Society* lxxxv (1963), 158–63. I am grateful to Dr Ian Roy for bringing this article, and many other items, to my attention.

would be loaded up in barrels and conveyed to the gunpowder factories while the petremen and their assistants moved on to a new locale.

The purveyance of this strategic resource was inherently unpopular. The petremen were patentees, monopolists and purveyors all rolled into one. They were never welcomed into an area since they represented central government interference at its worst, at least in the eyes of local residents. They were often officious in their demands, negligent about property rights, slow to fill in their excavations and quick to resent the less than total co-operation given them by the locals. Their habit of digging under dovecotes was particularly unpopular since the owners of these valuable properties – mostly gentlemen – complained that they scared away the birds. In addition, their levying of carts was disliked because they often forced the local farmers to drive them and their cargoes long distances for little remuneration and the carts were seldom in the same condition at the end of the duty as at the start.

The deep unpopularity of the petremen can perhaps best be seen in 1603 when many county residents refused to allow them to dig on their land for saltpetre at all, citing as their reason the death of the queen. Many citizens apparently felt that the queen's death invalidated the petremen's rights to purvey saltpetre and they seized upon this excuse to stand up against these hated purveyors. In response, the petremen petitioned the privy council to confirm their letters patent 'the validity of which has been vexatiously questioned, since the late queen's death'. The petremen stressed the need for their commodity and stated that they were saving the crown at least £1,000 per year in foreign saltpetre. They felt that many 'ignorant people and such as are obstinately minded' were bringing their vital business to a halt. They further stressed that they were not really monopolists since the mining of saltpetre was 'a matter of Royall prerogative inseperablie belonging to the imperial crowne'.[5] The fact that landowners and cart-owners so readily seized upon this supposed 'loophole' in the law provides strong evidence of the deep dislike felt for the saltpetremen in the provinces.

During the war years from 1585 to 1603, the pressing need for saltpetre naturally produced a high level of complaints. However, grievances about saltpetre did not go away during peacetime although the number of complaints initially dropped off when demand for the product was low. The activities of the petremen were mentioned as a grievance in parliament in 1606 and a commission was even established in October of that year to try to resolve some of the worst abuses.[6] The complaints may have had some result,

---

[5] PRO, SP 14/1/64, saltpetre and gunpowder patentees petition to privy council, Apr. 1603. Saltpetre and gunpowder production, like iron ordnance manufacture, was regularly exempted from statutes of monopoly as an essential royal prerogative.

[6] 'Abuse of such as have commission to make Salt Peeter is exceeding great to the Subject in digging up their Dove Houses at unseasonable tymes, and other Houses at their Pleasure; And in takeing their carts, and their wood up [to run their boilers] and other things in more violent and unlawfull sort now, then in tyme of warr': *The parliamentary*

since a new patent for gunpowder was issued the following year to the earl of Worcester, perhaps in an attempt to restrain some of the worst abuses. Even so, in 1617 the council again returned to the problem but this time without changing patentees. It concentrated primarily upon trying to restrain the earl of Worcester's men from seizing carts without cause. In the end, however, it was forced to admit that some men refused to rent the carts to the petremen at any price and certainly not at the going rate of 8d. a mile. The council decided that when such resistance was met, the petremen were entitled to seize the carts if, as the council told the earl, 'you cannot get carriages otherwise then at unreasonable and excessive prices'.[7] In the struggle between necessity and popularity, the council came down upon the side of necessity.

By the 1620s, when war was again imminent, new complaints about the petremen reached the privy council. However, the shortage of saltpetre (and gunpowder) which became apparent as the build-up to war continued, unsettled the councillors more than the grievances. Thus in May 1624 the council sent twenty-three letters of assistance to mayors, JPs, sheriffs and constables throughout the country asking them to assist the local petremen.[8] The council was deeply concerned about the shortage of petre and even doubled the amount to be brought into the Tower.

This, not surprisingly, increased the number of complaints about the activities of the petremen and in an attempt to control their excesses James I issued a proclamation on 26 December 1624 to justify the need for saltpetre and regulate its digging.[9] In general, the proclamation came down hardest not on the petremen but on 'the evill dealings of many ill disposed persons (who respecting more their own then the publicke good)' actually tried to prevent the growth of saltpetre in their barns and pigeon houses by paving those places or putting down boards, gravel, sand or brick.[10] In other words, the real villains, in the eyes of the government, were the landowners, not the petremen. The latter, however, were exhorted to take better care to replace

---

diary of Robert Bowyer 1606–7, ed. D. H. Willson, Minneapolis 1931, 131–2. For the saltpetre commission set up to deal with the issue see HMC, *Salisbury*, xviii. 335–6, Sir Robert Johnson to the earl of Salisbury, 31 Oct. 1606.

[7] APC 1616–17, 253–4, six open warrants, 22 May 1617.

[8] The petreman for Dorsetshire, Wiltshire and Hampshire was Thomas Hilliard, who was later involved in a major series of lawsuits concerning his 'unlawful digging' in many unseemly places. If the charges are to be believed, he was the epitome of the obnoxious petreman: PRO, SP 16/192/33, star chamber order against Thomas Helliard, 24 May 1631; SP 16/192/89, saltpetre reforms; SP 16/193/83, Mathew Goade's certificate against Hilliard, 14 June 1631; SP 16/197/6, Hilliard's petition to the commissioners of the Admiralty, 20 July 1631; SP 16/206/35, saltpetre division scheme.

[9] Ibid. SP 14/187/127, 'A Proclamation for the preservation of Grounds for making of salt-peeter, and to restore such Grounds which now are destroyed and to command assistance to be given to his Majesties Salt-Peeter Makers'.

[10] This may have been due as much to architectural change as to any conscious attempt to defraud the petremen. But the result was the same: less petre.

the earth they dug up, partly to keep the good will of the landowner, but mainly to insure the preservation of future saltpetre-bearing ground. The proclamation also prohibited the practice of taking money to spare certain stables or grounds from being dug up. It was an attempt to deal both with the problem of national requirements and with violations of property rights. It did not really solve either of these difficulties although the king at least made some attempt to provide a basis for the prosecution of the worst offenders among the petremen. Since there was no legislation which dealt with the procurement of saltpetre, the proclamation gave the problem at least some recognition in law and opened the possibility of prosecution in prerogative courts such as Star Chamber.[11]

By 1628 complaints about saltpetre had again reached parliament. The Commons was already deeply concerned about the cost of an unsuccessful war against France and Spain and about the social problems of billeting and controlling a standing army in England over the winter of 1627–8. When a war is going badly, soldiers and anyone involved in an unpopular war industry are prime targets for popular resentment. In one particularly colourful attack upon the petremen, parliament was told that they had at one point dug up a church so that the parishioners could not perform divine service. When challenged, the petremen 'answer[ed] the plaintiffs with obscene jest, that the earth in churches is best for their turns, for the women piss in their seats, which causes excellent saltpetre'.[12] Sir John Eliot probably spoke for many members when he said, 'I see a boldness in some men that makes them unworthy to live in a commonwealth.'[13]

The resulting bill for saltpetre attempted both to deal with the demand for the commodity and the grievances it caused but it was committed after the second reading on 25 April 1628, and died there.[14] In any event, the king could not have allowed any bill to pass which would prevent him from obtaining this vital military commodity.

The method of extracting saltpetre from the earth was cumbersome and unpopular but, on the whole, the semi-independent 'petremen' were able to provide sufficient quantities of the mineral to the gunpowder patentees for whom they worked. Between February and October 1589, for example, some twelve petremen brought over 650 cwt (72,800 pounds) of saltpetre into the Tower.[15] Two of these petremen alone, Robert and Thomas Robinson, were

---

[11] For a similar use of proclamations to create a mechanism for prosecution in star chamber see T. G. Barnes, 'The prerogative and environmental control of London building in the early seventeenth century: the lost opportunity', *California Law Review* lviii (1970), 1332–63.
[12] *Proceedings in parliament, 1628*, iv. 350.
[13] Ibid. iv. 347. For other complaints see ii. 71; iv. 82, 347.
[14] Ibid. iii. 78; 'An Act for the getting of Saltpeter, and for the furnishing of the realm with greater store than heretofore has been': CJ i. 888.
[15] The list of suppliers included John Ducke, William Deren, John Frye, George Sheppard, John Fox, Josias Pett, Alexander Pett, Hugh Maxon and Thomas and Robert

bound by contract to provide 200 cwt (22,400 pounds) of saltpetre per year to the London gunpowder makers.[16] In general, these small entrepreneurs operated under the general authority of the gunpowder makers' letters patent. George and John Evelyn and Richard Hill were granted the patent in 1589 for all saltpetre and gunpowder production in the country except for certain northern counties and London. The northern counties were covered by George Constable who was granted the patent in 1590 to dig petre in Yorkshire, Nottinghamshire, Lancashire, Northumberland, Westmorland and Cumberland for eleven years.[17] In 1592 Constable took Richard Hill on as his partner, perhaps to help in getting access to the gunpowder market since Hill had previously been associated with the Evelyns.[18] In addition Thomas and Robert Robinson were granted the patent for the areas around London and Westminster for ten years starting in 1591.[19] All these patents were invalidated in 1599 and the sole finding of saltpetre was granted to the powdermakers, John Evelyn, Robert Evelyn, John Wrenham and Richard Harding along with the merchant Simon Furner.[20] However, they delegated most of the actual work of obtaining the saltpetre to dozens of small scale entrepreneurs from year to year. From 1599 the close relationship between finding and processing saltpetre and gunpowder making became even closer, with the gunpowder patentees controlling both aspects of the industry.

Gunpowder production

The story of the early beginnings of gunpowder production in England falls outside the scope of this work and has moreover already been told.[21] The industry was centred around London, especially in Surrey, with numerous small storehouses and powder factories scattered about the region. Henry

---

Robinson: PRO, SP 12/227/3, amount of quantities and prices of the saltpetre brought into the Tower since the last composition; and the names of the saltpetremen supplying the same, 1 Oct. 1589.

[16] Ibid. SP 12/227/4, bond of Thomas and Robert Robynson for 200 cwt of saltpetre to John Evelyn to be made into gunpowder in London, 1 Oct. 1589.

[17] APC 1590–1, 21, repeat of letters patent of 26 Apr. 1590 granting the patent for 21 years, 11 Oct. 1590.

[18] In an interesting, possibly corrupt, move, Constable and Hill arranged to pay George Hogg, clerk of the deliveries, £30 per year to keep 'a true account of saltpeter delivered out or brought into the Tower by them': CSPD Eliz. I, 1591–4, 187 (16 Feb. 1592).

[19] PRO, patent rolls, court of chancery, C66/1496, mm. 8–12 (8 Jan. 1591). I am indebted to Mark Kennedy for this citation and for allowing me to look at his listings of numerous gunpowder and iron ordnance patents.

[20] Ibid.

[21] See especially H. E. Malden (ed.), *The Victoria history of the county of Surrey*, 4 vols, Westminster 1902–12, ii. 246. See also the introduction to *Royalist ordnance papers 1642–1646*, ed. Ian Roy (Oxfordshire Records Society xliii, 1979), and, for the later gunpowder industry, Tomlinson, *Guns and government*, 111–17.

VIII and Elizabeth I tried, as they had done with the armour, ordnance and gunmaking industries, to encourage the domestic production of powder to achieve some degree of national self-sufficiency in so vital a commodity. That this had not been achieved by the outbreak of the war with Spain was a matter of grave concern. By the 1580s, a host of small-scale producers and merchants provided gunpowder on an irregular basis to the ordnance office.

Domestic production capacity was limited with large quantities of powder being purchased overseas at relatively high rates. Powder merchants like Simon Furner, Henry Dale, Randall Symmes and William Hall brought in powder from Antwerp and Hamburg at 12d.–15d. per pound (the normal domestic rate was 8d. per pound) and stored it in various private warehouses in London.[22] All of these suppliers together could not produce or import enough gunpowder to satisfy the country's growing defence needs. This led to potentially disastrous consequences in 1588 when the fleet fighting the Armada was faced with a critical shortage of gunpowder.[23] Estimates by the ordnance officers in the spring of 1589 show how much powder was lacking from the stores even eight months after that event. They declared that the stores needed 188 lasts of powder to bring them up to their desired staple of 300.[24] The ordnance office was at least beginning to see the value of maintaining a standard quantity of powder in its stores. However, neither the domestic gunpowder industry in 1588 nor the merchants could quite keep pace with consumption. By September 1588, all the merchants in London were estimated to have only seven and a half lasts in their storehouses. In addition, England's involvement in war on the continent, especially in the Low Countries, made it essential that she encourage greater domestic production of gunpowder while also purchasing more from overseas.

Consequently, a patent of monopoly for the production of gunpowder was granted to George and John Evelyn along with Richard Hills on 28 January 1589. Gunpowder production was to be identified with the name of Evelyn

---

[22] At one point one of these merchants, Henry Dale, had over 800 barrels of gunpowder in a warehouse on Tower Hill, outside the walls of the Tower. The lieutenant of the Tower complained in 1586 that vagrants used to build straw fires in the ramshackle huts around the outer walls of this storehouse, with potentially disastrous consequences, but it was many years before the powder warehouse was centralised in the basement of the Tower: Cruickshank, *Elizabeth's army*, 69; CSPD Eliz. I, 1581–90, 311, petition of Sir Owyn Hopton to privy council to pay Sir Roger Dalison for Mr Dale to remove his 40 lasts of powder.

[23] See especially one of Howard's letters to Walsingham during the Armada battle pleading for as much powder and shot as possible to be sent to him: Garrett Mattingly, *The Armada*, Boston, Mass. 1959, 335. See also PRO, SP 12/214/28, 29, powder from Portsmouth to the fleet. Over 27,900 lbs. of powder were sent out to the fleet from Portsmouth alone.

[24] Ibid. SP 12/223/107, note of munition needed for the ordnance office, 30 Apr. 1589. The office also considered that it was short 3,900 muskets, 2,120 calivers and miscellaneous other items. They estimated that it would take at least £8,311 to bring the office up to its minimum level of preparedness.

for the next fifty years. The formal patents changed hands over the years, namely to the earl of Worcester in 1607 (renewed in 1617) and the duke of Buckingham and George Lord Carew in 1620 and 1624, but the production facilities remained in the hands of the Evelyn family almost up to the Civil War.[25]

George Evelyn and his sons John and Robert, maintained powder mills initially in Wooten, Surrey, and then later moved to Godstone and then to Kingston-on-Thames. The price and terms of their contract varied only slightly from year to year. Gunpowder prices stayed steady at 8d. per pound up to 1599 when the price actually dropped to 7d. a pound.[26] As late as 1626, the Evelyns' were producing powder for the government at 8½d. per pound.[27] This was much cheaper than the foreign product which was available at 10–12d. per pound.[28]

In August 1599 John and Robert Evelyn along with Richard Harding and Simon Furner were granted a new commission to provide at least 200 barrels a month at the lower price of 7d. a pound, or £583 6s. 8d. per month.[29] This team produced an average of 2,500 barrels (250,000 pounds) of gunpowder per year until the end of the reign of Elizabeth in addition to reworking almost 2,200 barrels of decayed gunpowder at a rate of 2–4d. a pound.[30]

Despite the increasing demand for powder, the government, controlling the grants for the monopoly on all the powder and saltpetre produced in the country, was able to set its own price and the price of this strategic supply actually went down. When the continuing low price of gunpowder is compared with the 18d. per pound being charged by the government for powder sent to the counties in 1640, after the collapse of the monopoly, questions are raised about the supposed dangers of monopolies.[31] Monopolies are harmful if they restrain competition to the point where one supplier has a stranglehold

---

[25] *DNB* xviii. 79–83. George Evelyn was the grandfather of the diarist John Evelyn (1620–1706). See also *Royalist ordnance papers 1642–1646*, 8–10, and Tomlinson, *Guns and government*, 111.
[26] PRO, WO 49/26, indenture book for 1601 reciting the terms of the 1599 agreement.
[27] Ibid. WO 49/56, fo. 77. The 1589 contract specified that they were to bring in 160 barrels (16,000lbs.) of the finished product to the office each month, at a monthly cost of £533 6s. 8d.
[28] Ibid. WO 49/21. This was certainly the government's 'special' price, since the Evelyns were allowed to sell any powder produced above the needs of the government to the merchant community at 10d. per lb.
[29] Ibid. SP 38/6, docquet, 24 Aug. 1599; WO 49/24. The Evelyns were paid by a special privy seal but the money still went through the hands of the lieutenant of the ordnance. See appendix 5 for further information on the lieutenants' accounts.
[30] Ibid. E 351/2808, account of John and Robert Evelyn for decayed powder, Jan. 1596–Sept. 1602. See also WO 55/1630 (1 Oct. 1602); WO 55/1633, delivery of decayed power to John Evelyn, 1605–6; WO 49/52, reworking of decayed powder, Aug. 1622.
[31] The government had to reduce the cost to 16d. and then 12d. per lb. before sales began to pick up: ibid. SP 16/461/35, report to the king of the commission for saltpetre and gunpowder, 28 July 1640.

Table 4
Comparison of gunpowder and total ordnance costs, 1593–1625

Years	Gunpowder purchased	Total ordnance expenses
1593–1603	91,300	192,800
1604–20	39,800	149,700
1620–5	27,050	85,700
Total	£158,150	£428,200

All figures are in pounds sterling to the nearest £50.

on the industry so that he can raise prices at will. In the case of a monopoly of a strategic resource, where the only legal purchaser of a product is the government, the ability of a monopolist to raise prices becomes subject to severe constraints. The monopoly for gunpowder production insured a regular and fixed supply of a vital resource without regard to economic forces such as market fluctuations. The industry was not allowed to collapse, as did many war industries in the years 1604–20, or exist in an unregulated fashion which might have resulted in an inferior product. Competition could theoretically have driven the price lower, but probably at the cost of quality and regularity. The governments of Elizabeth and James could not afford to take such chances.

The government's need for gunpowder, especially in time of war, was more constant than for most of the other ordnance commodities and consumed a large portion of the total ordnance office budget.[32]

As can be seen in table 4, from 1593 to 1625 a total of £158,150 was spent on gunpowder, making it the largest single expense for the ordnance office. This figure averages out to approximately £4,800 spent on gunpowder per year. Overall, this accounted for about 37 per cent of total ordnance office expenditures of £428,200, or an average of £12,975 per year for the years 1593–1625.

Gunpowder was a heavy expense, but the percentage of money spent on it varied as England shifted from war to peace and then back to a period of preparation for war again. Table 4 shows that the percentage of the total ordnance supplies budget spent on gunpowder declined from 47 per cent in the period 1593–1603 to 27 per cent in the years of peace from 1604–20. This decline is not surprising given that England was at peace and maintaining military supplies was not a high priority for James's government in those years. Less powder was obviously consumed in peacetime. From 1621–5, however, one can see somewhat of an increase in overall expenditure and

---

[32] The sums of money spent on gunpowder throughout this period compared with overall expenditure on ordnance can be seen in appendix 5.

gunpowder purchases. The average year from 1621 to 1625 saw £17,500 spent on total ordnance supplies, almost double the average of the years of peace, along with a corresponding increase in gunpowder purchases. Interestingly, the percentage of money spent on gunpowder (32 per cent) in these years is not dramatically higher than that of the earlier period of 1604 to 1620 (27 per cent). This indicates that gunpowder requirements for the military remained fairly constant during peacetime even when the state was beginning to think about preparing for war. This is even more clearly the case when one notices that most of the powder purchases in the period between 1621 and 1625 occurred in one year, 1624, when the ordnance office bought £13,600-worth of powder. This was 80 per cent of the total expenditure of the office for that year according to the listings in the indenture books. The following year a mere £5,100 was spent on powder, or only around 10 per cent of the £49,400 spent on military supplies in 1624–5 authorised by the parliamentary subsidy. If these 'abnormal' years are excluded, the ordnance office spent only an average of £2,800 per year in 1621, 1622 and 1623, not much above the average of £2,350 from 1604 to 1620. The ordnance office was not issued with sufficient money for the necessary powder purchases until war became almost inevitable in 1624 and then it was nearly too late.

Despite the increasing demand for gunpowder and all military supplies which became obvious after planning began for the abortive expedition to relieve the Palatinate, considerable amounts of powder were not purchased until 1624. According to the inventories of the ordnance office, from 1621 to 1624 an average of only around 40 lasts of powder were purchased annually by the ordnance office, barely enough to keep up with peacetime consumption.[33] As war became more likely in 1624 the situation changed with the purchase of some 160 lasts of powder from the royal powdermakers.[34] This massive purchase, costing around £13,600, was not enough to make up for years of small deliveries as is shown by the fact that the ordnance survey of 1625 (see table 5) showed only some 81 lasts in store. While the case that peacetime deliveries had satisfied peacetime consumption can be made, it is difficult not to accuse the government and the ordnance office of short-sightedness in assuming that this condition would last. The purchase of even 160 lasts did not bring the stores up to the hoped-for level of 300 lasts. Nor did the ordnance office buy much powder the following year after the subsidy

---

[33] PRO, WO 49/50 (1621), 52 (1622), 53 (1623); WO 55/1680 (1624). For 1620 see WO 55/1678. Ordnance office consumption of powder was 67 lasts from 1620 to 1621, 17 lasts from 1621 to 1622, and 45 lasts from 1622 to 1623. As the 1624 survey lists 131 lasts in stock as compared with 129 in 1623 and the indenture books show 41 lasts of powder delivered into the office, it seems that 39 lasts were consumed in the course of that year.
[34] Ibid. WO 49/54, subsidy supplies purchased by the ordnance office, 1624–5. The Evelyns were required by contract to deliver 20 lasts of powder per month at 8.5d. per lb. and managed to deliver 160 lasts in the space of a year, even though they were generally three months behind in their deliveries.

money was used up. In 1625, the office only spent £3,300 on gunpowder: a mere 37 lasts. With war against Spain on the horizon, why was such a small purchase made after the office had seemingly recognised the shortage the previous year?

The answer seems to be that the amount listed in the ordnance accounts does not include the large purchases of gunpowder by the financier and merchant, Philip Burlamachi. The size of Burlamachi's involvement in military matters can be seen at least in part when one notices that he was paid the huge sum of £713,364 for the years from 1620 to 1628. Much of the money paid to him was consumed by the pay, clothing and transport costs of English troops sent to the United Provinces and by Mansfield's abortive expedition to the Palatinate in 1625. However, the list of his expenditures includes the sum of £124,000 spent on saltpetre and gunpowder alone.[35] This was enough to purchase around 950 lasts of gunpowder, or slightly less than three times the total peacetime consumption of the English military from 1610 to 1620. The size of the powder purchases is even more startling when one realises that the amount of money spent by Burlamachi on powder was roughly equivalent to the entire amount of money spent on that product from 1593 to 1620. Deliveries of domestic gunpowder into the ordnance office from 1593 to 1603, during a major war, were less than 900 lasts. In addition, Burlamachi's purchases were meant merely as a supplement to the steady (but clearly inadequate) production of Evelyn's of 240 lasts per year under his contract. Clearly, the powder needs of an army and navy in the 1620s were far beyond those of earlier eras and the government, seemingly, was not prepared for this increase in scale before 1625.

Exactly how or where Burlamachi spent this money is unclear. He did not have to account for any of the money granted to him through the ordnance office accounts nor did much of this powder probably ever go into the stores where it could be accounted for. How much of it was issued directly to the forces in the Netherlands or trans-shipped to naval vessels bound for Cadiz or Rhé is also unclear. However, a portion of the gunpowder purchased by Burlamachi did make its way into the Tower in 1627 and from this the cost and origin of the other powder purchases can be determined. One of his declared accounts lists £7,368 to buy 56 lasts of powder through his factors in the Low Countries for the Rhé expedition at £131 the last, or 13*d*. a pound.[36] Clearly the Low Countries were the central powder market for the English forces in the 1620s with almost an unlimited supply of the important resource for those willing to pay for it. The cost was higher than the domestic product

---

[35] Ibid. SP 16/102/81, account of moneys paid or due to Philip Burlamachi on various accounts, [Apr?] 1628. For more on Burlamachi's financial dealings with the English government see Robert Ashton, 'The disbursing official under the early Stuarts: the cases of Sir William Russell and Philip Burlamachi', *BIHR* xxx (1957), 162–74.

[36] See Burlamachi's accounts in PRO, E 351/2709. His contract with the earl of Marlborough and others was made on 3 Apr. 1627.

by 4–5*d.* per pound or £40–50 per last. However, in war, with domestic production unable to keep pace with consumption, it was the only alternative.

The size of the purchases made overseas by Burlamachi proves quite clearly that domestic production was no longer adequate for the scale of warfare in the 1620s. John Evelyn could not produce enough powder to maintain the Tower stocks at an adequate level even during the period of the build-up to war from 1624 to 1625; it is obvious that only massive purchases by Burlamachi kept the Caroline military in gunpowder during war. The ordnance office system for powder production through domestic contractors was clearly inadequate and the government was forced to turn to a merchant and military entrepreneur with contacts on the continent and credit available virtually on demand. Domestic production and government planning alike in the 1620s could not keep pace with the new demands of war.

Money spent on gunpowder constituted a major part of the ordnance office budget and maintaining large stocks of gunpowder in the Tower was a high priority for the government for much of the period 1585–1625. However, stocks did fluctuate depending upon the amount of military activity or the efficiency of ordnance administration. The effect of military activity can be seen quite clearly by comparing a powder survey of May 1588 (before the Armada campaign) with one in November the same year. The official inventory lists 606 lasts of gunpowder in the Tower in May, and yet by November, after massive deliveries to the fleet, the stocks were down to 55 lasts.[37] This created a situation where powder was in desperately short supply, but by December of that year, stocks had recovered to the level of 152 lasts of powder.[38] As table 5 indicates, gunpowder stocks stayed fairly constant thereafter until they dipped in 1609 and then recovered in 1617. The supply level of 300 lasts on hand for 1617 implies that in the one area of gunpowder supply Sir Roger Dallison did not embezzle money or allow the contractor to go unpaid until the stocks were depleted as he had done with other suppliers.

Perhaps the reason why the staple of powder finally reached the hoped-for level of 300 lasts was because a combination of low demand and the fact that the Evelyns were protected by a special patent which deterred Dallison from interfering. From this high point in 1617, however, the stocks declined again until they levelled off to at 128–131 lasts from 1622 to 1624. The following year they declined to 81 lasts, which, given that war with Spain was almost inevitable by then, is quite alarming. Perhaps the stores had been drained to

---

[37] Ibid. E 101/64/19, a brief declaration of ordnance in the Tower, May 1588; SP 12/218/35, amount of brass and iron ordnance and other principal natures remaining in the ordnance office, 22 Nov. 1588.

[38] To a great extent this seems to have been due to the new contract with the Evelyns and the fact that some £5,753-worth of foreign powder had been purchased between July 1588 and March 1589: ibid. SP 12/223/12, brief note of ordnance office receipts and pay of the lieutenant general of the ordnance, Sir Robert Constable, 18 Mar. 1589.

Table 5
Gunpowder levels (in lasts) during selected survey years[39]

1589	112 (April)	1620	143
	129 (July)	1621	116
	144 (October)	1622	128
1595	191	1623	129
1603	240	1624	131
1609	105	1625	81
1617	300		

supply the ships at sea and had not yet recovered. This does not alter the fact that gunpowder stores were lower than they had ever been since the days following the Spanish Armada. This alone indicates that there was something seriously wrong in government planning for gunpowder in the 1620s.

While figures for overall gunpowder purchases by the ordnance office are not difficult to come by, reliable figures for the consumption of gunpowder by the army or navy in early modern England are less readily available. It is hard to discern whether powder was actually used in combat, lost due to dampness or embezzled and resold. The amount of powder used by the great ordnance, for example, varied greatly according to the size of the piece. Full cannons used as much as 27 pounds of gunpowder per shot, thus consuming a last of 2,400 pounds in approximately 85 shots. The bastard cannon (so-called because of its shortened barrel) would generally fire 120 shots per last (20 poinds per shot) while the more popular culverin and demi-culverin used 12 pounds and 8 pounds of powder per shot, respectively.[40]

Actual levels of gunpowder consumption in the field or at sea are more difficult to discover. During the war years from 1593 to 1603, for example, the ordnance office took delivery of over 890 lasts of gunpowder, or over 2.1 million pounds. The gunpowder stocks in the Tower had about 190 lasts in store in 1593 and yet had only 240 lasts left in 1603. The army and navy of Elizabeth had consumed over 840 lasts (in excess of 2 million pounds) of

---

[39] Inventories are taken from SP 12/223/107, 30 Apr. 1589; SP 12/227/2, powder remaining in her Majesty's storehouses, 1 Oct. 1589; Oxford, Bodleian Library, MS Rawl. A 207, fo. 1–10, ordnance survey, of July 1589; Note of munition needed by the ordnance office; WO 55/1672, survey of 1595 upon the entrance of Mr John Lee into the office of keeper of the stores; BL, MS Royal 17A XXXI, Linewray's survey, 3 May 1603; PRO, SP 14/53/20, ordnance in the Tower from the general survey of 1609 upon Sir Roger Ayscough becoming keeper of the stores, 17 Mar. 1610; WO 55/1680, the grand proportion of 1624 compared with 1617; WO 49/50, indenture book for 1621 comparing remains and issues with inventory of 1620; WO 49/52, indenture book for 1622; WO 49/53, indenture book for 1623; WO 49/55, indenture book for 1625.

[40] Ibid. SP 12/239/55, estimate of the shot of the great ordnance, 24 June 1591; James Sheriffe's table of ordnance, 1592, in Hogg, *Royal artillery*, 26.

gunpowder in those eleven years or an average of about 76⅓ lasts per year. Since the contract with the Evelyns was for eighty lasts per year, this was running things very close indeed. Much of this powder was apparently consumed by the navy which sent between one and four lasts of powder to sea with each ship. However, the army also used a great deal of powder in each of its various expeditions. It consumed especially large quantities in the long Irish campaign where troops and loyalist towns all had to be supplied from English stores.[41]

An example of how much gunpowder was expected to be consumed in battle can be provided by means of a brief examination of the Cadiz expedition of 1596. In this major amphibious raid on the mainland of Spain, eighteen royal ships and dozens of merchantmen and Dutch vessels took a land army of around 6,000 men to attack a fortified city. The ships were issued 43½ lasts of powder, or an average of around 2½ lasts per ship. This average is deceptive, however, since a major warship like the *Ark Royal* with 38 major guns and 17 smaller ones was issued four lasts while a pinnace such as the *Lion's Whelp* was given only 1¼ lasts for its 12 small guns.[42] The figures for the land forces are even more interesting. Fifty lasts of powder were issued for the land forces, more than for the entire royal element of the fleet. Most of this was meant to be issued to the soldiers, implying that planners for the expedition were either expecting a series of major land engagements or else that the English presence at Cadiz was going to be more permanent than it turned out to be or than most modern historians believe was intended. The expedition only took along four cannon and two culverin as a siege train with 1,000 rounds for each weapon. At the normal consumption rates, these guns could only use up around 16 lasts of powder between them leaving 34 for the ground forces. There were only 3,000 calivers issued for the expedition which, at the rate of an ounce of powder per shot, meant that each weapon had available to it 27 pounds of powder or 435 shots. Given that the standard issue of gunpowder for each man in the field was probably only 2 pounds or 32 shots, this was a very large stock of powder to have on hand. A major action was obviously anticipated and the ordnance office planned accordingly and was able to send the necessarily large supply to Cadiz.

Powder consumption during peacetime, as would be expected, seems to have been much more modest. Powder seldom seems to have been used during peacetime except for saluting other ships and flags or fighting off the occasional pirate.[43] When the excess was returned into the stores after a

---

[41] It is difficult to say how much was sent to Ireland because the delivery books of the period are even less complete than the indenture books. They often consist only of lists of ships supplied even in active years for land campaigns.
[42] PRO, WO 55/1626, delivery books, 1596.
[43] Oppenheim comments on the initiatives to reduce excessive saluting and courtesy firing of naval ordnance. It was apparently perceived as a major source of powder wastage. He cites one instance in 1628 when the fleet lying off Plymouth fired £100-worth of powder in one day in drinking healths: Oppenheim, *Royal navy*, 213–14.

voyage, the resulting dampness often made it essential that it be reworked. Far more was probably ruined by dampness or poor storage than was consumed in action. Most of the issues of powder during peacetime were to ships. For example, from 1610 to 1620, only 379 lasts of powder were issued out of the Tower for any purpose, about 34 lasts per year on average. Of this amount 140 lasts (over one-third) were issued to ships, 66 lasts (17 per cent) were sent to forts, 36 lasts to Ireland (less than 10 per cent), with almost as many (26 lasts) issued for 'entertainments'.[44] Domestic powder production was easily able to keep up with such low rates of consumption until the beginnings of the war with Spain in 1625. However, lack of planning for the increased need for powder during wartime left England critically short of this vital commodity at the worst possible moment.

The failure of domestic production to keep up with wartime demand should have been apparent to the government even before 1625. In 1621, when Evelyn was approached to provide powder for the proposed expedition to recapture the Palatinate, the committee which consulted him reported that Evelyn and the other arms makers were: 'able to supply soe litle in any kind upon soe short a warning as three mounthes, that the greatest parte of powder and of arms both for horsse and ffoote must be provided in the Lowe Cuntrys where (wee conceave) it may be best had'.[45] Nor did this warning galvanise the government into action: gunpowder shortages continued to be a problem.

In 1623 James issued a proclamation in an attempt to deal with this shortage 'by which the king's ships and subjects are endangered'. This reiterated that all gunpowder was to be sent to the king's powdermaker, proofed and stamped with a mark of its quality. These drastic steps were deemed necessary, as the text of the proclamation plainly states, because of the poor quality of the foreign powder coming secretly into England. In addition, the pressing need for any foreign powder at all demonstrates an increased requirement for powder which Evelyn was not able to meet.[46] However, the proclamation does not seem to have had any dramatic effect on the supply of gunpowder, although it may have assisted in the administrative handling of stocks once they were in the Tower.

Complaints of powder shortages were to reappear regularly. John Evelyn could not keep up with his contracts and there were rumours that what was brought into the Tower was wasted or sold for personal profit. For example, in 1624, Sir John Coke complained that Evelyn was not fulfilling his contract. He said that Evelyn had supplied only 100 lasts of powder since 1621, a fact generally borne out by the records. However, Coke must have meant 'new' powder since the Evelyns brought in at least 132 lasts of reworked, 'decayed',

---

[44] PRO, SP 14/115/61, deliveries out of the ordnance office, 1610–20.
[45] HMC, *Salisbury*, xxii. 140–4. The expedition was to consist of 25,000 foot and 5,000 horse.
[46] PRO, SP 14/187/110, gunpowder proclamation, 16 Jan. 1623.

powder between 1621 and 1623. Coke claimed that Evelyn was 135 lasts below his promised deliveries.[47] Evelyn, on the other hand, claimed in May 1624 that he was fulfilling his contract of 20 lasts per month. They both could have been right since Coke's attack in March of 1624 probably referred to an old contract with Evelyn that had been voided due to the government's failure to pay promptly. Most contracts had a clause that allowed the gunpowder maker to stop bringing in powder if payments were over 90 days in arrears, which apparently occurred during the financially straitened circumstances of the 1620s. Evelyn defended himself shortly after he had begun bringing in supplies of gunpowder under a new contract to be paid for out of the parliamentary subsidy of 1624.[48] Coke was referring to a situation that was serious from 1621 to 1624 but which improved, belatedly, soon after his attack.

The neglect of gunpowder stocks for the years 1621–4 could not be remedied overnight and Tower stocks remained dangerously low. In this, the gunpowder industry was similar to other defence industries of the period. It was difficult to expand production capacity in armament industries without a great deal of warning, prior planning and expense. The government may have received and even recognised the warning, but could not plan adequately and could not come up with the money to improve the situation quickly enough. The government virtually stopped the purchase of gunpowder from 1621 until early in 1624 and found itself in the position of having to turn to foreign sources and merchant suppliers for this vital strategic resource. Self-sufficiency in gunpowder for England in the early seventeenth century was virtually impossible. This same phenomenon, to a smaller degree, can be observed in even the lesser ordnance supplies: the handguns, pikes and other so called 'habilliments of war'.

---

[47] Ibid., SP 14/161/13, 21 March 1624. Evelyn was to bring in 6½ lasts per month for the king and 40 additional lasts per year to be resold to the public. The king was to pay only 7*d*. per lb. for all of it, but would resell 40 lasts at 10*d*. per lb. thereby clearing a nice 3*d*. per lb., or £1,200 per year profit. For an example of a contract for reworking decayed powder see WO 49/49, indenture book for 1620, contract to rework over 42 lasts of gunpowder and return to store.

[48] He even requested an advance of £2,000 on his contract so that he could put up new buildings: *CSPD James I, 1623–5*, 246, Evelyn to Carew, 15 May 1624.

6

Hand Guns, 'Habilliments of War' and the Arms Merchants

Falstaff: 'Oh, give me the spare men, and spare me the great ones. Put me a caliver into Wart's hand, Bardolph.'

Bardolph: 'Hold, Wart, traverse. Thus, thus, thus.'

Falstaff: 'Come manage me your caliver. So. Very well. Go to. Very good, exceeding good. Oh, give me always a little, lean, old, chapped, bald shot.'

– Shakespeare, *Henry IV, Part II*, act III, scene ii

In addition to its responsibilities for the great ordnance and gunpowder, the ordnance office was also the agency for the procurement, storage, maintenance and issuance of smaller firearms such as calivers and muskets. The office of the keeper of the small guns maintained these weapons, but they were made by independent artisans. The fact that there was a separate officer in charge of the office of small guns whereas there was no such office for the management of the great ordnance, may indicate that the smaller and more numerous handguns posed a greater administrative challenge than did the cannons. Moreover, there was the additional office of Her Majesty's master gunmaker.

This post was held by one craftsman at a time, paid at the rate of 6*d*. per day or £9 2*s*. 6*d*. per year,[1] and the two known occupants of the office were William Hoappe in the 1590s and Henry Rowland in the 1620s. The master gunmaker co-ordinated for the ordnance office the issuance of weapons to the other gunmakers for repair and the distribution of gunpowder to the gunmakers who often proofed their own weapons; he was also the contact point for the various contracts made with the gunmakers. In a sense he was first among equals and also an intermediary between the government and the ill-organised craftsmen who made the weapons for the government.[2]

The small weapons brought into the office varied over time as older types

---

[1] PRO, SP 12/221/13, book of crown offices, [1588?]. Probably early Jacobean.
[2] Ibid. WO 49/19; WO 55/1626. In this last document Hoappe is also referred to as the proofmaster for small ordnance: WO 55/451; WO 55/1629, fo. 61. It took approximately 2oz of gunpowder to proof each weapon in this instance. Muskets normally used only 1oz of powder per shot so probably two rounds were fired from each gun.

of guns became obsolete and were replaced by newer models. By the 1590s, the old-fashioned harquebus (or arquebus or hackbutt), a crude and heavy gun, was obsolete and those which remained in the store had deteriorated virtually beyond repair. The newer caliver, on the other hand, was a lighter, smaller-bored gun which was still much in use in England and Ireland although passing out of use on the continent. New calivers cost, on the average, 12s. 6d. to 13s. 4d. each in the early 1590s but had declined in price to 11s. by the end of the reign of Elizabeth. This decline was due in part to the larger quantities purchased by the government during the war years since the caliver was ideal for the small unit skirmishes typical of the conflict in Ireland. Between 1598 and 1602 the Elizabethan government was increasingly tied down by the O'Neill rebellion in Ireland and was forced to expend enormous sums to suppress it. This had the beneficial side effect of forcing the government to buy weapons in bulk and with such steady employment the number of gunmakers increased over the years of war. In order to compete for the lucrative government contracts, the gunmakers also seem to have been forced to lower their prices. It helped that there were few other legitimate outlets for their products, and the government, as the primary consumer, could virtually set its own price.

The calivers produced by the gunmakers generally came equipped with a flask which held the powder for the main charge, a touch-box for the finer 'serpentine' powder for the priming pan, and a bullet mould so that the soldier could cast his own bullets. In many cases this last item was essential since each gunmaker made the bore a slightly different size due to the imperfection of their manufacturing equipment. Often a bullet cast in a standard size would not fit a weapon and the soldier, out of prudence, generally made his own shot out of the lead issued to him. A small amount of pre-cast shot was made by the office's plumber (worker in lead) each year. As a crude proof, he would roll the musket balls onto a large board with holes drilled in it the size of the musket bore. The correctly sized balls and those smaller than needed would fall through. The larger balls would not. The smaller ones were not a problem since they could be dealt with in the field by wrapping them up in extra wadding before ramming them down the musket barrel.

The caliver makers also carried out any major repairs on the weapons for the office of keeper of the small guns was only large enough to do routine maintenance. Even weapons in poor condition could generally be restocked and repaired for under 5s. This was a great saving and the ordnance office issued thousands of weapons to the caliver makers in the 1590s for repair.[3] Only after all these old weapons had been repaired and issued did the thrifty government contract for new weapons. However, by the end of the Spanish

---

[3] Many of the calivers sent to Ireland at the start the O'Neill rebellion were those that had been procured by Sir Thomas Gresham in 1560, and were by then almost 45 years old: ibid. WO 49/20; E 351/26.

and Irish war in 1604, the caliver was virtually obsolete and the government had turned increasingly to the musket.

The musket had a heavier bore than the caliver and required slightly different ancillary equipment. It was either 5 feet in length, costing 21s. in 1596, or 4½ feet in length costing 20s. in that year.[4] The length of the musket was gradually reduced until by the start of the Civil War, the musket had been standardised at 4 feet.[5] Furnished muskets included a bandoleer of a dozen or so wooden or leather 'bottles', each containing one charge of powder, which was worn over the shoulder of the musketeer. This item was generally subcontracted out by the gunmakers to a girdler, that craft being virtually a monopoly of the Wright family of London. (See the list of craftsmen in appendix 2.) The office also dealt directly with the girdlers for their replacement bandoleers. Other 'furnished' equipment for the musket generally included, as with the caliver, a touch-box for fine powder and a bullet mould. However, the heavy musket, unlike the caliver, also needed a rest which was generally provided separately by the pikemakers or carpenters. This, a metal tipped wooden stick with a 'U' shaped top, was considered necessary for holding up the heavy, long weapon while firing it. It was in common use through the 1620s although was discontinued in England by the start of the civil war, as the length and weight of the musket had considerably reduced; it had been abandoned on the continent during the Thirty Years' War.[6] The variance in prices for muskets in the same year often depended less on which gunmaker provided it then on how many extra furnishings were included with each piece. By 1602 the price for a furnished musket had fallen on the average to 16s. each but occasional deals were made for larger quantities at short notice for which the government apparently paid a premium. In 1599, for example, Sir George Carew was issued a warrant for £2,000 to buy 2,000 muskets to replenish the stores.[7] The price of £1 per musket was somewhat unusual by 1599, however, and the average price continued to be between 16s. and 18s. 6d. each up to the start of the war with Spain in 1625. Between 1624 and 1625, over 1,600 muskets and 1,344 calivers were purchased for the stores at a cost of £2,500 paid out of the parliamentary subsidy of 1624.[8]

Both the muskets and the calivers which were provided to the office were commonly matchlocks which required the infantryman to carry burning lengths of nitre-soaked rope (match) on his person when going into battle.

---

[4] Ibid. WO 49/20, agreement between the gunmakers and privy council for 213 muskets at 5ft and 256 muskets at 4½ft, at a total cost of £479 13s., 26 Feb. 1596. Sixteen gunmakers are listed producing between 9 and 71 muskets each.
[5] C. H. Firth, *Cromwell's army*, London 1902, 80.
[6] Ibid. 79–80.
[7] CSPD Eliz. I, 1598–1601, 278, warrant, 6 Aug. 1599.
[8] PRO, WO 49/54, 55. An estimate for the cost of 3,102 muskets in 1628 was £3,260, or 21s. each, but this included 3,000 bandoleers which normally cost 4s. each so the muskets themselves only cost around 17s.: BL, MS Harl. 429, fo. 49, 3 Sept. 1629.

This was attached to the cock of the musket when firing. The soldier would open his priming pan full of touchpowder and pull the 'tricker' or trigger to push the match into the pan. Earlier muskets and calivers were also made with 'sear-locks' rather than 'tricker-locks' but the difference between their actions was minimal. There were also a few wheel-locks purchased for the stores. However, these were expensive devices with many moving parts. The spring of the wheel-lock was wound with a device like a key and when the trigger was pulled the spring moved a wheel with pyrite on it which struck a piece of metal causing a spark in the pan. They were not regularly issued due to their unreliability and expense. The more common of the weapons of this firelock family was the 'snaphaunse' or snaphanse lock. This was an early type of flintlock which had fewer parts than the wheel-lock and needed no key to wind it. Common by the time of Civil War, their more reliable and faster action caused them eventually to be preferred to the matchlock which, first purchased by the ordnance office at least as early as 1601[9] initially was by far the more common weapon.[10]

Extensive or sophisticated equipment was not needed to make the muskets and calivers required by the ordnance office. Virtually any craftsman with a forge could make a crude firearm which would conform to the lax government standards of the time. Moreover, since there was no gunmakers company until 1637, the manufacture of firearms was not restricted to any body of craftsmen.[11] Nor was the craft subject to much in the way of internal regulation or specified standards. Virtually the only method of checking up on the gunmakers' work was by proofing each weapon before it was received into the office. These problems were not adequately addressed until the formation of the first gunmakers company in 1637 although some attempts at establishing city responsibility for quality control were made as early as 1600.

Thus in July 1600, a letter from the privy council to Mr Wilbraham, master of requests, and Sir John Peyton, lieutenant of the Tower, referred to the problem of quality control. The council had had brought to its attention a dispute between the Blacksmiths' Company and the Armourers' Company over the 'serch of muskettes, gonnes, armor and other warrlyke weapons'. This dispute had prevented any effective quality control at all:

> whereby soch counties of the realme as do make great provicion of armor and weapon for publicke service were often tymes greatly deceaved in those

---

[9] PRO, WO 49/26, ordnance indentures, 1601.
[10] Firth, *Cromwell's army*, 88–9. The matchlock was still being used in the English army during William III's wars in Ireland in the 1690s, but by 1700 variations of the firelock had entirely superseded it.
[11] L. O. Boynton, 'The charter of the Company of Gunmakers, London', *Journal of the Society of Army Historical Research* vi (1927), 79–92.

provicions they made, her Majesty's service dysappointed and the souldier many tymes grevyouslie hurt and endangered by the breakinge of their peeces.[12]

Clearly this affected the military preparedness of the entire kingdom since the local militia or private arms procurers probably did not have any specialised proofing system like that of the ordnance office. The Lord Mayor was asked to look into the problem and find out why the warden of the Blacksmiths' Company refused to perform the service as a previous act of the council had required. But unfortunately little seems to have been done.

Partly as a result of the lack of any effective supervision or craft discipline, gunmakers could be found all over the country, with fairly well developed small arms industries in Bristol and Wales. In 1593, for example, William Grosvenor of Bellaporte, Salop, offered to provide 1,000 muskets and 1,000 calivers yearly to the stores in London and thus to save the government some £15 for every 100 muskets ordered and £3 6s. 6d. for every 100 calivers. In addition, he offered to supply the forces in Ireland with whatever they needed in the way of small arms and armour. The goods would be delivered to Chester to save the transport costs and he would be able to keep together his workmen who were already supplying the surrounding counties with arms.[13]

The true centre for the production of handguns was London however, and it was here that most of the gunmakers lived and worked.[14] Their forges and workshops were set up in the districts near the Tower: the Minories, Southwark, Holborn, East Smithfield, Tower Wharf, Towerhill and St Katherines. It is difficult to say how many gunmakers there were at any one time, since the numbers fluctuated according to demand. In 1594, for example, there were only three individuals manufacturing weapons for the ordnance stores: Philip Dier and William Hoppe, musket makers, and Gosson Harrison, blacksmith. They were mainly involved in the repair of weapons and the manufacture of flasks and touchboxes, since of the 335 muskets or calivers purchased that year, fully 320 were not made by London gunsmiths at all but rather were purchased from Randall Symes (or Symmes), an arms merchant.[15] However, in 1596, a busy year because of the ambitious expedition to Cadiz, there were at least thirty-eight gunmakers, blacksmiths or armourers supplying small guns to the ordnance office or repairing those guns. Each of them must have received a small proportion of the business of the office since only 1,000

---

[12] APC 1599–1600, 541 (29 July 1600).
[13] See HMC, *Salisbury*, iv. 459, offer to supply ordnance by William Grosvenor, [1593]. There is no evidence that this particular offer was accepted, but men going to Ireland were often provided with equipment and arms manufactured in or near Chester and Bristol so if this offer was not accepted, another similar one probably was.
[14] Walter M. Stern, 'Gunmaking in seventeenth-century London', *Journal of the Arms and Armour Society* i (1954), 55–100.
[15] PRO, WO 49/18.

new muskets or calivers were made during the year and 500 sent out for repair.[16] By far the busiest of the war years for the gunmakers was 1599, the year in which the earl of Essex launched his lavishly-supplied expedition to Ireland. In that year over forty gunsmiths manufactured almost 4,000 calivers and muskets for the stores at a cost to the government of around £3,000.[17]

However, 1599 seems to have been the peak year of production. With the coming of peace in 1603 the number of gunmakers diminished almost immediately, with only eleven known gunmakers still providing weapons to the office in 1605 and five by 1607.[18] The subsequent lack of skilled gunmakers by the 1620s, although doubtless disturbing to those on the council who advocated military preparedness, was not as serious as the decline in the number of gunfounders. It took many months, almost years, to create a new forge with the skilled workmen to build great ordnance, but much less time to retrain enough blacksmiths to make small arms. In addition, small arms can be made very quickly and stores can be replenished with a minimum of advanced warning. This point is borne out by the fact that when the office needed to make larger purchases of small guns again in 1620, they were able to distribute the order to twelve gunmakers. By the following year, there were at least twenty-six craftsmen (an increase of over 100 per cent) involved in the manufacture of handguns for the government of which only five were in the trade in 1605.[19] The number of gunmakers continued to expand during the build-up to war, reaching thirty-one by 1625. By the time of the formation of the Gunmakers' Company in 1637, there were sixty-three craftsmen involved in the manufacture of muskets in London alone.[20]

Despite the increasing importance of firearms on the sixteenth- and seventeenth-century military scene, much more than great ordnance and small arms were required in order to prepare an army for an expedition. There were a host of smaller items necessary for any major military campaign which fell under the general heading of 'habilliments of war'.[21] Many of these were provided by craftsmen working for the government and paid a regular salary by the ordnance office. The ordnance office carpenter built field carriages and gun chests. The master smith made crow bars, iron nails and shovels. The plumber provided lead and cast some lead shot for muskets.

---

[16] Ibid. WO 49/20. For a fairly complete list of suppliers of small arms to the office see appendix 2.
[17] PRO, WO 49/24. Among the gunmakers listed were Jane Staunton, widow, Isabel Hopkins, Janes Bowers and Anne Addis. They were probably carrying out their late husbands' trade since women were generally not admitted as members of any accepted craft.
[18] Ibid. WO 49/31; Stern, 'Gunmaking', 55. The number of gunmakers for 1605 may not be accurate since the office bought so few weapons that year that they only needed to approach a few craftsmen.
[19] Ibid. WO 49/49, 50. The five men still engaged in the trade were Christopher Bird, John Harrington, Thomas Laverocke, Jr, Roger Holder or Howlder, and Richard Berrowe.
[20] Ibid. WO 49/54, 55; Boynton, 'Company of Gunmakers', 80–1.
[21] See appendix 3 for a sample list of such 'habilliments' for the army and for the navy.

The bowyer and fletcher built hundreds of longbows, most of which were never issued to troops. The office also continued to produce sheaf after sheaf of arrows, although it seems that they were seldom issued to anyone. Occasionally one finds five or ten bows sent to a ship where they would be useful in sending fire arrows into the enemy's rigging, but they were almost never issued to any land forces. Instead longbows, crossbows, bolts and arrows were mainly stockpiled in the Tower.

There were other supplies, however, which were only obtained from independent craftsmen. For example, pikes, both long (16 feet) and short (8–10 feet) were made by Her Majesty's pikemaker. The standard pike prices were fairly constant at 2s. 6d. each for long pikes and 20d. each for short ones unless they were covered with gilt as were the ceremonial pikes.[22] Bandoleers for musketeers were made by Peter, Robert and Anne Wright for 4s. each.

Armour, like the bow and arrow, was also going out of fashion, but stores of body armour were maintained in the ordnance office and the armoury through to the Civil War. Much of it, primarily the corslet or pikeman's body armour, was purchased overseas or from the Armourers' Company of London. A complete set cost from 18s. to 30s. for the standard issue 'Brest' (frontpiece), 'Back' (backpiece), gorget (metal collar) and helmet.[23] Prices for armour stayed very constant throughout the late sixteenth and early seventeenth centuries. In 1586, for example, there were complaints that foreign merchants were 'dumping' their corslets in England for 18s. while local craftsmen were charging 28s. The fact that the armoury bought their corslets for 18s. in 1586 and the ordnance office was still paying just 18s. each in 1625 indicates both that the government took advantage of the foreign goods and that the competition helped keep the prices down.[24] There were also severe complaints in 1621 when Sir Dudley Carlton, the ambassador to the States General of the United Provinces, tried to buy armour for the proposed 12,000-man expedition to the Palatinate in the Low Countries instead of at home. He had already made some tentative agreements when the privy council told him to stop, saying that in their consultations with the king, the ordnance officers, the armourers and the cutlers, it had been decided to 'buy English'. It was hoped that the goods would be lower in price, of better quality, available in the time required and would have the inestimable benefit of 'gayneinge manufacture and affoarding imployment to [the king's] owne subjects'.[25] The small English arms industry did not relish competition.

---

[22] PRO, WO 49/17, 1593. John Edwards, his Majesty's pikemaker in 1625, charged 3s. 8d. for pikes with Spanish steel heads as did Robert Thacker of London in that same year. For other price comparisons on key military supplies see appendix 4.
[23] PRO, WO 49/54.
[24] HMC, *Salisbury*, iii. 132–3 (Feb. 1586). See also PRO, WO 49/55, fo. 101b. Armour was being produced in London at more reasonable prices by 1625, primarily by the armourers John Francklyn, William Crowch, John Ashton and Thomas Stephens.
[25] *APC 1619–21*, 384 (15 May 1621). The council further asked Carlton to assure the

However, there were problems other than foreign competition which were developing from the early years of James I. Local armourers had begun to see their trade shrink after 1604, partly due to the peace itself and partly due to the decline of the domestic market in the counties. It was probably in that year that armour makers petitioned the House of Lords to save their ancient trade. Their petition mentioned that there had been some thirty-five armour makers in London and the suburbs during the reign of Queen Elizabeth whereas that number had even by 1604 shrunk to only five. They blamed parliament for this state of affairs more than foreign competition, since they complained that with the repeal of 4 and 5 Philip and Mary, a key statute requiring the provision of arms to local militiamen, there was no longer any fixed domestic market. They did not actually call for the statute to be renewed, but instead asked that some course be taken by parliament to encourage the health of their trade.[26] The armour industry did not vanish, but it did suffer the same severe constriction as other armaments industries after 1604. Unlike them, however, it did not recover again in the 1620s since body armour slowly but surely vanished from the arms inventories and the battlefields of Europe.

Swords, however, were still very much a part of each soldier's basic equipment. The pikeman and musketeers had, in addition to their own main weapons, swords and daggers at their sides to use when the fighting got too close for them to use the ungainly pike or the cumbersome, slow-firing musket. During the 1590s swords were purchased from cutlers of the London Cutlers' Company or from overseas sources through the office of the armoury.[27] The cost, depending upon quality and type of hilt, varied from 6s. 8d. to 10s. each. Between 1590 and 1603, the armoury purchased over 8,400 swords at a cost to the government of more than £3,500. The craftsmen who made these blades are not listed and it is possible that many were produced overseas.

There were problems with the foreign supply of swords, however. In 1590 there were complaints that such blades were defective 'made of sleight stuff ... and vented into dyvers counties to suche as in these doubtfull times have been injoyned to furnish themselves with armour and weapon'.[28] The Lord Mayor was requested by the privy council to investigate this complaint and to appoint wardens of the Cutlers' Company to search the warehouses for defective blades and to seize them. Since the blades were in direct competition with the Cutlers' Company's own products, it was like putting the fox to

---

king's son-in-law, Frederick, the Elector Palatine, that this new twist would not alter the king's resolution to relieve the Palatinate.
[26] HMC, *Salisbury*, xvi. 401–2, [1604]. See also *Statutes of the Realm*, 4 and 5 Philip and Mary, c. 2 and 3 'An Acte for the havinge and keeping of Horse Armour and Weapon' and 'An act for the taking of musters'. These were repealed by 1 Jac. I, c. 25.
[27] PRO, E 101/64/11, declared accounts of the master of the armoury.
[28] APC 1590, 35, privy council to lord mayor of London, 9 Apr. 1590.

guard the henhouse. The mayor's appointees would certainly conduct a diligent search, but the Cutlers' Company inspectors were probably not unbiased authorities on what constituted a defective blade.

Most of the swords purchased by the central office of the armoury in the 1590s were intended for the troops in Ireland as replacements since the initial levies of troops for all overseas expeditions were issued with swords in their counties of origin. The smaller and shorter-term expeditions did not need such replacements and one looks in vain through the armoury records for any large-scale purchases for the expeditions to Normandy, Brittany, Cadiz or even for the forces in the Low Countries. In the latter case, the troops probably had local sources for the purchase of swords since the Netherlands (especially Amsterdam) was renowned as having one of the best arms markets in Europe.

The procedures for buying swords changed considerably with the renewal of war in the 1620s. The procurement functions of the armoury were gradually taken over by the ordnance office, with the result that swords were purchased through that office rather than through the armoury. By the outbreak of war in 1625, the names of cutlers, number of swords purchased and cost of swords began appearing in the ordnance records. Between 1624 and 1625 Thomas Cale, Thomas Cheshire, John Porter, John Harmer, Thomas Rogers, Robert Smith, John Cooper and William Cave, all London cutlers, provided at least 7,169 swords at a cost of over £2,200 to the ordnance office.[29] The average price of each blade was 6s. 2d., which was lower than the price charged in the 1590s. This seems to indicate that the cost of at least some war supplies was not increasing despite a booming market for arms on the continent. To a certain degree this also demonstrates the small scale of the arms production industry in England at the end of a long period of peace. There were apparently only a few cutlers providing swords to the ordnance office. If the craftsmen had also been producing for the wider European market, there would almost certainly have been more of them.

The arms merchants

The role of the independent craftsman in the arms procurement system was crucial to the long term self-sufficiency of the English military establishment. However, there were times when the state required vast quantities of arms and supplies at short notice which either the craftsmen could not provide quickly enough, or were not able to supply at all. At that point the ordnance personnel had no choice but to deal with the handful of London merchants who could provide these supplies at short notice. This was especially true of those various merchants (some of them ordnance officers and clerks) who provided the 'emptions' for the ships – oil, tallow, sheepskins, canvas, nails,

[29] PRO, WO 49/54, 55.

rozen, sulphur and a host of other minor, yet necessary, supplies.[30] The ordnance office would have found it a very time-consuming job to accumulate these supplies directly from individual craftsmen or merchants. Instead, it contracted with dozens of chandlers to gather them together from the petty merchants involved. In these instances, convenience was as much a consideration as price. Since many of the chandlers were also ordnance personnel, there was perhaps the added attraction of the profit which was made by officers and clerks of the ordnance office.

Generally speaking, the merchants providing supplies to the ordnance office fall into two categories. The first type of merchant was one whose financial and trade contacts on the continent were so extensive that they could conjure up as much war matériel as was needed merely by spreading the word to their overseas factors. An early example of the use of commercial contacts to obtain arms was Sir Thomas Gresham, whose trading contacts allowed him to purchase over £139,000 worth of arms and munitions between 1558 and 1562 when England was in desperate need of them.[31] These purchases indicate both the need for huge quantities of supplies at short notice and the poor state of England's own arms industry at the time. In the 1620s, Philip Burlamachi, a noted and powerful London financier, provided money, credit and arms to the crown thanks to his continental connections.[32] In both instances, the arms deals were only a small part of the merchants' dealings with the state. They were not arms merchants *per se* but rather merchants who used their contacts to obtain some arms on an irregular basis when England was desperate for them at short notice.

There were also merchants who specialised in weapons procurement and the purchase of war supplies, a growing category throughout the late sixteenth century as the wars of Elizabeth showed no sign of ending. The market existed, and the number of competitors who wanted to service it increased. These merchants concentrated on high volume supplies such as muskets, pikes, gunpowder, rope and match. The office purchased large quantities of these goods, especially rope and match, to provide for the forces in Ireland and those at sea. William Beale, a London merchant, specialised in providing large quantities of rope to the ordnance office in the 1590s from a variety of overseas sources.[33] The scarcity of rope also affected the supplies of match which was a vital commodity for musketeers and naval gunners alike and thus was constantly in demand. Match was often ruined soon after issue by

---

[30] See appendix 3.
[31] PRO, E 351/26, declared accounts of Sir Thomas Gresham.
[32] Stearns, 'Caroline military system', 209–12. See also BL, MS Harl. 429, fo. 63, 24 July 1629.
[33] Even his sources did not provide anywhere near enough rope to satisfy the needs of the service. In one instance in 1601 the navy was forced to contract directly with the Muscovy Company to provide almost £15,000-worth of cables and rope to the stores in Deptford and Chatham: PRO, E 403/2560 fo. 223b–4.

Table 6
Merchant suppliers to the ordnance office, 1593–1603

	Supplier and value of supplies provided		
Year	Randall Symmes	Simeon Furner	Others
1593	0	0	60
1594	190	0	60
1595	990	1,605	305
1596	600	2,340	2,350
1597	*	*	*
1598	80	0	125
1599	40	0	2,495
1600	0	640	1,440
1601	0	1,350	270
1602	0	1,595	5
1603	0	740	0
Total	£1,900	£8,270	£7,110
Grand Total			£17,280

All figures are in pounds sterling to the nearest £5.
* Ordnance books for 1597 are missing.

dampness, an obvious hazard on a ship. It was also consumed in great amounts by land forces since it was regularly lit by the musketeers or gunners even if they were only anticipating action. No veteran soldier or sailor went into action without his burning match by his side, just in case. Match was provided primarily by two men in the 1590s, Randall Symmes, who also provided guns, pikes and ordnance, and Simeon Furner. In 1601 Furner, a London merchant, who was also a partner with the Evelyns in the manufacture and supply of gunpowder, was made the patentee for match which he provided at 17s. per hundredweight.[34] Furner was one of the busiest of the merchants in the late sixteenth and early seventeenth centuries, providing over £2,000 of match and £6,000 of other supplies to the ordnance office between 1595 and 1603.

As is shown in table 6, out of the total amount of supplies brought into the office by merchants from 1593 to 1603, almost half was provided by Simeon Furner. He provided £8,000-worth of supplies out of a total of £17,280. Of this, he supplied £2,060-worth of match, £985-worth of rope and £2,580-worth of gunpowder. Doubtless there were other merchants who provided other arms supplies, since clothing and food contractors can occasionally be found providing some arms for new levies as well as those goods, but most

---

[34] APC 1601–4, 289, privy council to the ordnance office, 18 Oct. 1601.

Table 7
Breakdown of merchant supplied items, 1593–1603

Item	Value
Rope	3,300
Match	4,475
Ordnance	1,320
Powder	3,635
Shot	945
Handguns	840
Pike	145
Lead	635
Misc	1,965
Total	£17,280

All figures are in pounds sterling to the nearest £5.

such instances are poorly documented and the extent of their activities is unknown. As table 7 shows, merchants concentrated on providing match, gunpowder, rope and ordnance.

One other important merchant, who provided literally thousands of sets of armour, swords and calivers for the troops going to Ireland, does not appear in the official records of the ordnance office at all. This was Edmond Nicholson, of London, who at least from 1598 to 1604 was involved in the provision of arms to the troops from his own storehouses. Nicholson offered to provide arms for pikemen and calivermen 'of better sort than used heretofore, and at as reasonable rates' and the council took him up on it.[35] Each year from 1598 through 1604, Nicholson was directed to provide from 500 to 2,000 sets of arms at a time to supply the levies going to Ireland. In the years from 1598 to 1601 alone, he provided £9,597-worth of arms, armour and supplies to the Irish forces.[36] None of these supplies or the money to pay Nicholson went through the ordnance office; the contract was made directly with the privy council and Nicholson was paid directly from the exchequer. The ordnance office was far from having a monopoly on government purchases of weapons.

The counties were also involved in providing arms or cash in lieu of arms for their levies going overseas. Since the drain in manpower on the counties was so heavy, and since their own arms had left with earlier levies, seldom to return, the counties often sent cash to London and the council arranged for the arms directly.[37] In February 1601, one of the conductors of a unit bound

---

[35] PRO, SP 12/275/105, list of arms offered to be supplied by Mr Nicolson, 29 Oct. 1600. See also *APC 1601–4*, 65, 469, 472, 487.
[36] PRO, SP 15/34/55, account of moneys paid out for levy, apparelling and arming soldiers, [24 Mar.] 1603.
[37] *CSPD Eliz. I, 1601–3*, 179, Robert Bowyer to Thomas Edmondes, clerk of the council,

for Cork in Ireland was told to take his men to Bristol unarmed, there to arm 350 of them with weapons provided by Nicholson while another 150 men were to be provided with equipment from the county of Gloucester where they were pressed.[38]

Nicholson maintained extensive storehouses in London and shipped his goods overland to Bristol or Chester which were the two main ports for men and supplies going to Ireland. He was something of an 'official' merchant and thus obtained assistance from the government in moving his goods. In December 1601 the privy council issued open warrants to all public officers to assist Nicholson in moving these supplies overland by providing him with horses and carts.[39] In effect Nicholson was an arms patentee and on numerous instances, with the council concerned that the counties provided high quality arms for their troops, he was even recommended to the counties as a man to be trusted with their supply.

It is possible that Nicholson was the individual referred to in an undated petition in the Salisbury papers as having requested all arms supply from the various companies in London to go through him. This petitioner supported his proposal by stating that he could provide quality arms at a steady price. This, he claimed, was better than allowing workmen, at the hint of government purchases, to raise their prices and sell shoddy goods to fulfill the large government orders.[40] Whether Nicholson was indeed the ambitious patentee in this instance or not is immaterial, since by the end of the war he was fulfilling that role anyway.

The role of 'official' arms patentee was not an unalloyed benefit for Nicholson. In late 1603, with the war winding down, Nicholson was begging to be reimbursed for some of his now surplus stores:

> Praying that he may have recompense for large stores of arms furnished by him in the late Queen's time for the use of the trained bands in Ireland and left on his hands owing to the conclusion of peace and the cessation of a demand for warlike provisions.[41]

For the arms merchant, peace was often an event to be lamented.

By the 1620s the ordnance office tended to rely less and less on merchants for supplies. England seems to have achieved at least some measure of self-

---

26 Apr. 1602. See also *APC 1601–4*, 222–3, council to lords lieutenants of the counties. The offer was that either the counties would arm the men themselves, at their own expense, or that they were to send 30s. per man to London for the government to provide for them.

[38] PRO, E 407/12/6, miscellaneous papers, orders, etc., relating to the expenses of troops, garrisons, etc. in England, Ireland and abroad, 1559–1777.
[39] *APC 1601–4*, 469 (31 Dec. 1601).
[40] HMC, *Salisbury*, xiii. 328–9. This proposal should probably be dated sometime in 1601 since that was the year Nicholson made a similar proposal to the council which prompted them to establish a special commission to investigate its impact.
[41] Ibid. xv. 303, [Nov. 1603].

sufficiency although this was probably due to reduced demand rather than to any expanded arms industry. Although still forced occasionally into the open market to buy war supplies, most notably rope and match, the value of supplies purchased by the ordnance office from merchants between 1620 and 1625 was lower than at the height of Elizabeth's wars. In the 1620s, the ordnance office primarily relied upon one merchant, John Fletcher of London, who from 1620 through 1625 provided only slightly less than £5,000-worth of supplies. This averaged out at about £815 *per annum*, or slightly less than half of the £1,727 *per annum* spent on merchants' goods in the years 1593–1603. Most of the money spent in the 1620s was on rope and match, which still remained in short supply. In particular, there is no record in the ordnance office accounts of any mass purchases of gunpowder, ordnance, guns or shot from continental sources from 1620 until 1625. Of course, there was no need for mass purchases in time of peace, but even the war scares of the early 1620s do not seem to have prompted any large scale dealings with merchants. However, if the expedition to the Palatinate had actually been launched, such large scale purchases may well have been required.[42]

In general, the ordnance office preferred to deal with individual craftsmen for the larger items – ordnance, handguns, pikes, ironworks, gunpowder, shot – while only dealing with merchants for batches of small items such as ships' emptions, or for imported goods such as rope and match. This was not a hard and fast rule, for when 2,000 muskets with swords, match, shot, powder and rests were needed at short notice, the ordnance office and the privy council turned to whatever source had it most readily available.

Merchants could supply at short notice, but in the long run, the health of the military establishment in England depended upon the dozens of craftsmen and suppliers in London and other centres of production. As such, the number of craftsmen expanded to meet the needs of the growing war effort of the 1590s and drastically shrank during the period of peace from 1604 to 1620. Only as James, and later Charles, began to see that it was impossible to stay out of continental affairs did the number of craftsmen begin to expand again. From 1620 until war was declared in 1625 more craftsmen begin to appear in the ordnance accounts, not least of them being cutlers and armourers who began to provide their goods through the ordnance rather than the armoury. This period, involving as it did numerous war scares and at least one sponsored expedition, that of Count Mansfield, did much to prepare the arms production establishment for the increased orders of 1625. If the quality was not as good as it could have been – and there were always complaints on this score – at least England did not have to scrape together weapons from a dozen different foreign sources at the very beginning of the war. Compared with the crisis of the first few years of Elizabeth's war with Spain right

---

[42] Philip Burlamachi purchased large quantities of stores for the military, but he did not work through the ordnance office.

through to the defeat of the Armada, the domestic arms production industry had made great strides even though it still had a long way to go.

The arms industries of England

The pattern of the production of ordnance, gunpowder, arms and other supplies in England from the 1580s to the 1620s and the relationship of that production to the government of England demonstrates wide variations. In general it is possible to see that the government of Tudor and Stuart England and specifically the privy council, was deeply involved in the basic defence industries of the period, but that results were not altogether beneficial. Government control extended to protecting some industries from potentially ruinous foreign (and in some cases domestic) competition and to setting some general standards for the goods brought into the national stores. The monarch and the council were particularly concerned to preserve and control the gunfounding and gunpowder industries as essential elements of national defence. This was based upon the monarch's belief in his or her essential rights under the prerogative as the ultimate defender of the realm.

The control of war industries by the government was accomplished with a light hand and was by and large successful in ensuring their survival. Most industries, especially the gunfounding and gunpowder monopolies, seemed to benefit from government control, although in the former case overproduction and over-control restricted potential markets. In part this was the result of a government policy which set prices and, during wartime, provided a steady market. However, concern with national defence could not preserve war industries at an artificially high wartime level. The rigours of peace shrank basic defence industries very quickly with no government thought to the possible consequences. But what else could the government have done about it? No Tudor or Stuart government was wealthy enough to maintain a fixed level of military purchase during peacetime which would keep the suppliers of military equipment busy without bankrupting the kingdom. Patents and monopolies preserved some industries from disintegration, but not even a centralised (and comparatively wealthy) regime like that of Habsburg Spain could afford to do more. However, England paid the price for allowing her military industries to shrink to the low level they had reached by 1625 for they were decidedly unprepared for war. A little more money, a little more forethought and some additional administrative supervision of some basic defence industries might have been of great value. But as Joan Wake has said about the English militia system in peacetime: 'It is an old story, but have Englishmen at any period ever spent money or trouble in peace so as to avoid greater charges in time of war?'[43]

---

[43] *A copy of papers relating to musters, beacons, subsidies, etc. in the county of Northampton A.D. 1586–1623*, ed. Joan Wake (Northamptonshire Record Society iii, 1926), p. cxvii.

7

The Wider Ordnance Establishment

> 'Tis time to leave the Books in dust,
> and oyl th' unused Armours rust:
> Removing from the Wall
> The corslet of the Hall.'
> – Andrew Marvell, *An Horatian ode upon Cromwell's return from Ireland*

There is no question but that the London ordnance office was the chief warehouse of arms and armaments for the kingdom. However, several other, smaller, ordnance offices and storehouses maintained stocks of supplies with a certain measure of independence from the London office. In two of these, at Berwick and in Dublin, the head of the office was even called the master of the ordnance and was expected to account independently to the privy council and the exchequer for his administrative and financial responsibilities. The master in Dublin, in particular, was virtually autonomous as befitted a major officer in a separate kingdom. In the case of the smaller storehouses at Chatham, Rochester, Deptford and Portsmouth, some local responsibility for the accountability and maintenance of supplies was held by a clerk. However, these regional storehouses were little more than satellites of the central office. In addition, each of the castles and forts along the coast maintained some stores on hand, not least of which were hundreds of pieces of heavy ordnance, but these were under the control of their own governors or captains. In none of these castles was there anything which could be considered a major supply depot, and the items which were to hand and usable were generally for the defence of the castle rather than for issue to any major force. Each of these establishments added to the military potential of the realm and to the financial and administrative burden of the ordnance office. Each will be examined in turn in order to assess the size of their stores and their role in the defence of the kingdom.

The north

The master of the ordnance in the north was responsible for ordnance supplies in Newcastle, Tynemouth, Berwick, Warke Castle, Norham Castle and on Holy Island. Thomas Sutton held this office from 1570 until 1591 when his deputy, Sir Simon Musgrave, took over.[1] It is interesting that this post was held for so many years by Sutton as he was in the process of amassing one of the largest fortunes of any commoner in England at the time.[2] According to his declared accounts from 1591 through 1604, Musgrave was held accountable for more than 91 pieces of brass ordnance worth some £8,141 as well as for £3,344 worth of gunpowder, 290 muskets, 1,100 calivers, 692 corslets and 2,500 pikes. The office also had a store of the usual 'habilliments of war' such as baskets, sheet lead, salt petre, ladles and other miscellaneous supplies.[3] In 1604 Sir Simon was succeeded in the office by his son, Sir Richard, who had been granted the reversion in 1594.[4]

The ordnance office in the north consisted primarily of the master, who was paid £146 per year, two servants, one clerk, and two labourers all at 12d. per diem. One of the servants probably held the title of comptroller of the office of the ordnance. In 1596 this post was held by William Selby whose responsibilities included taking annual surveys of the ordnance in the north and making up the books of remain, deliveries and quarterly charges for the office.[5]

The office did not maintain the extensive staff of artificers of the London office, so the duties of the office clerks were generally restricted to accounting for the supplies they had and arranging for the disposition of new shipments of arms from London. There seems to have been little or no armaments or ancillary industries in the north at this time. Almost all the military supplies seem to have been sent out from the central office in London. Gunpowder, lead, ordnance, small guns, horse harnesses and even iron goods and timber planks were all sent to Berwick and Newcastle from London. Most of the

---

[1] *CSPD Eliz. I, 1581–90*, 215, account of ordnance received out of the Tower for Berwick, Newcastle and the north from 20 Mar. 1584 to 29 Sept. 1587. This officer was also called the keeper of the ordnance in the north.

[2] According to Nef, his fortune was based on coal. No officer could get rich from so small an office. Sutton moved to London in 1580, so Musgrave was probably *de facto* master from that date: Nef, *British coal industry*, i. 151–2.

[3] For Sir Simon Musgrave's declared accounts see PRO, E 351/2606 (1583–91); E 351/2610 (1591–1604). Many of the figures seem suspicious, but they still give at least a rough estimate of the size and value of the office.

[4] *CSPD Eliz. I, 1591–4*, 508, docquet, 17 May 1594. Sir Richard held the office of master until 1617 when, on surrendering it, he was granted a pension of 8s. per day: *CSPD James I, 1611–18*, 443, sign manual grant, 10 Mar. 1617. Since the last (surviving) account taken of the office only runs through to 1609, it is probable that the office fell into disuse after that date. For Sir Richard's account see PRO, E 351/2613A.

[5] *APC 1596–7*, 184–5 (18 Sept. 1596). Selby was instructed to try to locate some missing arms which had been issued to the earl of Huntingdon, then lord lieutenant of the north, in 1588. In addition, he was to survey the munitions at Carlisle, technically out of his area of responsibility, by (tactfully) informing Lord Scrope of the need to see the supplies and muster the gunners.

goods were sent by sea to Newcastle or Berwick and then either placed in the storehouses there or else loaded on carts for the overland journey to Carlisle.[6]

Once in the north, goods were stored in warehouses inside the walls of the respective towns or castles. The storehouse at Newcastle, known as 'The Manors', was extensively repaired at the cost of some £218 in 1597. This included reroofing the great hall to make an armour storehouse and repairing the floor of the Arrow House.[7] Unfortunately the storehouse had again fallen into such disrepair by 1614 that the munitions were rusting through exposure to the elements. In Sir Richard Musgrave's account for his stewardship of the office from 1604 to 1609, it was noted that most of the munitions were now unserviceable or 'have been stollen and ymberilled by evill disposed persons by reason of the greate decay and fall of the Stoarehowses at Newcastle which have lyen open ever since his Ma[jesty's] coming to the crowne'.[8] Since the account was not taken until 3 May 1612, and since the realm had been at peace for nine years under a king not inclined to spend his money on military matters, it is likely that the storehouses had been in bad shape for some time.

There were other storehouses and castles which were under the general supervision of the master of the ordnance in the north, although the governors of these establishments maintained a considerable degree of independence. Tynemouth Castle maintained a substantial store of munitions and it managed to keep its storehouse in slightly better shape than those in Newcastle. However, an inventory in 1606 listed only nine major pieces of ordnance (most on rotting gun carriages), thirteen decayed muskets, nine halberds, and fifteen pikes.[9] Lord Sheffield had reported this neglect to the government earlier that year along with his fears that parts of Northumberland were 'overrun with papists'.[10] This comment probably prompted the government to take an inventory the next year with an eye to improving the stores at Tynemouth. If the government of James was not very interested in potential foreign enemies, it was still concerned with defending itself against the enemy from within. Newcastle and Berwick had originally been fortified for defence against Scotland, now united with England under James VI and I, whereas the Gunpowder Plot of the previous year pointed to a much more obvious internal threat.

---

[6] This was a fairly expensive undertaking, as the freight charges from the Tower to Berwick, in 1595 for example, were 13s. 4d. per ton. One consignment of goods that year, worth some £1,639, weighed 65 tons and cost £44 to ship.
[7] *CSPD Eliz. I, 1595–7*, 460, account of works to be done in 1597 at the queen's storehouse in Newcastle called the Manors. The privy seal was granted for £200 on 10 July 1595 and repairs were completed by 16 July 1597.
[8] PRO, E 351/2313A, declared accounts of Sir Richard Musgrave.
[9] HMC, *Salisbury*, xviii. 366–7, inventory delivered to Thomas Cuthbert, deputy to Sir William Selby the younger, by William Whitehead, deputy to Sir Henrie Witherington [called in this inventory, Woodrington], governor of the castle, 30 Dec. 1606.
[10] Ibid. 333–4 (30 Oct. [1606]).

The garrison and ordnance stores at Berwick, the major fortress on the border with Scotland, were quick to feel the cold winds of neglect which blew after the accession of James I. With the two crowns united, James was convinced that the ancient enmity of England and Scotland would evaporate into the historical mist. One of his top priorities upon his summoning a parliament was the legal and absolute union of the two kingdoms into one. What better way to begin this process than by dismantling the now 'obsolete' fortress at Berwick?

Perhaps the original obviously anti-Scottish function of the fortress had unwittingly been demonstrated all too well for James when he and then his queen passed through Berwick on their way to London in 1603. They were greeted with massive salutes from the heavy ordnance along the walls as the English welcomed them by expending over £500-worth of gunpowder.[11]

James's new advisors, especially Sir Robert Cecil, doubtless looked upon the dismantling of the garrison as a means to save some money. With peace with Spain an imminent possibility and peace with Scotland assured, why should the government 'waste' money on expensive fortifications? The king apparently agreed that no further money should be wasted on 'useless' fortresses and he ordered the establishment of a commission to take an inventory of the garrison and the ordnance with a view to its reduction.[12]

The commission quickly concluded that, with the dissolution of the ordnance office of the north, the major officers in Berwick, including the surveyor of victuals, the master of the ordnance, and the governor, would cease to draw their pay while the gunners were to go on half-pay: over £10,000 per year would be saved by these drastic measures.[13] As part of the process of dismantling the fortress most of the serviceable pieces of brass ordnance would be dismounted and shipped to London together with most of the ordnance supplies.[14] Between 19 August and 1 September 1604 some 43 major and 24 smaller pieces of ordnance were dismounted, loaded onto ships and transported to the Tower in London. In addition, all the field carriages

---

[11] PRO, E 351/2610. Sir Simon Musgrave's account for 1591–1604 lists 6 lasts and 318lbs. of gunpowder (14,718 lbs. in all) expended on welcoming the king and queen to Berwick. Gunpowder cost an average of 8*d*. per lb. at this time.

[12] By Christmas Day 1603 James I had ordered that the garrison be reduced to 100 of the oldest soldiers, who could retain their posts for life. The younger men could choose to serve in the cautionary towns in Flushing or Brill, or else in Ireland: ibid. SP 14/5/5, the king to Sir William Bowes and others, commissioners for dissolving the garrison at Berwick, 4 Dec. 1603.

[13] Ibid. Around £15,000 was to be saved according to one report: HMC, *Salisbury* xv. 351, 336–8, 354. This seems a high figure, but it was claimed that yearly wages bills for military establishments in Berwick, Holy Isle and the Castle of Wark amounted to £13,400 and that the commissioners were to reduce it to around £3,000.

[14] Ibid. xvi. 27–8, Captain William Bowyer to Cecil, 16 Feb. 1604.

for the guns, hundreds of rounds of shot, 900 pikes, and almost 400 muskets and calivers were sent from Berwick to London.[15]

The dissolution of a major garrison in the north was accomplished fairly quickly and painlessly, except, no doubt, for the garrison members and their families. Captain William Bowyer, the garrison commander during the transition, petitioned Sir Robert Cecil to ask if the king was really resolved to remove all the ordnance from the town except for a few old and unserviceable iron pieces. He further hinted that Cecil had originally been in favour of leaving at least fifteen major pieces in Berwick so as not to leave Berwick prey to 'the turbulent spirits of home bred or foreign practisers'. According to Bowyer, there were some who might be encouraged to violence if 'they understand the nakedness of the mounts and no ordnance left for defence'.[16] Cecil, perhaps bowing to the wishes of the king, had obviously revised his original opinions for he now moved swiftly to ensure that all the serviceable ordnance was taken to London.

One cannot help wondering along with Captain Bowyer at the hastiness and completeness of the dissolution. Did James really believe he would thus save a great deal of money? Was that his chief motivation? Why leave Berwick so completely defenceless? Even a peace-loving monarch would have recognised the need for defences in the border area between the two parts of his dominions, not to mention the obvious need to maintain ordnance in any major town along the coast. Yet the fortress was stripped. Why?

One possible motivation is that the speedy and thorough dissolution of the garrison at Berwick was meant as a political statement, a symbolic act, which had its own logic separate from either military considerations or those of common sense. Berwick had been the point of departure for numerous invasions of Scotland. It had dominated the lives of all who lived along the borders for generations and as such it was a symbol of the power of England which could be, and often was, used against Scotland.[17] Its reduction would demonstrate more clearly than any other act that England and Scotland were now to be considered by all the king's subjects, just as he considered them, as one single kingdom. Union of the two kingdoms was near to James's heart and doubtless the actions taken to strip Berwick were meant to convey to his subjects on both sides of the border that the old political realities had changed. Perhaps no other single action in all of James's reign better high-

---

[15] PRO, WO 49/30, fo. 165–9, 177–9, 203. This list included 8 large cannons, 14 demi-cannons, 7 culverins, 3 demi-culverins and 11 sakers, weighing over 185,000 lbs. It took three ships to carry all the supplies back to the Tower at a cost of more than £270 in freight charges alone.

[16] HMC, *Salisbury*, xvi. 171 (11 July 1604).

[17] The symbolic importance of Berwick should not be confused with its actual military usefulness. Marcus Merriman and John Summerson claim that the fort at Berwick was 'almost useless militarily': 'The Scottish border', in H. M. Colvin (ed.), *A history of the King's works*, London 1982, iv. 607–94. They quote Lord Willoughby, the new governor in 1598, as saying that Berwick was 'a meere showe and opinion of a stronge thinge'.

lights the political and symbolic importance of arms and armaments to the early seventeenth-century mind. Castles, stores or armour, heavy ordnance and stocks of gunpowder spoke volumes to other nations and to a king's own subjects about his intentions. As such, each aspect of arms procurement, storage locations, castle fortifications and military preparedness had profound political consequences.

Ireland

The maintenance of stores for the army in Ireland posed a continuing challenge to Tudor and Stuart monarchs. Elizabeth faced a major rebellion in Ireland from 1594 to the end of her reign. James had to maintain a garrison there which was, for all intents and purposes, virtually his only professional military force. The trials and tribulations of keeping Ireland supplied with ordnance stores, while not on the scale of the legendary 'getting a pike to Flanders', were formidable.[18] Once supplies actually reached Ireland, there were continuing problems associated with storage, issue and account.

When military supplies arrived in the country, they came under the control of the ordnance office of Ireland, headed by its own master of the ordnance. During Elizabeth's Irish wars, that master was Sir George Bourchier. He kept a clerk, assistant clerk, seven gunners and eight artificers on his permanent staff. The Irish ordnance office was neither as large, nor as centralised as the main office in the Tower. However, it receipted for stores sent from England by ship or initially moved overland from London to Bristol or Chester, moved those stores into a central warehouse in Dublin, maintained them and issued them as needed.

The master had the additional task of controlling numerous smaller storehouses in garrisons throughout the countryside. As with masters of the ordnance in the field, accounting for all the weapons in these stores during time of war was a difficult task. In addition, much of the ordnance supply was carried over to Ireland by private merchants and delivered directly to the towns or persons requesting it. This made accountability a nightmare since the privy council still held Bourchier responsible for supplies even if he had never seen them. For example, in April 1599, after Essex arrived with his lavishly-supplied army, Bourchier complained that almost three-quarters of the equipment was issued directly to the soldiers without his knowledge and without being controlled by his store.[19]

---

[18] See Parker, *Army of Flanders*. For similar problems in supplying Ireland see Richard Winship Stewart, 'The "Irish Road": military supply and arms for Elizabeth's army during the O'Neill rebellion in Ireland, 1598–1601', in Mark Fissel (ed.), *War and government in Britain, 1598–1650*, Manchester – New York 1991, 17–37.

[19] PRO, E 101/690/31; APC 1601–4, three open warrants to assist Edmund Nicolson and John Allen 469, 31 Dec. 1601; APC 1599–1600, 144, lord treasurer to Mr Nicolson to

By 1599 several smaller storehouses had been set up in Waterford, Clark, Limerick, Athlone, Carrickfergus and Newry in order to provide prompt supply to the field armies and garrisons throughout Ireland. This followed an earlier experiment at setting up decentralised storehouses, or 'staples', for food near various garrisons. Each munitions' store had at least one clerk to supervise it, a labourer to assist him and often a gunner or two. The main office at Dublin, however, was still the central workhouse and storage facility for Ireland and retained its existence throughout the reign of James while many of the smaller storehouses vanished as soon as the need for them had disappeared. Only the main office can be considered a permanent ordnance office.[20]

Castles and coastal defences

Maintaining credible defences throughout the realm had financial as well as political consequences. Perhaps in no other area did the long-term costs of a military establishment strike home during peacetime so much as in the need to maintain continuous supply to the castles and fortresses along the coast of England. These fortifications mainly dated from the massive building programme of Henry VIII and included at least thirty castles, sconces (small redoubts), towers, blockhouses or bulwarks in widely varying states of repair.[21] In 1580 and the decade following, money tended to be diverted to the more urgent requirements of the navy. Only after 1588 was there an attempt to rebuild some of the neglected forts and even this half-hearted effort dropped off severely after 1603.[22]

In an inventory of twenty of these forts taken around 1603, it was reported that there were over 156 pieces of brass ordnance alone in these fortifications, ranging from twenty-two pieces at Portsmouth Castle and nineteen at Newcastle, down to two pieces in a decayed gunhouse near Rye. By that year, most of the forts in question had sadly deteriorated. In part this was due to their use as strategic reserves for supplies. In 1589, for example, the surveyor of the ordnance was authorised to pull brass ordnance out of some of the castles in order to supply seven new ships under construction. The navy had greater priority for supplies during this crucial phase of the war, especially

---

provide weapons at £3 10s. for each soldier, 9 Mar. 1600; PRO, WO 49/26, fo. 162; SP 63/206/50. In the period from 1 Mar. to 1 Sept. 1599, while Essex was roaming ineffectively around Munster, the Irish ordnance office issued 459 calivers, 142 muskets, 429 pikes, 993 swords and 360 barrels of gunpowder: ibid. 50i.
[20] Ibid. SP 63/194/23i–x. For staples of victuals see E 403/2560, fo. 166.
[21] See J. R. Hale, 'Tudor fortifications 1485–1558', in his *Renaissance war studies*, 63–98.
[22] Colvin, *The king's works*, iv. 402.

since the defeat of the Armada in 1588 seemed to assure safety for the coasts of England for some time.[23]

The state of the forts in 1603, however, was far superior to their condition in 1623 when, after a long period of peace, another survey of the forts was taken. This time the survey was more comprehensive, and it emphasised the increasingly decrepit condition of the nation's defences. It listed only seventy-eight major pieces of brass ordnance and slightly over 300 iron pieces as being ready for firing. In addition, most of those were mounted on rotting gun carriages and placed on decaying firing platforms.[24] The total stock of powder in all the forts amounted to slightly over twelve lasts (30,000 pounds). Given that a large cannon used 40 pounds for one shot and even a smaller demi-culverin (throwing a 9-pound) took 9 pounds of powder per shot, a very minor engagement would drain the forts of stores. The same was true of the stocks of small arms, there being only 900 muskets overall, one-third of which were unserviceable. Of the 2,000 long pikes on hand, almost half were decayed beyond use. Even the walls of the castles were in some cases in total disrepair. In the case of Camber Castle, the survey stated that its main walls were almost completely submerged by the sea. The surveyors called it a 'wholly unprofitable' fort, and stated that it would take £2,500 to repair it.[25] The officers of the ordnance who had been chosen to carry out the survey estimated that as a minimum it would take £13,318 to repair the forts and castles of the kingdom, and this would not include supplying the storehouses with massive amounts of munitions. Large capital investment on this scale was not beyond the resources of England at the time, but given the neglect of the military establishment since the accession of James and the peace with Spain in 1604, such expenditure was unlikely.[26]

The case for continued military preparedness, even during peace, was put very forcibly by Sir Ferdinando Gorges, governor of Plymouth and a close protegé of the earl of Essex.[27] In 1584 Plymouth had been well stocked with heavy ordnance and supplies and it received substantial supplies and cash for

---

[23] PRO, SP 15/35/70, account of brass ordnance remaining in his Majesty's castles, forts etc., [1603?].

[24] Generally it was the gun carriages which reduced the preparedness of the forts. The timber had to be replaced every few years or the gun would dismount itself at its first firing: HMC, *Salisbury*, iv. 441, Sir George Carew to Sir Robert Cecil, 21 Dec. 1593.

[25] BL, MS Harl. 1326, 125 fos, survey of forts. By 1623 only 9 pieces of decayed ordnance, 20 old muskets and 500lbs. of gunpowder were left in this fortress which in 1542 had been described as being immensely strong: Colvin, *The king's works*, iv. 447.

[26] The survey also covered ordnance and armoury establishments in the same year. The estimated cost of repair could have been reduced by some £2,500 merely by omitting the reconstruction of the swamped Camber Castle.

[27] Gorges had been knighted by Essex at the siege of Rouen in 1591 and had been named as one of the conspirators in 1601. However, he remained as governor of Plymouth under James I: *DNB*, 22, 241.

repairs throughout the war with Spain.[28] By 1607, however, its defences had deteriorated to such an extent that Gorges wrote a long letter to Salisbury pleading for assistance. His belief was that 'the only means to continue a peace inviolable is always to be sufficiently provided both to defend and to offend, in which case none will dare to attempt for fear of procuring their own loss'. In particular, he complained that Plymouth's defences had never been completely finished nor furnished with ordnance and what had been finished had now deteriorated. What few supplies had been sent to the fort had long since been spent on 'triumphs or ordinary customs of entertainments'. Gorges feared that the town lay completely open to the real enemy, who were, according to the traditionally-minded Gorges, the French. As for the fort being able to rely upon the assistance of nearby county forces, Gorges proclaimed in a succinct and scathing indictment that 'the [forces of the] country are out of use, and their arms out of order, their minds unwilling, and their bodies unapt'. The present peace, which Gorges saw as but a breathing-spell, was to be no reason for allowing the defences of the realm to collapse. He wrote:

> Considering that the reasons which commonly are most prevelant between princes and states in conclusion of peace (if victory be not accomplished) are the necessities of either part not longer able to pursue the wars, and no sooner are the conditions concluded on but the last day of the confirmation thereof is the first beginning to make preparation to supply those defects and to hasten the means to encounter with all occurents that time, occasion, or men's nature shall present . . . the negligent and unarmed are always a prey to the vigilant and powerful.[29]

Gorges's voice was probably not the only one raised in favour of continued military preparedness, but James's financial problems did not permit long-term investment.

Some of the other strategic ports were luckier than Plymouth. Portsmouth, for example, had enormous sums of money poured into its defences in the 1580s and 1590s and this flow did not stop even after the conclusion of peace in 1604.[30] According to the accounts of Sir Francis Vere, governor of Portsmouth from 1606 to 1609, the garrison and fortress were still in reasonably good condition. Less than one third of the ordnance had been dismounted or become unserviceable; this was a lower percentage of derelict weapons than in other forts where most of the guns had been lost. In addition, the fort still had over 10,000 pounds of gunpowder on hand along

---

[28] *CSPD Eliz. I, 1581–90*, 150.
[29] HMC, *Salisbury*, ix. 87–8, Gorges to privy council, 7 Apr. 1607. Plymouth did receive some supplies in 1617: the ordnance office shipped £442-worth on 25 Feb. 1617: *APC 1616–17*, 162–4.
[30] For the build-up in Portsmouth see *CSPD Eliz. I, 1581–90*, 416–17, remembrances and notes of material for the completion of the works at Portsmouth, 12–14 Jun. 1587; HMC, *Salisbury*, iv. 440–1.

with 10,000 pounds of match, 200 muskets and 749 calivers.[31] Portsmouth had even received large supplies of ordnance carriages (more than sixty-four field-carriages, implying that there were sixty-four pieces of dismounted artillery waiting for them at Portsmouth), powder, shot and other miscellaneous supplies in 1615 and 1621.[32] Although not on the scale of the storehouse in the Tower, Portsmouth maintained a stock of war supplies far above that of the average coastal fortress.

However, the poor condition overall of the country's castles and forts during the inter-war years of 1604–25 points to a lack of interest during peacetime in the nation's defensive position. The coastal forts were the nation's first line of defence, and yet were allowed to decay while James I went deeper and deeper into debt on other, comparatively non-essential, expenditures. The ordnance officers, of course, could not be held responsible for the lack of fiscal responsibility shown by the crown, yet as overseers of the supplies for castles and forts, they must have been concerned with their weakened condition. But there was little they could do without money or the support of the monarch. Thus, despite occasional flurries of interest in resupplying a few forts, nothing major was done to repair and re-equip the majority of them until the war years of 1625 to 1627 when expenditure on a huge scale was required in order to prosecute the new war with Spain.[33]

The ordnance annexes

The ordnance office was directly involved in the management of coastal fortifications only to the extent that it was to issue and account for the supplies drawn by those forts and, in the case of the master gunner of England, account for the number and training status of the gunners. However, the office was directly responsible for several smaller storehouses where items were stored, primarily for ease of supply to the navy. These ordnance annexes were located in Woolwich, Rochester, Chatham and Deptford. They were particularly useful because ordnance office policy required that each time a ship returned from a voyage, all the ordnance stores (and sometimes even the guns themselves) were to be removed from the ship and returned to the control of the ordnance office so that the master gunner of that ship was relieved of responsibility. The ships then rode empty at their harbour anchorage until spring. Only when ships were appointed as harbour guards did this

---

[31] PRO, AO 1/161/434. The account was taken of Dame Elizabeth Vere in 1611, two years after Sir Francis's death. It showed the account to be £17 in debt, but this was offset by a previous surplus of £72.

[32] Ibid. WO 55/452, 16 July 1615, June 1621.

[33] For the increasing interest in supplying castles, and even the construction of new forts at Harwich see ibid. WO 49/56, fos 23, 35, indentures for 1626; WO 55/452; HMC, *Salisbury*, xxii. 242, Sir John Heydon and others to Captain Arthur Harris, St Michael's Mount, Cornwall, 2 Jan. 1625.

routine vary. These procedures were meant to maintain accountability for valuable supplies and prevent loss at anchorage but they could also consume a great deal of time and effort, especially if all the supplies had to be returned to the central storehouse in London.

The ordnance annexes were established at least as early as 1578, but probably much earlier, to expedite the issue and return of supplies. Since most of the ships sailed out in March or April and returned in October and November, storing their supplies in warehouses nearby prevented a potential administrative bottleneck for the ordnance office and saved time and money on lighterage up and down the Thames.

Despite the paucity of evidence about the operations of the annexes, it seems apparent that there was considerable variation in the way they were administered. In Rochester, for example, from 1587 to 1595, a storehouse was rented from one Walter Heathe for £6 a year, although office accounts indicate that he was not paid for much of that time.[34] Its use probably did not survive the war, since an indenture made out in June 1603 mentions 32s. to be paid to one of the clerks of the ordnance office, William Barroway, for 'fetchinge up all the munition from the late Storehouse' in Rochester.[35]

In Deptford and Chatham, the storehouses were probably made of government materials and sited on government property, since there is no mention in the ordnance record books of rent being paid. However, since the storehouses handled mostly naval stores, perhaps the navy picked up the bill. Chatham had very few stores of its own so it required only one clerk in permanent residence. During the peak spring and autumn seasons, when it was necessary to issue and take remains of large quantities of supplies, an additional ordnance officer generally came down from London to assist.

Woolwich, however, was a different matter. The site of an ancient armoury, its storehouse was alternately repaired and then abandoned as the need arose or subsided. In 1586, over £133 was spent on repairing the old armoury and making it into a storehouse and £2,027 on 148 pieces of brass and iron ordnance and carriages to be placed in the store.[36] More money was spent on the storehouses in 1596, but by 1603 most of the stores had been moved back to London. A survey in 1614 confirms that the storehouse had been abandoned, since by that time little was left there except some old wheels and abandoned carriages which the surveyors sold in bulk for £71. Despite this, the storehouse still had a keeper, one Samuell Holles, and the surveyors maintained that the storehouse was still salvageable.[37] By 1620 the

---

[34] PRO, WO 49/19, 11 Dec. 1595.
[35] Ibid. WO 49/29, by warrant of the lord high treasurer.
[36] Ibid. SP 12/186/39, estimate for provisions for the office of the ordnance for the seas; also for new building and other reparations to be done at the storehouse at Woolwich, 31 Jan. 1586. For later developments of Woolwich as a major arsenal see Hogg, *Royal arsenal*; Tomlinson, *Guns and government*, 12–23.
[37] The surveyors believed that without work 'his Ma[jesty] shoulde loose that whole

old storehouse had been taken down, board by board, by the master carpenter of the ordnance, William Wheatley. However, a new one was built shortly thereafter and Woolwich has maintained some connections with the ordnance almost ever since.[38]

The convenience for the ordnance and navy and the savings in time, money and manpower, made Woolwich and the other annexes important and cost-effective parts of the wider ordnance establishment. However, there were other storehouses which did not fall under the ordnance office but which also had a role to play in the supply of arms to England's military. One of the oldest of these was the armoury.

The armoury

The office of the armoury was the senior of the two permanent armaments storage and management facilities. Like the ordnance office, it had grown out of the establishment of the king's privy wardrobe during the fifteenth century, but the title of master of the king's armoury was created before that of master of the ordnance and thus had some official precedence.[39] However, by the end of the reign of Elizabeth, the armoury and its various storehouses and workshops had been over-shadowed by the larger and busier ordnance, just as the expansion of firearms had driven bows, bills and halberds into relative insignificance. But this trend did not follow a constant course. The office of the armoury at the death of Henry VIII had only 160 sets of 'demi-lances' (horse armour), two corslets, 456 maces, and less than 3,000 'Almaine Rivetts' (early German body armour). However, in the 1560s, the stores in the armoury expanded to include 1,138 demi-lances, 7,719 corslets (which replaced the 'Almaine Rivets'), 23,629 morrions (headpieces) and 4,397 'skulls' (rounded, obsolete headpieces).[40] In addition, over 4,000 corslets and other pieces of armour had been issued from the armoury to Berwick, Hampton Court, Greenwich and to several counties over the years. Thus, despite the decline in the need to keep huge amounts of heavy, ceremonial armour

---

grounde the storehuses and all which very shortly wythout present help wilbe eaten into the Thames': PRO, WO 55/452, report of Sir Francis Morice, Sir Roger Dallison, Sir John Kay and Sir Robert Johnson to Lord Carew, 29 Mar. 1614.

[38] One interesting sidelight to the discussion on the storehouses was the sudden need for ensuring their security against possible enemy attack in the late 1590s and early 1600s: ibid. WO 55/1629, fo. 218, 17 Apr. 1600. There were obviously risks involved in the policy of maintaining annexes of war supplies outside of London.

[39] Hogg, *Royal arsenal*, i. 78–81. In 1601, however, Sir John Peyton, lieutenant of the Tower, considered that the office of master of the armoury was in his gift but that it was 'otherwised disposed' of to his regret. He also considered that the importance of the office was 'never so great' as then: HMC, *Salisbury*, xi. 169, Peyton to Cecil. 17 Apr. 1601.

[40] BL, MS Harl. 7457, the state of the armoury from the death of Henry VIII to the reign of Elizabeth, Jan. 1546–31 Dec. 1561.

for the heavily-armoured knight, the armoury expanded in the mid sixteenth century primarily to meet the increased need for more suits of corslets, or pikeman's body armour. It is easy to forget that the pike was, in its time, almost as revolutionary a weapon – returning the battle to the disciplined infantryman – as was the musket later on in the century. It was not until the firearm assumed the dominant role on the battlefield and the need for highly mobile armies became critical that body armour became obsolete.[41] Only then did the armoury suffer a serious and this time irreversible decline in terms of budget, influence and function.

The head of the various armouries throughout the kingdom was the master of the armoury who maintained his main office in the White Tower. He was paid a fee of £31 18s. 9d. a year, with an additional fee of £66 13s. 4d. for maintaining the armour in the Green Gallery in Greenwich.[42] In addition to Greenwich and the Tower, the master was also responsible for the much smaller storehouses and workshops at Woolwich, Windsor Castle, Hampton Court, Portsmouth and Westminster. These varied in size from Greenwich, which maintained a large collection of ceremonial armour and some corslets, down to Westminster and Windsor Castle, which are seldom mentioned at all in the surveys of the office (taken in 1587, 1588, 1596, and 1611) and appear only fleetingly in other accounts. They continued to exist, but probably simply as a result of bureaucratic inertia since their stores grew smaller and less serviceable as the years of peace under James continued.[43] Sir Henry Lee, master of the armoury from 1581 until his death in 1610, complained bitterly in 1601 that the armouries in Hampton Court and Windsor Castle, which had been well furnished at the start of his time in office, now had next to nothing in the stores and no armourer appointed to keep them.[44]

To assist in the management of these far-flung assets, the master of the armoury had a deputy master and a clerk, both of whom served in the Tower, and a keeper of the armouries at each of the smaller offices.[45] Work in each

---

[41] On the continent the use of body armour came to an end during the Thirty Years War, as a result of the need for increased mobility. England was somewhat behind the times, but its wide-scale use did not survive the Civil War: Firth, *Cromwell's army*, 78–88; Stearns, 'Caroline military system', 394; Hogg, *Royal arsenal*, i. 78.

[42] BL, MS Harl. 7457; Hogg, *Royal arsenal*, i. 80.

[43] By 1611 most of the supplies were in the Tower, but the commission appointed to conduct the survey found a dwindling store of armour for the tilt and large stocks of rusting rivets and plate in Woolwich and Westminster: PRO, SP 14/64/71, 72, report of the commissioners of the survey of the armour left in the Tower, Greenwich, Woolwich, etc. late in the charge of Sir Henry Lee, taken at the transfer of the office to Sir Thomas Monson, June 1611. For other surveys see SP 12/198/79; 211/83; 261/61.

[44] HMC, *Salisbury*, xiv. 181–2, Lee to Sir John Stanhope, vice-chamberlain to the queen, 29 July 1601.

[45] The clerk at the Tower from 1589 until at least 1601 was William Sugden who also held the keepership of Greenwich for a while. He was paid 2s. 6d. per day and 26s. 8d. per year for livery. Most of the keepers had similar perquisites of office such as livery or a house. The master, of course, had the most lucrative 'perks' of all including the grant of

place was carried out by a team of armourers headed by a master craftsman. In the Tower there were eighteen armourers, one paid 10d. a day, two at 12d. a day, and a master craftsman paid 16d. a day. At Greenwich the keeper, paid 20d. per day, was assisted by a yeoman and maintained, according to one source, an additional twenty craftsman at salaries ranging from £15 to £36 per year.[46] On the whole, the craftsman were mainly occupied in maintaining the rich armour and tilt armour left in their keeping by the monarch or by various noblemen. Office accounts show that most of the money directed to that office was spent on repairs to existing equipment and on purchasing swords, armour and headpieces from contract armourers in London or from overseas sources. By the late sixteenth century the armourers did little or no manufacturing of plate armour or swords on their own. The office received an ordinary allowance of only £400 per year which was barely enough for the armourers' wages with a little left over for oil and varnish for the armour.[47]

The shrinking influence and budget of the armoury from the middle of the sixteenth century onwards was a matter of some concern for the master of the armoury. He was deeply sensitive to any infringement on his office especially when it emanated from the rival office of the ordnance. A key example of this sort of bureaucratic conflict occurred in 1601 when the privy council authorised George Harvey, deputy lieutenant of the ordnance, to supply a certain proportion of arms including swords for Ireland. Lee immediately complained that the provision of swords was the responsibility of his office. The council was forced to explain that no prejudice was intended to his office, and added, rather unconvincingly, that Harvey had acted in his private capacity (as entrepreneur) rather than as an ordnance official. In addition, they claimed that since the supply needed was so large, and so much haste was needed, they 'did require the healp of a man of somme credite and of skill wee thought him a fitter person than a marchant to deale in it, and if he had not undertaken it some marchant had been appointed to make this provision'.[48] This does not speak well of the council's view of Lee's ability to organise a supply of arms for Ireland.

The armoury did provide over £3,500-worth of swords and armour for Ireland between 1597 and 1602. However, on at least two other occasions, in

---

the income from some tenements and gardens on Tower Hill: *CSPD James I, 1603–10*, 512, docquet, lease of certain gardens and tenements in reversion after Sir Henry Lee, master of the armoury, to Sir Thomas Monson, 11 May 1609.

[46] Ibid. 96, 584, commission to Thomas Lincoln, yeoman of the king's armoury at Greenwich 31 Jan. 1610, 16 Apr. 1604.

[47] The master's accounts are about the only substantive source for the activities of the armoury. They can be found in PRO, E 101/64/11, E 351/2963 and AO 1/2299/3–5, 2300/6–9, for Sir Henry Lee (1581–1610), Sir Thomas Monson (1602–22) and Sir William Cope, Bart. (1622–6). However, they are very vague about the number of employees at each facility and even more vague about the exact annual expenditure of the armoury.

[48] *APC 1601–4*, 108–9 (28 July 1601).

1598 and again in 1601, the council tried to obtain swords for overseas levies from other sources rather than through the armoury. In a letter to Sir Robert Cecil in 1601, John Lee mentioned that the earl of Essex had tried to buy 3,000 swords for his expedition to Ireland without going through the armoury. In the same letter he asked Cecil to ensure that arms going to the Low Countries be purchased through his cousin, Sir Henry Lee, since the provision of swords was traditionally a function of the master of the armoury.[49] The fact that Lee had to write a special letter to Cecil to plead for what should automatically have taken place through the office of the armoury strongly indicates that the delineation of tasks between the ordnance and the armoury was no longer as clear as it had been.

The decline of the armoury had become even more apparent by the 1620s when the ordnance office regularly began supplying swords, lances and even corslets for the army. The struggle over spheres of responsibility was not, however, won by the ordnance office immediately. As late as 1631 there were complaints that the master of the armouries had 'from time out of memory' provided swords and armour for the king's armies. The writer in this case, one Roger Falconer, complained to some royal commissioners for the armoury that Sir Richard Morison, then lieutenant of the ordnance, was bringing armour and swords into the ordnance stores directly without going through the armoury. He further charged that ordnance personnel did not know how to test their strength or store them properly.[50] While complaining of their ignorance, Falconer did not, however, recommend that the armoury be restored to its old task. On the contrary, he complained that there were more than nineteen armourers in the Tower and at Greenwich who drew their wages but had not made any armour since long before the accession of James I. He recommended that the armoury be abolished completely and all the armourers pensioned out. Armouries at the Tower, Greenwich and Portsmouth alone should be retained under his plan, probably with a skeleton staffs responsible for repairs.[51] However, despite its dwindling responsibilities, the armoury was not abolished.

The decline in the armoury becomes even more obvious when the expenditure of the office throughout the whole period from 1590 to 1625 is examined. From 1590 to 1594 it spent £2,087, only slightly more than their current ordinary allowance of £2,000 for this period. From 1595 to 1603, however, mainly because they were providing swords and armour for Ireland, it spent over £11,000 including some £2,400 in each of two years, 1596 and 1599. These years, especially the latter, saw peaks in armoury expenditure. The office thereafter spent only its ordinary allowance of £400 per year until 1625, with exceptions in the years 1607 and 1621.

---

[49] HMC, *Salisbury*, x. 550–1 [1601].
[50] PRO, SP 16/206/30, Roger Fawkenor [Falconer] to commissioners of the armoury, [1631?].
[51] Ibid. SP 16/206/31, abuses in the armoury, [1631?].

In 1607 the armoury spent £937 on swords for Ireland during the O'Dogherty uprising, while in 1621 it spent £120 for swords for the general store.[52] It is clear from these figures that the armoury was losing its role as a major arms supply facility of the crown. The ordinary allowance let it maintain the ceremonial armour it had on hand, but money to procure and ship armour, swords, lances or even head-pieces was seldom routed through the hands of the master. Arms procurement was increasingly being taken over by the ordnance office. The armoury had lost its traditional responsibilities almost entirely by 1625; it was soon more a museum than an office taking an active part in the growing military supply establishment. In 1671 it was abolished by Charles II, and the present office of the armoury in the Tower bears little relationship in size or responsibilities to the original.[53]

The county stores

The ordnance office served as the main repository for military stores in England and as the centre for the procurement of the huge quantity of supplies needed for major overseas expeditions. However, in no sense was it the only mechanism for arming and equipping the military forces of the kingdom. Levies of troops moving to coastal towns for transport overseas were generally expected to arrive with some equipment procured in their counties of origin. Each soldier was to be provided with pike, musket or sword, some form of headpiece and a coat. Each of the 'shot', or musketeers, was supposed to have a basic load of bullets and powder in his bandoleer or flask and pouch. All these items were to be provided locally by a general assessment of those in the county who were liable to taxation and the local leadership – constables, sheriffs, deputy lieutenants – were held accountable by the privy council for their quality and quantity. The county leadership was also responsible for arming and training the main manpower reserve of the nation, the local militia.

The political impact of the procurement of arms and armaments in the counties was immense, on numerous occasions reaching the halls of Westminster. The need for the central government to enforce such expenditure, both for overseas levies and militia forces, inevitably led to tensions between the counties and central government up until the Civil War period. Any examination of the cost of war in Tudor and Stuart England must not neglect the fact that much of the expense for the initial issue of equipment for any expedition was borne by the county. The ordnance office was generally responsible for the supply of replacement arms to those expeditions and for other miscellaneous military equipment needed by the forces. This situation

---

[52] These figures are compiled from the master of the armoury's accounts: ibid. AO 1/2299/4–5, 2300/6–9

[53] Hogg, *Royal arsenal*, i. 81.

changed over time until, by the time war broke out in 1625, the central ordnance stores were providing the bulk even of initial arms.

Militia arms

There is a general consensus among historians that the arms of England's militiamen were generally of dubious reliability. This is often borne out by the facts. For example, despite the imminence of military engagement in 1588, a survey taken of the 9,088 militia mobilised in Southampton reported 'many of the men being very rawly furnished, some whereof lacketh a headpiece, some a sword, some one thing or other that is evil unfit or unbeseeming about him'.[54] If the preparedness of this critical county was typical of the other maritime counties, Elizabeth must have been very grateful that the Spanish army did not come ashore. Nor did the situation improve over time. The arms of the Somerset militia in 1602 were 'very defective', while the muster of the trained bands in Shropshire in 1605 was delayed partly due to bad weather and partly to 'the defective state of the arms'.[55]

Complaints about the poor state of the arms in almost every county in early modern England could be cited virtually indefinitely. One reason for this was the fragmented nature of the arms supply system in each county. Each county militia found its arms in its own way, and the problem was compounded by the different types of weapons within a county and the different ways individuals were held accountable for them.

There were three types or categories of arms at the county level. The first, and oldest, was that of private arms and armour. The aristocracy had always maintained stocks for their own retainers and the militia act of 1558 had continued the principle while trying to ensure that the arms were used for the government's purposes rather than for resolving private disputes or starting rebellions.[56] Private warfare, a major problem in the early sixteenth century, had virtually vanished by this time but memories were long. The arms and armour of private individuals were kept in their residences or halls and they were responsible for keeping them clean and available in the quantity mandated by the statute of 1558.

After the militia statute lapsed in 1604, the levels of each type of weapon were often arbitrarily set by the lord lieutenant and his deputies. This led to resistance among private owners who did not wish to buy new equipment or change over from one type of weapon to another. But, even before the repeal

---

[54] CSPD Eliz. I, 1580–9, 485, certificate upon survey taken of the county of Southampton by Captain Nich. Dawtrey, 30 May 1588.
[55] HMC, Salisbury, xii. 478–9, Hertford to privy council, 20 Nov. 1602; CSPD James I, 1603–10, 238, Sir Francis Newport and Robert Nedham to privy council, 1 Nov. 1605.
[56] Boynton, Elizabethan militia, 20–4.

of the statute, forcing each landowner to keep his arms up to any standard was a monumental task.

There were a few county gentry who took their responsibilities seriously. In 1599 Sir Edward York, of Wisbeach Castle in Yorkshire, wrote to Sir Robert Cecil that he had spent a great deal of his own money in acquiring private arms: 'I have been at great expense since coming in arming myself, buying horses and maintaining my people, besides my great toil and charge in Yorkshire, in viewing arms.'[57] In Hampshire, in that same year, Captain Hampden Poulet was sent to the Isle of Wight with the trained bands to defend against a threatened Spanish landing. He took with him four corslets, three muskets, three calivers and two demi-lances (armour for light horse) to arm himself and several retainers. This was apparently just a small part of the private store of weapons to be found at his house in Basingstoke from which he could outfit from eight to ten men.[58] Landowners such as York and Poulett took their duties seriously and provided arms for themselves and their neighbours. Not everyone was so public-spirited, and the provision of arms by private individuals was very much a hit or miss affair. Many prosperous landowners tried to obey the letter of the law, or the letter of the lieutenant's orders, by providing little more than rusted, obsolete suits of armour or an antique lance. On the whole, private arms were increasingly becoming an anachronism and more money was being spent on the purchase of public arms for the county.

Virtually every parish maintained a stock of publicly-owned weapons. These were paid for by the local militia rate or private subscriptions raised by the gentry and were maintained at some central point. They might be kept in church porches, churches being one of the few 'common' buildings in a parish, or in a special armoury. Churchwardens' accounts regularly list expenses for maintaining arms and armour although the bills were doubtless paid by the county militia rate.

In some cities, special centralised armouries, such as the gatehouses in Hereford, were established for public arms,[59] but in most counties there was resistance to their being established. Sir John Smythe, a die-hard conservative known for his ardent championing of the longbow, feared that a distant, centralised armoury would cause much disorder with the troops. In any emergency, the soldiers would be forced to run to the armoury, '& there in a hubbledehuffe disorderlie to arme themselves; whereof... little men doo put on great or tall mens armoure, and leave litle mens armours unfit for grat men to put on; according to the old saying, first come, first served'.[60] A more common fear was that a central location would be the first target in a civil

---

[57] *CSPD Eliz. I, 1598–1601*, 318, York to Cecil, 1 Sept. 1599.
[58] Hampshire Record Office, MS Herriard/Jervoise, XX 58, 8 Aug. 1599; XX 51A, 11 July 1599.
[59] Boynton, *Elizabethan militia*, 20–4.
[60] Ibid. 23.

disorder, turning a mob into a formidable army while effectively disarming much of the local militia.

There were also active supporters of the centralisation of weapons in a county armoury. Sir Henry Cocke, deputy lieutenant of Hertfordshire, believed that keeping the weapons in one place 'will be the readiest for all manner of employments, either for musters or training, and will be best for keeping [maintaining] it'. As for the objection that it would incite or assist a rebellion, he believed that it was more dangerous to have weapons scattered all over the countryside in the custody of 'simple constables and others'.[61] Efficiency and security were probably the decisive arguments for a centralised armoury with tradition and conservatism weighing against it.

The arguments for and against a central armoury, in this instance in York, were considered in 1600, by an unidentified writer (possibly Thomas Cecil, Lord Burghley, president of the council of the north), in a note which argued that the advantages far outweighed the disadvantages. One of these advantages was that the armour would be better maintained 'whereas now it is spoiled in two or three years'. This alone would relieve the county of the estimated expense of £200 which was spent for every muster in replacing old or unserviceable equipment. In addition, the weapons would be under the eye of the county authorities. This would preclude the apparently common practice of captains sent from London (presumably muster masters or conductors) 'who for money allowed and disallowed what they thought fit, to the prejudice of the country'. (For the word 'prejudice', read greater cost and trouble.) It would also mean that the weapons would be in the hands of the local representatives of central government (the lord president of the council of the north and the lord lieutenant in this case) rather than in the hands of the constables where 'it is at the commandment of their landlords, or such justices as dwell next them, as witnessed in the last rebellion'. As for the objection that an armoury would be too tempting a target for rebels, he answered that the armoury could not be opened unless the lord president or lord lieutenant were taken prisoner, which 'if they do, then they have the whole country at command, in whatever place the armour shall be'.[62]

While some of these arguments seem somewhat specious, the location of an armoury in a strongly fortified place such as a castle or citadel of some sort would probably have enhanced county security and cost the gentry less in the long run. This is demonstrated by what happened in 1607 during a rising in Northamptonshire. The 1,000-odd followers of John Reynolds, nicknamed

---

[61] *CSPD Eliz. I*, 1595–7, 136, Sir Henry Cocke to Lord Burghley, Hertfordshire, 30 Nov. 1595. Sir Henry recommended that the armouries be located 'in good towns, near to the houses of justices' and that the powder be kept in some remote place, a good way from the armouries. See also BL, MS Lansdowne 79, fo. 14, 23 Dec. 1595

[62] PRO, SP 12/274/26, note of reasons for providing at York a magazine of armour for Yorkshire, Jan. 1600. This is not signed, but seems to reflect many of the views and concerns of Thomas Cecil, son of William Cecil, lord treasurer under Elizabeth.

'Captain Pouch', were able to arm themselves only with a few bows, pitchforks, pikes and a handful of firearms, while most of the county weapons and most of the county gunpowder were safely stored in the city of Northampton and in Barnwell Castle. The rising fizzled out after a short battle with the local gentry who, 'fynding great backwardnes in the trained bandes', gathered their own retainers and friends on horseback to quell the disturbance.[63] Keeping crucial ammunition in central armouries and therefore out of the hands of the rebels helped prevent what could have been a serious uprising. However, the training and reliability of the trained bands seems to have been seriously deficient and this, more than anything, demonstrates the sorry condition of the early Stuart militia system even in a county as generally conscientious as Northamptonshire.

Armouries were apparently established in several counties, but there was no consistent, rationalised policy on the part of central government to hold them to any standards. The privy council did encourage the central storing of powder and shot, especially in London and the main cities. In 1616 the council complained to the Lord Mayor and aldermen of London that the city was 'altogeather unprovided of armes' and should at least provide a 'competent stoare of powder' of 100 lasts.[64]

The documentation on county storehouses is very poor, but one of the best was apparently in Bedfordshire. In 1589 Henry Grey, earl of Kent, lord lieutenant of the county, informed the council that he had established storehouses of powder and equipment in the three principal towns of Bedford, Ampthill and Shefford. His boast that 'I do thinke ther is not anye other sheire (for that number) better appointed and furnished then this smale and poore sheire of Bedforde' seems to have been justified. Each soldier knew which set of armour was his, and every county resident contributed to a 'reasonable composicion' set by the earl to pay for some armourers who maintained the weapons and furniture under the watchful eye of the cost-conscious justices of the peace.[65]

For a non-coastal county, Bedfordshire was very well prepared for any possible service. Of course, the year 1589 was certainly far from typical and many counties worked harder at providing a better armed militia in that year and the previous one than in earlier, less threatening times. But, a report in 1623 that the armouries in Bedfordshire's three principal towns were still 'well stored', and that the men were being provided with the best of modern equipment, indicates that 1589 was perhaps not an unusual year for this county.[66]

---

[63] *The Montagu muster book 1602–23*, ed. Joan Wake, Peterborough 1935, pp. xlvi–xlviii.
[64] APC 1615–16, 501–2, privy council to lord mayor, 24 Apr. 1616. At 2400lbs. per last, this was a request to buy and store 240,000lbs. of gunpowder. They were to buy it out of the Tower stores.
[65] PRO, SP 12/227/25, earl of Kent to privy council, 18 Oct. 1589.
[66] CSPD James I, 1623–5, 110, earl of Kent to privy council, 14 Nov. 1623. Much of the

WIDER ORDNANCE ESTABLISHMENT

There was probably a gradual increase in the number of armouries from year to year, but it was not a nation-wide phenomenon nor is it known exactly how many such armouries there were. Each county reserved for itself the right to decide how much was to be spent on arms and their maintenance. This naturally resulted in widely varying standards of armaments and storehouses. Wales was apparently faster to establish armouries than England, beginning in 1569, while Lancashire, Bedfordshire, Hampshire and Northamptonshire were among the counties which must be considered more 'advanced' in the public storage of weapons in England. Worcestershire, on the other hand, seems to have neglected to build up a substantial arms store. In 1607 a county resident wrote to the earl of Salisbury that 'No part of the kingdom is further out of frame than this country, which stil swarms with multitudes of dangerous papists, who though they go to church for form's sake, conceal in their houses priests and others of most dangerous dispositions.' He complained that

> so bare and disfurnished was the whole city of Worcester and the store house there, that there was not in both to be found forty pounds of powder and shot to furnish the king's subjects to suppress so devilish an attempt; yet there has been a round sum of money levied upon the country to provide such thigs; all which the country hardly brooks, and groans under the burden thereof.[67]

The role of the militia in internal security together with the sorry state of the county's defences can be seen very clearly barely three years after the end of a major war. It is also apparent that even when, as in Worcestershire, money was collected for weapons, it was not always spent as intended. It was only after the Gunpowder Plot that the council began to turn its attention to revitalising the public arms of the nation, and even then the task was not undertaken in any systematic fashion.

If anything, the storage procedures for another vital commodity for the county militia, gunpowder, were even more haphazard than those for arms and armaments. If militiamen were to receive any kind of realistic marksmanship training on muster day, a few pounds of gunpowder per man had to be stored in a convenient place near the muster grounds. The powder would then be taken from there, divided into individual charges and issued. Thus, the musters in 1588 emphasised the use of live rounds in training. If Northamptonshire is any kind of an example, each county probably expended around 800 pounds of gunpowder in five days training costing around £25. This was a fairly heavy expenditure of powder, yet even the normal peacetime allowance for training seems to have been 2 pounds per man per day of

credit for this situation should probably go to the earl who was a member of a powerful and militarily-oriented family.
[67] HMC, *Salisbury*, xix. 307, Humphrey Wheeler to the earl of Salisbury, 31 Oct. 1607.

training by 1614.[68] Little wonder that the privy council encouraged the establishment of a staple, or central store, of powder in all the major county towns.

The establishment of county powder storehouses was not a new development in the 1580s. In 1575 the county of Devonshire had between 300 and 2,400 pounds of powder and a proportion of bullets and match stored in Exeter, Totnes, Dartmouth, Plymouth, Barnstaple, Tavistock, South Molton, Torrington, Bideford, Tiverton and Cullompton.[69] However, the need for such stores increased in the war years and even the coming of peace did not prevent the stockpiling of gunpowder in the larger towns of each county. Northamptonshire was charged by the privy council in 1585 to store powder in Peterborough, Northampton, Daventry, Oundle, Kettering, Towcester and Wellingborough.[70] When it tried to consolidate its stores in 1592 by moving almost all the powder to a central location in Northampton (the county had an east and a west division, each with its own storehouses) the privy council objected and forced the county to give the powder back to the eastern division. In some counties the privy council obviously recognised the virtue of decentralised stores.[71]

The storage of powder was a constant drain on county resources. It had to be constantly replenished whether used in training or not. During the war years it would be used up in exercises and given to the levies as an initial issue when sent on overseas service. During peacetime, on the other hand, it often became damp, depending on the storage conditions, and needed to be reworked or replaced every few years. In 1622 the earl of Southampton wrote to the council complaining of a very poor muster that year in his county of Hampshire. Not only did many soldiers not show up (and even more were 'wilful refusers' in showing arms), but the county powder store was also in bad shape. He had to contract it out to an unnamed craftsman to be reworked, but the man did not perform his task satisfactorily. The earl reported that he was forced to order another batch of powder at a proportion of 6 pounds of powder per firearm in the county along with 2 pounds of match and forty rounds each.[72]

The third category of weapons in the county militia system combined

---

[68] *Musters, beacons and subsidies*, 23, 11 (an interesting description of the progression of a soldier from 'dry' fire without powder, to powder only in the pan, to powder in the pan and barrel without a bullet and finally to a fully-charged piece). See also *Northamptonshire lieutenancy papers, and other documents 1580–1614*, ed. Jeremy Goring and Joan Wake (Northamptonshire Record Society xxvii, 1975), 13.
[69] BL, MS Royal 18D, III, fo. 12.
[70] *Northamptonshire lieutenancy papers*, 18, 36, 98–101. By 1590 Higham Ferres, Rothwell and Thrapton were included.
[71] *APC 1591–2*, 522–3, privy council to Sir Edward Montague and Sir Richard Knightly, 11 June 1592.
[72] PRO, SP 14/132/98, earl of Southampton to privy council, 15 Aug. 1622. See also HMC, *Buccleuch and Queensberry*, iii. 201, muster expenses at Kettering, 1 Oct. 1617.

aspects of both private and public ownership. That is, the arms were purchased by one individual or group of individuals for someone else to carry on muster day. Rather than providing a substitute for their service, some individuals would satisfy county requirements by purchasing their exemption in the form of a weapon or suit of armour. This sometimes resulted in a ludicrous mixture of arms such as in the case of Robert Norman, of Thingoe hundred, Suffolk. Norman was equipped with 'a caliver, flask and touchbox from the widow Norman, a burgonet [headpiece] from John Bartylmew, a sword from widow Norman, and dagger and girdle from John Lynge, Thomas Barnard, and Robert Gooday'.[73]

The 'private/public' arms often included those which were confiscated from recusants during various crack-downs on Catholics both during the war with Spain and after the Gunpowder Plot. In Lancashire in 1612 the deputy lieutenants were warned by the privy council to make lists of all recusants and then 'to repair to the dwellinge houses or places of the said convicted Recusants or non-commicantes, and take from them all armes and weapon other than shalbee necessarie for defence of their howses'.[74] This occurred again in 1619, with the privy council adding as a rider to their instructions that the arms 'by long lying and rust are much decayed, and will in a shorte tyme become unservicable and of no use unlesse some course be taken for the scouring and amendinge of the same'. As a result, the deputy lieutenants were ordered to have the arms cleaned at the expense of the recusant owner, have the recusant drill with them at the muster (despite the recusant supposedly being a dangerous threat) and then ensure that the arms be stored in a public place away from the owner. Thus in one order the council pointed out the dangers of armed recusants, while admitting that the arms were of little value, then ordered the recusants to be trained with those arms (which they had to maintain at their own expense), and ended with a demand that they be not trusted to keep them in their own houses.[75] The resulting confusion led the council to decree in 1625 that they could not readily distinguish between the 'well and worse affected' and so the trained bands were ordered to confiscate all weapons for their own use rather than allowing recusants any role at all.[76]

Except in the case of the confiscated weapons, it is very hard to discover how the counties procured their arms. There does not seem to have been a very substantial small arms industry in the provinces since the market was

---

[73] Boynton, *Elizabethan militia*, 71.
[74] *The Lancashire lieutenancy under the Tudors and Stuarts*, ed. John Harland, 2 vols (Chatham Soceity xlix, 1859), 260. For earlier examples of the confiscation of recusant arms see APC 1592, 40–2, privy council to the lords lieutenants repeating directions of 1585, 21 July 1592.
[75] APC 1619–21, 11, privy council reporting on letters from her Majesty's lieutenants, 11 July 1619.
[76] APC 1625–6, 188–9, privy council to lords lieutenants touching disarming of recusants, 4 Oct. 1625.

rather small, but one cannot discount the possibility that some local blacksmiths made extra money by hammering out corslets or an occasional musket. In 1596 the deputy lieutenants of Northamptonshire made an agreement with Parr Lane, one of their militia captains, to supply coats, armour and weapons to the militia. He provided 47 corslets at 40s. each, 23 muskets at 35s. each, 24 at 30s. each and 94 coats at 13s. 4d. each. It is not clear where he got them, but since the price he charged was almost double what the London arms makers were charging, either he purchased them from a small, low-volume craftsman in the area or else he made a profit of close to 100 per cent on the deal.[77] In a later example of private purchase, the earl of Exeter offered in 1617 to buy muskets for the bands of Northamptonshire from a London gunmaker at a cost of 26s. 8d. each.[78]

There were certainly some arms producers in the counties, although the evidence is very sketchy. The JPs of Lancashire wrote to the privy council in 1603 in response to the council's query regarding 'extraordinary provision made of arms by recusants in those parts'. The justices reported that they had examined all the armourers in the county as to the quantity of armour, weapons and gunpowder purchased by any known recusants and had discovered 'all depose that to their knowledge they have not so sold any'.[79] Although this indicates that much of the Catholic menace was in the minds of the council, it also shows that there were probably a number of local sources (if not manufacturers) for small arms in that county and probably in other too.

Somerset and the environs of Bristol seem to have had a small but flourishing arms industry, doubtless because of the need to keep merchant ships supplied. However, the industry also relied heavily upon the rebellion in Ireland to stay profitable. Sir John Cowper reported to the council soon after the death of Elizabeth that he had set up a battery works in Somerset to furnish enough plate for 4,000 sets of armour a year. For him, like his London counterparts, the coming of peace was hard. He complained to Cecil in 1604:

> In this time of peace the stock will grow so great that he must discontinue the works, except the king will receive some competent numbers of armours into the Tower of London where always has been the store to supply all parts of the land upon any sudden need which is not now furnished with many that are of any use.[80]

Sir John's offer was probably not taken up since the armourers in London and Greenwich were more than able to keep up with the peacetime demand for arms and at less cost.

---

[77] *Musters, beacons and subsidies*, 32.
[78] HMC, *Buccleuch and Queensberry*, iii, 199–201, Exeter to his deputy lieutenants, 28 Apr. 1617.
[79] HMC, *Salisbury*, xv. 88 (13 May 1603).
[80] Ibid. xvi. 418 [1604].

Since Bristol was also a major port of embarkation for soldiers travelling to Ireland, there was probably a small weapons industry in the city to provide equipment for the troops who occasionally showed up without arms from their county stores or with arms of poor quality. In 1598 and 1600 two bands of soldiers going to Ireland were provided with small arms in Bristol, although in the second instance they were provided by Edmund Nicholson, a London merchant who had probably purchased them in London.[81] There is every indication that most purchases of arms and armour occurred through arms merchants in London who had bought the arms directly from the producers in that city. In 1599 Thomas, Lord Burghley, wrote to his brother, Sir Robert Cecil, that one of his men was going to London 'to prepare for sending the whole provision of armour for better furnishing this country; though the charge will be £4,000 it will scarce furnish half the wants such has been the small care taken since my Lord of Huntingdon's death'.[82]

London's dominance in the arms trade increased during the 1590s, with the privy council even recommending by 1602 that the counties buy arms through one individual, Edmund Nicolson. The council had problems with defective arms and recommended to the sheriffs and commissioners of musters that when repairing the 'general defectes' of the militia arms 'you will rather choose to buy of his Armers then of another; If he shall offer you the same at so reasonable rates as you shall thincke fitte to agree on according to the severall Pattrons [patterns] of Arms' located in the Tower in London. Nicholson was to supply arms and armour for all the counties, if possible, and his 'approved' equipment was to be marked with a 'specyall stamp' as proof of their quality.[83] The council, in desiring to standardise the county arms and ensure their quality, thus contributed to the central role of London in the arms market.

The counties began to conduct most of their arms business in London. In Northamptonshire in 1617 the earl of Exeter asked John Kettle, a London gunmaker and armourer, to provide 50 new muskets for his county. Kettle took the muskets up to Northampton by cart and distributed them at the muster held that year; he also took additional orders for the following year.[84] In Yorkshire, the lord president of the council of the north, Lord Scrope, wrote to the privy council in 1620, saying that the trained bands had not been exercised in five years and that 'arms must be provided from London,

---

[81] PRO, E 407/12/6, privy council to lord mayor of Bristol.
[82] *CSPD Eliz. I, 1598–1601*, 332 (18 Oct. 1599). The county is probably Yorkshire, since Burghley had just been appointed lord president of the council of the north: R. R. Reid, *The king's council in the north*, London – New York 1921, 230–9.
[83] *Montagu muster book*, 216–17, letter from the council to the sheriff and commissioners for musters, 29 Apr. 1602. Nicholson was charging the reasonable price of 32s. for a complete set of footman's armour. Other prices included 70s. for each light horse (armour and lance) and £5 for each heavily armoured cavalryman.
[84] HMC, *Buccleuch and Queensberry*, iii. 199–201, Exeter to deputy lieutenants and deputies to the constables of the hundreds, 28 Apr.–19 Sep. 1617.

before all can be completed'.[85] In a similar instance, this time in Hampshire in 1623, the county made provision of their arms from John Ashton, a noted London armourer.[86]

London was probably the source of most of the weapons and armour purchased by the counties for their own use, but the local deputy lieutenant is occasionally to be found searching farther afield for weapons. In 1626 Sir Thomas Jervoise of Hampshire, despite his London contacts, paid £144 3s. 6d. for arms purchased from the Low Countries for his county.[87] The type of armour and weapons bought indicate that this was a special order for the county horse, and not common armour for the average soldier. The status-conscious gentry (most mounted units were composed of the well-off) presumably felt that they could afford to buy the more elaborate armour available overseas.

Despite the occasional luxury of expensive weapons, there was often very strong resistance to any large-scale arms purchases, and many counties held on to unserviceable or obsolete weapons far beyond their useful lives. There were a number of reasons why this was so. The most obvious was cost. County taxpayers were notoriously allergic to paying their militia rates to support the militia and to buy arms.[88] In Hampshire in 1588, on the eve of the Spanish Armada, the people seemed to fear the cost of weapons and the precedent such purchases would set more than the Spanish invasion. They complained that 'The thing the people fere most is that this new increase of Furnyture or Armour shalbe a contynuall charge uppon them selves, and their posteritie herafter.'[89] In 1597 the privy council complained that Bristol was slack in arming its men because of the cost of weapons. The city leaders left the trained bands 'altogether unarmed and [were] unwillinge to be at the chardge to be furnyshed as they ought to be' to the detriment of their own security.[90]

Complaints about militia rates were often based upon the professed or real inability of the assessed individual to pay. The rate was based loosely upon the subsidy lists but the requirement for individuals to provide arms or parts of arms was often grounded upon the ownership of certain pieces of property. When that property changed hands, either through sale or death, the

---

[85] *CSPD James I, 1619–23*, 195 (30 Nov. 1620).
[86] Hampshire Record office, MS Herriard/Jervoise, XXXV. 13 (18 July 1623). The 'special' arms of great value were carefully packed in hampers covered with preservative and the other armour was stored in 'drifatts', or barrels for dry goods.
[87] Part of the expense included paying £4 to a gentlemen to go to the Low Countries, procure the goods, ship them and unload them at Whitehall in London for overland transport to Hampshire: ibid. XXXVII. 130.
[88] See especially Hassell Smith, 'Militia statutes and militia rates', 93–110.
[89] Boynton, *Elizabethan militia*, 47–8; PRO, SP 12/208/75, 76, Captain Nicholas Dawtrey's report on state of all able men in Hampshire, 21 Feb. 1588.
[90] *APC 1597–8*, 111, privy council to Captain Dockwrey, 9 Nov. 1597.

previous owner's arms generally disappeared. The new owner was often unaware of the requirement to provide a weapon or was unwilling to buy one.[91]

Sometimes the militia officers felt compelled to use their own money to buy arms and armour for their men when local landowners had been particularly neglectful of their responsibilities. This was especially the case when they had to lead such poorly armed men overseas. When some troops of Sir John Borough's company in 1587 were discovered to be lacking uniform headpieces, Borough's lieutenant, Captain Crosbie, supplied them with matching Spanish morions out of his own armoury despite the protestations of Lord Buckhurst. Buckhurst wrote to Lord Burghley that Crosbie had viewed his troops and 'found grete fault wt them that they were not sutably armed some having Burgonnets while some Burgonnets lacke + some morions of the first fashion wt a hie crest wch now they utterlie mislike'. Crosbie wanted them to match, whereas Buckhurst said, reasonably, 'though they were of divers fashions, yet they wold serve the turn in the field (the braveness of the show excepted) as well as the Spanish morion'. Crosbie, pressured by his sense of military fashion, issued 148 morions to his men so that he could lead them to the Low Countries in style.[92] In a similar incident in 1601, this time concerning the provision of coats, the council had to intercede with the deputy lieutenants of Somerset to prevent them from spending excess money on unnecessary equipment. Sir Francis Hastings and his partners in the office had planned to buy 4,000 new coats for the county militia on their own initiative. Although the council praised his good intentions, it went on to state that the county should not 'be at this tyme unnecessarilie burthened with a non-essential expense'.[93] The pleas for better equipment did not always come from the central government, nor were they always based upon true necessity.

The problem of collecting money for weapons was certainly compounded by the lapsing of the militia statutes in 1604 which removed the legal basis for the collection of the militia rates. The only authority for forcing inhabitants to provide weapons or money for weapons thereafter was the king's prerogative. This tool had to be used with very great care and due respect for the sensitivities of the counties. When the earl of Hertford was opposed by his own deputies in the collection of a militia rate in Somerset in 1604, he wrote to the king to intercede since he perceived that this was a direct attack upon the king's prerogative. Hertford stated that the authority to levy the

---

[91] Boynton, *Elizabethan militia*, 21. According to Boynton, armour was regarded as a capital investment, and was often divided among the heirs to an estate. In Hertfordshire much armour was 'lost by the death of sundry person, who have divided their livings amongst their wives and children, and by removal of others into different shires': *CSPD Eliz. I, 1595–7*, 108, Sir Henry Cock, Sir John Brockett and Sir Philip Boteler to Lord Burghley, lord lieutenant of Hertfordshire, 6 Oct. 1596.
[92] PRO, SP 12/226/73, Buckhurst to Burghley, 28 Sept. 1589.
[93] APC 1601–4, 91, privy council to Hastings, 26 July 1601.

rate proceeded 'onely from kingly prerogative, not assisted with any statutes or lawes in that behalfe'.[94] The following year, residents of Wiltshire (also part of Hertford's lieutenancy) refused to pay their militia rate on the grounds that it lacked a legal basis.[95] The lack of a statutory basis for the collection of militia rates was indeed a continuing problem throughout the reign of James I and contributed greatly to the poor quality of county arms.

Even when militia rates were peacefully collected in the 1590s there were occasional complaints about the way in which the money was spent. In 1596 in Cheshire, the muster commissioners had apparently collected heavy rates for the militia 'which hath bin gathered on the inhabitants and come to the handes of certaine persons that have not imployed the same to the use and furnishing of the county, and there hat bin no trewe accompt yealded of the same'.[96] Even collections sanctioned by statute went astray very easily in so decentralised a system and made such rates unpopular.

In lieu of a law which fixed the amount and type of contribution owed by each household in each county, the Jacobean privy council established guidelines for a more equitable assessment for arms. In May 1619 the council stated that arms were 'to bee assessed rateably accordinge to the value of those launds they [property-owners] hold in the same, nothwithstaundinge they fynd armes, either in London or anie other countie where they dwell or reside'.[97] This was a major departure from a system which, as with the subsidy collection, had major landowners pay their rates only in the county of actual residence even though they might possess larger, tax free, estates in other counties. The earl of Bath immediately put this system into operation and was congratulated by the council for assessing arms according to landholdings in his county whether the owner lived there or not.[98]

While the expense of weapons was a major source of irritation to many of the county inhabitants, an additional complication was the fact that so many of the arms that were purchased for the trained bands ended up in the hands of levies sent overseas. Unfortunately, very few of these weapons returned.[99]

There were constant complaints from the counties during the war years of Elizabeth that they had purchased weapons for the overseas levies and wanted them returned to the county stores. However, weapons were regularly lost in service or sold or pawned by the soldiers or their officers. As a result, many counties grew reluctant to purchase any new weapons for their troops

---

[94] *Earl of Hertford's lieutenancy papers: 1603–1612*, ed. W. P. D. Murphy (Wiltshire Record Society xxiii, 1969), 102.
[95] Ibid. 63.
[96] APC 1596–7, 61–2, privy council to the commissioners of the musters in Cheshire, 26 July 1596.
[97] APC 1619–21, 218, privy council to lords lieutenant and muster commissioners, 31 May 1619.
[98] APC 1621–3, 89–90, privy council to the earl of Bath, 19 Nov. 1621.
[99] See any of the expeditions to the continent between 1589 and 1595 in Wernham, *After the Armada*.

for fear that they would be taken off for foreign service. They presumably did not mind losing the rogues and vagabonds who were commonly pressed into the army, but expensive weapons were another matter.[100]

Counties also faced the difficulty and expense of properly maintaining county arms and armour. The privy council was fairly consistent in its attempts to establish strict standards for the wearing and maintenance of arms in order to improve overall levels of efficiency and, in the long run, save everybody money. Lord Burghley took particular interest in all such matters during the early war years. In 1589 and 1590 he issued specific instructions to the county of Hertfordshire to 'Looke verie stricktlie to the armour and to the weapons and to all other furn[iture] for the shire that the armour be fit and readie for s'vice and the weapons the Lyke for execucion.'[101] The county militia leaders were to ensure that the armour fitted the soldiers and looked good as well as being serviceable. On the march the soldiers were to wear the armour rather than throw it into the backs of carts or stuff it into sacks to be carried by horses as was the common practice. The equipment was to be well scoured and dressed to eliminate rust and inspections were to be made by the leaders of the bands every six weeks to see if any repairs were needed. As an incentive to careful treatment of expensive equipment, Burghley recommended that each sergeant was to draw 3d. per year for the upkeep of every firearm or pike. This general charge was to be collected by the constable of each town.[102]

Burghley's standards were somewhat optimistic since there was virtually no way he could enforce a nation-wide programme of such detail and complexity when the cost had to be borne by the local ratepayer. It remained for each county to decide how much was to be spent on maintaining arms and armour and the result was that each county remained a law unto itself.

There was one abortive attempt in 1620 to enforce a national maintenance scheme by granting a patent to one Edward Sheldon for the dressing, repairing and inspecting of county arms. Sheldon and his workmen were to travel from county to county inspecting arms stores and dressing the arms at set prices. They were to receive 5d. to clean each 'white' (uncoated metal) corslet, 12d. for each 'black' (metal painted black) corslet and 12d. for each caliver or musket repaired. Their patent included the right to force the county to bring its arms to whatever central location the patentee chose and then they were to be permitted free rein to order the replacement of old arms. Any county which did not allow the patentees to inspect or dress its arms was to be regarded as being in contempt of council and punished accordingly. The grant was to last for twenty-one years, but it was named as a grievance in

---

[100] *CSPD Eliz. I, 1595–7*, 108, deputy lieutenants of Hertfordshire to Lord Burghley, 6 Oct. 1596.
[101] PRO, SP 12/224/94, notes by Mr Humphrey Coningsby for the muster of the trained bands in Hertford, 14 June 1589.
[102] HMC, *Salisbury*, iv. 15–19, Burghley, orders for the musters, 15 Mar. 1590.

the parliament of 1621 and was revoked.[103] Laudable though the goal was, no county wanted an agent of central government (and a hated patentee at that) to be given the right to force the county to take their arms to him at his whim to be forcibly cleaned at fixed rates or even scrapped along with a command to buy new ones. The scheme had all the disadvantages of centralisation with virtually no redeeming features, from the counties' point of view at least.

The wider ordnance world

Although the Tower and Minories storehouses in London were undoubtedly the chief arsenals of the realm, the fact that the English state and its Irish counterpart were essentially decentralised made multiple stores of weapons inevitable. Subordinate ordnance offices, such as those in the north and Ireland, annexes in Woolwich, Rochester, Chatham and Deptford, stores in castles and forts, and finally the hodge-podge weapons stores of the counties made up a patchwork of overlapping and confusing systems and standards. All attempts at producing one national system of weapons procurement, or regulating quality and type of equipment and standard of maintenance were doomed to failure. The counties did not want such a system, which was sure to be expensive, and central government did not have the money or the administrative expertise to impose it. The privy council had to be content with using the arms stores which had evolved over the centuries as best they could. When the need was less, during time of peace, stores were allowed to decay and fall into disuse. During time of war, various local and national initiatives were undertaken to establish the rudiments of a standard system of arms storage for England and Ireland. The mixed results of such attempts virtually ensured that when Charles I needed to activate the military establishment in 1625, after twenty years of peace, he had virtually to strip his kingdom of arms in order to launch his expeditionary forces to Cadiz and Rhé.[104]

---

[103] *Commons debates 1621*, vii. 329. I have found no evidence of attempts to enforce this patent. It was probably in existence for too short a time.
[104] For the ordnance problems and disastrous results of both Charles's expeditions in the 1620s see my articles in Fissel, *War and government in Britain*, 112–132.

8

Conclusion

Judgements about the relative effectiveness of the Elizabethan military establishment compared with that of Stuart England have, over the years, been harsh. C. H. Firth utterly condemned the Elizabethan military system. Considering it from the perspective of the admittedly effective Cromwellian military machine, he stated that 'The military system which the Tudors bequeathed to the Stuarts was completely inefficient. It had broken down long before the Tudor period ended.'[1] But the evidence demands a reconsideration of this statement. The Elizabethan military system in general, and the supply of arms in particular, can actually be said to have reached a high point of military effectiveness in the last years of the sixteenth century. The military expeditions of Elizabeth on the continent, while hardly flawless in planning or execution, generally achieved their broad aims of sustaining the Dutch rebels and the French crown against Spanish encroachments. The more spectacular amphibious raids on Spain itself were less successful because of the unrealistic expectations of their planners, the waste of supply and failures of leadership. But England was able to defend herself against three major attempts at invasion on the part of the Spaniards, including a landing in Ireland in aid of Tyrone, which was initially sucessfull. The sternest test of the military logistics system was Ireland – where the English forces were totally dependent upon support from home for food, pay, clothing and arms – and, by and large, it is clear that problems with the supply system had been corrected. The Irish campaign alone confounds the contention that the Elizabethan military system was 'completely inefficient'. The leadership and logistical machine of the army had matured through experience in war to the point where it was able to concentrate on winning in Ireland. As a result in great measure of almost constant warfare from 1585 to 1603, the military machine that the Tudors bequeathed to the Stuarts was a well-oiled and remarkably effective one.

The supply system of the English land forces made great strides in the course of the war with Spain. This owed much to the growing power of the navy, which made it possible for successive Spanish armadas to be fended off, while still maintaining a flow of supplies to the ground forces in the Low Countries, France and Ireland. The use of contract merchantmen was also important since many of the supplies were loaded into commercial ships for

[1] Firth, *Cromwell's army*, 1.

the voyages to the theatres of war. The importance of this naval lifeline, merchant and military, cannot be overstressed, especially for the campaigns in Ireland. Control of the sea, or at least the ability to maintain unbroken contact by sea with Ireland and the continent, was a critical factor in England's ability to supply her forces. Logistics depend not only upon the quantity of supplies that can be produced or administered, but also upon having the means available to move them promptly when required. In the context of the times, and especially when one looks ahead from the Elizabethan period to Charles's failures in the war with Spain and France between 1625 and 1629, the Elizabethan military supply system stands out as superior to that of the Stuarts.

The role of the arms supply system, especially the part played by the ordnance office, in the Elizabethan military success story is clear. When compared with the contractor system which provided food and clothing to the troops, the more centralised arms procurement process run by the Elizabethan ordnance office was generally more efficient. This should not blind us to the fact that the privy council could rely upon the counties to provide most of the initial arms needed for military expeditions. Towards the end of the war, the government also began to rely heavily upon arms merchants and monopolists to provide occasional infusions of arms. This mixture of systems highlights the pragmatic character of Elizabethan government while also indicating that the arms supply system was not yet ready for complete centralisation. Even with heavy demand and a large, well-developed arms industry, a centralised system could not have coped with massive demands made upon it. The result was that Elizabethan arms procurement involved a mixture of methods with the privy council orchestrating switches from county procurement to contractor to ordnance office for the armaments needed by the military as the situation and resources allowed. The system worked even if its complexity baffles most modern observers. The expeditions to the continent or to Ireland often ran into trouble because of shortages of food or a failure of leadership, but seldom because of a lack of arms or other ordnance supplies.

Despite administrative, financial and political difficulties, the Elizabethan system worked and achieved its limited goals. The same cannot be said of its Stuart successor. The Stuart ordnance office in peacetime was saddled with corruption and inefficiency to such an extent that it was ill-prepared for war despite adequate warning and large infusions of cash. The failure of the Cadiz expedition in 1625 and the later disaster at Rhé in 1627, while the result of many factors, cannot but cast doubt upon any favourable judgement of the Stuart military system. When one looks even farther ahead, to the period from 1639 to 1642, it becomes even more difficult to declare that the Stuart military establishment compared at all favourably with that of the Tudors. Why should this be so? What differentiated the Stuart arms supply system from that of the Tudors? In order to isolate those differences, it is necessary to examine five aspects of the procurement system and to discuss their military and political consequences: the growth of bureaucracy and the changing level of administrative efficiency in war and peace; changes in the financial burden and financial management techniques in the ordnance office; the shifting relationship between government and the war industries of the realm; changing standards of the central government and the pressure upon the localities to conform to those higher standards; the changing nature of warfare in early modern Europe.

The various arms supply and storage establishments in England in the Tudor and Stuart period were small, yet they had a major role to play in the development of bureaucracy. Under pressure of war from 1585 to 1603 the size, complexity of procedures, and range of duties of the ordnance office expanded to meet the increasing requirements of England's military establishment. This expansion was neither anticipated nor planned, rather it was a a consequence of the increased quantities of goods and money going through the office. The number of official clerks in the office grew, the duties of the officers became more clearly defined under pressure of work, and office reformers gradually perceived how the office ought to function. Official and unofficial descriptions of how the office ought to function were increasingly contrasted to the reality of how it did function. Increasing consciousness of how a bureaucracy should work was caused by the pressing need for a better, more efficient office to supply the military. The various instructions to the ordnance office drawn up by the earl of Warwick and the queen, and the reform projects of 1598 and 1601 were all limited attempts to place the office on a rational footing, not for the sake of rationalisation *per se*, but rather as a means to deal with specific shortcomings. When the urgent need for the more efficient delivery of supplies vanished in 1604, the urge to rationalise lost its driving force. Under the Stuarts the supply network suffered from all the diseases of what might be called a prerational bureaucracy: corruption, poor organisation, domination by personalities and absence of any system of appointment or promotion by merit. There was no high-road to a centralised state or to a rational bureaucracy.

It is thus possible to trace the development of increasing efficiency through experience in ordnance office administration from the outbreak of war in 1585 through to its conclusion in 1604. The path was far from smooth and the rise in effectiveness far from inexorable, but despite occasional setbacks and isolated mistakes, the ordnance office at the end of the first war with Spain was far better able to supply a major land army than at the beginning. The fact that this relatively successful performance was not translated into institutionalised terms and incorporated into office procedures in order to build on this experience in time of peace says much about Jacobean bureaucracy. The institutional memory of the office failed. In an age before rational conceptions of organisational management, there was simply no way to utilise past performance for future success. When the office was forced to prepare for war in the 1620s, it had to begin all over again, painfully reassembling precedents and reinventing procedures in order to succeed even as well as it did. The ordnance office suffered an administrative gap between 1604 and 1620. The arms supply system for the English army, so laboriously built up over twenty years of warfare, vanished so completely after 1604 that in 1621 ordnance officers and suppliers alike could not, even with three months notice, assemble enough arms for a medium-sized field army to recover the Palatinate. Even after the war scare of 1621, the office did not effectively prepare for war. In part, thanks to a penurious monarch, they lacked the finances to maintain even a low level of military expenditure. Thus the purchases of 1624–5 had to be so huge and the need so urgent that there was considerable wastage and little effective quality control. This was complicated by the fact that the office was forced to provide all the supplies for the expeditions rather than relying upon the counties or even the armoury to share the burden.

The ordnance office during wartime learned slowly, and having learned, had no mechanism to retain and use that knowledge without the constant practice provided by war. Peace inevitably eroded what relative efficiency had been acquired during war.

Any harsh judgement on the failure of the institutional memory of the Jacobean ordnance office should be tempered. Some of the problems which occurred between 1603 and 1625 may be attributed to the disappearance of experienced personnel from the ordnance office. The turnover of experienced personnel – especially in the offices of surveyor of the ordnance, keeper of the stores and clerk of the deliveries – doubtless had an effect on the efficient running of the office. During that period most of the key offices changed hands from two to eight times and this was almost certainly a key factor in the difficulties the office experienced in coping with the renewal of war in 1625. The miracle was that these inexperienced officers did as well as they did, coping with over £65,000-worth of ordnance supplies purchased in 1624 and 1625 with fewer complaints than might have been expected. However, the stores were depleted by the Cadiz expedition, the quality of items provided was often suspect and many key items (such as gunpowder) had to be purchased from abroad. The office was certainly less self-sufficient. One is forced to conclude that the ordnance office under the Stuarts was no longer as efficiently administered as it had been during the last years of the Irish rebellion under Elizabeth. A failure to learn from the past played a vital role in its decline.

The different financial problems faced by the ordnance office in this period also had considerable effect on the relative efficiency of the Tudor and Stuart arms supply systems. Despite severe financial pressure and increasing debt, Elizabeth managed to find the money to sustain the purchase of the weapons and war matériel needed to fight the greatest power in Europe to a stalemate. This was partly because she was able to spread the burden around to the counties. The involvement and support of the counties, specifically of the county leadership, in the entire war effort, and in the arms supply system in particular, was crucial to England's performance. The fact that Elizabeth

CONCLUSION

and her ministers were able to elicit it was certainly a key to her success. However, it was also crucial that the ordnance office continued to draw its ordinary allowance in addition to the huge sums granted by special privy seal for the war. The 'external' factor of how much money was given to the office by the government was critical as can be seen in the years from 1618 to 1626 when most of the ordinary allowance was not paid. This cutback severely limited the ability of the office to perform routine purchases and maintenance of its stores, both of which were vital activities which would have helped preserve its effectiveness. The attempt at direct management of the office by the privy council, with its method of granting special privy seals for almost all routine expenditures, made efficient, regular management of the ordnance's finances from 1618 to 1626 virtually impossible. The large sums granted to the office in 1624 and 1625 helped, but that money came too late and was too much to spend effectively in the time available.

The third aspect of comparison between the Tudor and Stuart arms supply systems was the growing importance of the state's relationships with the network of arms craftsmen and merchants. The three-way relationship between the government, the ordnance office and the arms suppliers is fraught with consequences for early modern England. The beginnings of today's military–industrial–political complex can be seen in the close relationship of government, bureaucracy and suppliers which was present in a rudimentary form even in early modern England. Virtually the entire range of products supplied to the ordnance office as the storehouse for the realm fell under the direct or indirect influence of the government. The privy council, as the chief executive agency of the government, was heavily involved in encouraging, protecting and controlling the iron and brass ordnance and gunpowder industries. These were vital to the kingdom's security and thus could not be left to the vagaries of market forces. Monopolies, although unpopular on many levels, were one way in which a financially strapped government – and what early modern governments were not in this condition? – could insure the survival of necessary industries. The cost of monopolies went beyond popular disapproval. Monopolies were a 'half-way house' between independent industries and direct control by the government which often led to poor quality goods and a limited production capacity. Greater government control of war industries would probably not have lessened the unpopularity of its actions (especially in the saltpetre industry) but it could have helped control the quality of the items produced while restraining the worst of the excesses. Seeking to save money and preserve essential industries, the government adopted a middle course and accepted a share of the responsibility for the disruptions of the industries without the compensation of a better product or more efficient production.

In the area of relations between government and industry, there was more continuity than discontinuity between the Tudor and Stuart regimes. Elizabeth and James faced many of the same problems in assisting and sustaining vital industries despite popular or rival industrial detractors. They responded in much the same way by granting patents, monopolies and licences. However, the Tudor arms industries flourished while those of the Stuarts virtually vanished. This was mainly because Elizabeth was at war and James was not. Government could not begin to provide sufficient support for war industries during peacetime to enable them to maintain a large and expandable productive capacity adequate to meet all the demands of an early modern state. Despite the same political and economic pressures and the same basic responses, Tudor England gradually became virtually self-sufficient in military supplies and arms because of its constant state of war while Stuart England, after twenty years of peace, had to rely upon foreign suppliers for many of its needs.

The slow reaction time of an early market economy simply could not be trusted to provide, unaided, all the many goods that an activated military establishment would need at a time of crisis. A key example of continuing dependence upon foreign supplies making up for a lack of domestic productive capacity occurred in 1620 and 1621 with the plans for the Palatinate expedition. Evelyn and many other suppliers professed their inability to provide the amount of supplies the government needed at such short notice. They recommended – and the council had no choice but to agree – that foreign supplies be purchased through merchants or other contacts overseas. Domestic productive capacity, despite governmental protection on a limited scale, could not respond quickly enough. As a result, the role of the arms merchants who had access to foreign sources continued to be important throughout this period despite the crown's continual hopes (unmatched by sustained interest and funding) of self-sufficiency in arms production.

The merchants were able, although often requiring government assistance, to supply any short-fall of war matériel at short notice. There were risks, but the potential profits were just too attractive. As there was no effective means to maintain a peacetime arms industry, the government had little choice but to turn to the merchants.

The plain fact was that the Stuart government simply could not afford to maintain an easily-expandable arms production capability in peacetime. It could not purchase large quantities of war supplies for storage in the Tower when it was chronically short of cash, nor could it allow arms producers uncontrolled access to foreign markets which would allow them to maintain production levels and sell their excess overseas for a profit. Some government protection and support was lent to the major industries, such as gunpowder and ordnance, with their high overheads, skilled employees and lengthy start-up time but even this was barely enough to keep them alive. It could not provide such protection to the majority of the smaller industries without incurring great expense which, during peacetime, would have been difficult to justify to the nation. The relationship between industry and government was still ill-defined and *ad hoc*, with the government concerned to maintain some control of certain key industries on grounds of national security. The suppliers benefited from this to a certain extent too. They could turn to the

CONCLUSION

government to support their survival and as a permanent market for their goods. Such support was far from being guaranteed; the government did not bail out the majority of arms producers in 1604 who suddenly found themselves without a market. However, for a lucky handful of industries, government protection in the form of monopolies and letters patent saved them from total extinction. With the government often the only legal market for those items, its relationship with the suppliers was clearly a symbiotic one with each benefiting from, and unable to do without, the other.

The development of an effective, centralised bureaucracy in England was a long and slow process. It involved no less than a change in the very conception of government and its role in the lives of its subjects. The process was accelerated by war in the early modern period with the government needing to marshall all its resources to survive. This was especially true as England found itself involved in a new type of warfare that demanded larger armies, heavily armed ships and more ancillary military equipment for sieges. The stress upon relations between the central government and the counties was correspondingly greater as the need for more men and more money grew at an unprecedented rate. Soldiers were increasingly being armed with expensive firearms as well as pikes and were also supported in the field by a growing and sophisticated array of other weapons and supplies from axes to wheelbarrows. Although it is perhaps too early to talk of any revolution in tactics and weaponry such as occurred in the mid-seventeenth century, warfare was taking on a decidedly more technological aspect.[2]

England, of course, was not the only country to face the pressures of a new, more technological type of warfare which required more elaborate administrative means of control. It is instructive to compare, briefly, England's halting steps towards greater uniformity, standardisation and central control of the military with the means used by England's great enemy of the period: Spain. Without doubt Spain had the largest, most experienced, most centrally controlled and most expensive military system in Europe. It seemed that the latter two items – central control and expense – went together since it literally took the wealth of the Indies to hold the system together. Even so, as I. A. A. Thompson has shown, Spain's military–administrative system swung wildly between the two poles of *administracion* or direct royal control, and *asiento*, indirect control by contractors or private entrepreneurs.[3] Even in the wealthiest state in Europe, centralised control of a growing military establishment without an efficient, rationalised, systematic, civil service bureaucracy was simply too expensive to maintain for long. By the 1630s Spain had turned its back on the centralised system of Philip II and 'practically the

---

[2] For more on the military revolution of the seventeenth century see Michael Roberts, *The military revolution 1550–1660*; Geoffrey Parker, 'The "military revolution", 1560–1660 – a myth?', *Journal of Modern History* xlviii (1976), 195–214, and *Military revolution*.

[3] Thompson, *War and government*, 1–5.

whole of the war machine, of the high seas fleet, the arms industries, the victualling of the galleys and the African garrisons, and the recruiting process also, had passed into private hands, contracted out to entrepreneurs and local authorities'.[4] The Spanish state, constantly at war to protect its huge empire, was forced to decentralise its administrative network because of its great cost and lapsed into virtually total reliance on *asiento*.

In Spain's struggle between administrative methods, many of the same forces were at play as in England's slow movement towards a centralised bureaucracy. However, the timing and result were vastly different. Elizabeth, her ministers and her officers were never committed to the notion of centralisation and only adopted elements of central control when the situation required it. When circumstances changed, as at the end of war in 1604, the measures were dropped as well. The Tudor regime remained a mixture of direct administration and decentralised management through contractors even under the pressure of war. To be sure, England did not have the wealth and could not therefore afford the luxury of direct control on the Spanish model; as a result the English state was able to weather its financial and military crisis from 1585 to 1604 while Spain went broke. It would be overly simplistic to suggest that the English 'mixed procurement' system was the key to the fiscal and political survival of the state, but it seems a distinct possibility when viewed in the light of the crippling financial burden of centralised management in Spain. When England did begin to move towards greater standardisation of arms and centralisation of military bureaucracy in the 1620s and 1630s (after Spain had virtually given them up) the results for England were not totally beneficial either. Tensions between central government and the counties, disputes in parliament, military failure, political unrest, all occurred as Charles I attempted to establish a more centralised, 'modern' state. War and the preparation for war, as the underlying reason for many centralising initiatives, was to have severe consequences for the state in the years to come. The tax resources and administrative means of the state could not yet support a highly centralised military establishment.

This detailed study of the arms supply system in war and peace in early modern England demonstrates the complex nature of the impact of war upon the state. It is true that war has always been considered one of the strongest driving forces behind the development of a centralised bureaucracy, but the details of how a state dealt with the specific needs of war show just how complicated this was. From 1585 to 1603, centralising forces were encouraged by almost constant warfare which drew heavily upon England's resources and forced the state to subordinate all other considerations to the need to survive. However, when England, relatively isolated from the maelstrom of continental politics, returned to a state of peace, those forces could not be sustained. Circumstances rather than a commitment to any over-

---

[4] Ibid. 7.

CONCLUSION

arching, intellectual ideal of the powers of the state enlarged the bureaucracy and created the climate for increased state involvement in the lives of its subjects. Subsequent financial and political pressures in early Stuart England were such as to suspend centralisation of the state and its arms procurement system. It was not until war became more likely from 1620 onwards that increased administrative interest in standardised arms and more efficient bureaucratic organisation forced the government to press harder for one national arms policy. Necessity brought renewed attempts to centralise the arms supply network: the need for higher quality, more modern, standardised arms – and larger quantities of them – for the forces of the kingdom. The failure of that system in battle highlighted the fact that realisation of the need for better arms was not matched by the administrative and bureaucratic mechanisms to procure them. The older Elizabethan system, a mixture of private-, contractor- and government-supplied weapons was discarded in favour of supply almost exclusively by the central government in 1625. There was, however, inadequate administrative support for this. War created the climate for centralisation, but for the system to provide the necessary items to the battlefield required adminstrative and bureaucratic mechanisms by means of which a centralised arms procurement system could be implemented. But these – a rationalised bureaucracy, established office procedures, a merit-based appointment system for officers, effective supervisory techniques to insure probity in office and a dedicated and adequate office budget as a minimum – did not yet exist.

APPENDIX 1

Ordnance office personnel and salaried artificers, 1585–1625

Master (or master-general) of the ordnance
Ambrose Dudley, 1st earl of Warwick	1560–89
Sir Philip Sidney (joint)	1585–6
Robert Devereux, 2nd earl of Essex	1597–1600
Charles Blount, 1st earl of Devonshire	1603–6
George Carew, 1st Lord Carew of Clopton (afterwards 1st earl of Totnes)	1608–29

Lieutenant (or lieutenant general) of the ordnance
Sir William Pelham	1576–87
Sir Robert Constable	1588–91
Sir George Carew	1592–1608
Sir Roger Dallison	1608–16
Sir Richard Morisson	1616–25
Sir William Harrington	1625–6

Surveyor of the ordnance
John Powell	1583–95
William Partheridge	1595–9
Sir John Davis	1599–1602
Sir John Linewray	1602–6
Sir Roger Dallison [Hogg lists Joseph Earth]	1606–8
Sir John Kay	1608–23
Sir John Ogle	1623–4
Richard Kay	1624–5

Clerk of the ordnance
William Paynter	1554–95
Sir Stephen Riddlesden	1595–1603
John Riddlesden (joint)	1603–7
Francis Morice	1608—>

Keeper of the stores
Richard Bowland	1572–89
Thomas Bedwell	1589–95
John Lee	1595–1603
Sir Amias Preston	1603–9
Samuel Hales	1609–12
John Hammond (joint)	1609–12
Sir Roger Ayscough (joint)	1609–12
Nedtracy Smart	1614–20
Shackerley Tracy (joint)	1614–20

APPENDIX 1

Thomas Powell   1620–7
John Colding (joint)   1620–7

Clerk of the deliveries
Brian Hogge   1578–95
George Hogge (joint)   1578–95
John Linewray   1595–1602
George Hogge (joint)   1595–1602
Sir Robert Johnson   1602–4
Robert Johnson, Jr   1604–10
Ralph Freeman   1610–18
Edward Johnson   1618–40
Henry Johnson (joint)   1618–40

Clerk to the lieutenant/master
William Cudnor   [1595]–1603
John Pavy   1603–8
Richard Paulfreyman   1609
George Hooker   1609—>

Master gunner of England
Stephen Bull   [1595]–1608
William Bull   1608–10
William Hammond   1610–22
John Reynolds   1622—>

Keeper of the rich weapons
William Ridge   [1595]–1614?
Nedtracy Smart   1614?–20
Thomas Powell   1621—>

Keeper of the small guns
William Fookes   [1595]–1598
Henry Halder   1598–9
Richard Paulfreyman   1599–1611
James Paulfreyman   1612—>

Proofmasters
Stephen Bull   [1595]–1607
William Hammond   [1595]–1623
William Bull   1607–11
John Reynolds   1612—>
John Dwarris   1623—>

Furbishers
Martin Hopkins   [1595]–1606
William Ridge   [1595]–1615?
Thomas Plasse   1606–15?
Henry Gisbourne   1615?–23

ORDNANCE OFFICE PERSONNEL, 1585–1625

Henry Gotobed	1615?–20
Thomas Vasey	1621–2
Lewes Tayte	1623—>
John Norcot	1622—>

Ordnance clerks

Anthony Paynter	[1595]
John Bagnall	[1595]
Thomas Wates	[1595]
Edward Partheridge	[1595]–1598
William Scott	[1595]–1601
Thomas Lucas	[1595]
John Squier	[1595]–1598
Richard Paulfreyman	[1595]–1608
Richard Haynes	1598–1605
Thomas Lincon	1598–1605
Richard Lentall	1598–1606
Tristram Slader	1598—>
Thomas Lynde	1600
Francis Kinniston	1600–1
Richard Birche	1601–4
Jarvas Westcot	1601–2, 1604–5
Richard Long	1602–5
William Cudner	1603–14?
John Pavey	1603–14?
Edward Cooke	1605–7
Robert Bevis	1605—>
William Forster	1605—>
John Bristowe	1605—>
Roger Warmall	1606–7
Richard Bowen	1607–9
John Parrey	1607–13
William Barroway	1608—>
John Jerman	1612–20
Simon Drawater	1614?–18
Randalle Downing	1614?–17
Andrea Bassano	1614?—>
Edward Merriweather	1618–23
Richard Phillips	1618–19
William Barker	1620—>
Nathanial Edwards	1620–3
Robert Selby	1620–1
Henry Collingwood	1622—>
William Gilden	1624—>
James Cardiffe	1624—>

Messenger

Richard Ffarrar	[1595]–97
Moses Winchell	1598–1609

APPENDIX 1

Richard Birch	1604–7
Hugh Price	1607–8
Richard Cooke	1609–22
Samuel Cox	1622—>

Blacksmith
John Skinner	[1595]–1599
Stephen Stephens	1599–1614?
Robert Bowers	1614?—>

Cowper
Richard Goad	[1595]–1597
Humphrey Harrison	1598–1624
Alexander Norman	1624—>

Wheeler
William Smeaton	[1595]—>
Thomas Aldridge (joint)	1602–19

Carpenter
John Hedland	[1595]–1609
William Wheatley	1610–21
John Horton	1621–2
Mathewe Banks	1623—>

Plumber
James Pilkington	[1595]–1610
Richard Davison	1610–17
Joseph Day	1617—>

Fletcher
William Reynolds	[1595]–1597
John Powell	1597—>

Bowyer
Richard Bowlte (Bolte)	[1595]–1607
John Jefferson	1608—>

Sources: Hogg, *The Royal arsenal*, ii. 1036–45; Ordnance Office quarter books, PRO, WO 54/1–10. The quarter books do not begin until 1595 and those officers, clerks or artificers listed at that date had probably been in the office for an unknown number of years previously. The records for the second quarter of 1614 through to the second quarter of 1616 are missing, so personnel who are not recorded in the third quarter of 1616 are presumed to have died or left office sometime in the interim. Those personnel not listed in Hogg, who were in office after 1625, have not been given a termination date: the symbol '—>' indicates continuance in office beyond that date.

APPENDIX 2

Craftsmen and suppliers to the ordnance office, 1593–1603 and 1620–5

Craftsmen	1593–1603	1620–5
Armourers (javelins, halberts, corslets)		
William Ridge	x	
Henry Foster	x	
John Perilow	x	
Joseph Hayes	x	
John Franklin		x
William Crouch		x
John Ashton		x
John Harmer		x
Thomas Stephens		x
William Saunders		x
John Cooper (armoury)		x
Richard Nash (armoury)		x
Rowland Foster		x
Basketmakers		
Adrian Adrianson	x	
William Wheatley		x
Blacksmiths		
John Gurre	x	
Martin Hopkins	x	
Isabel Hopkins (W)	x	
Marie Hopkins (W)	x	
Christopher Oswine	x	
Stephen Stephens	x	
James Waters	x	
Thomas Manninge	x	
Geoffrey Baker	x	
Margaret Bucke (W)	x	
John Skinner	x	
Thomas Yardley	x	
Lewes Tayte		x
Henry Gisbourne		x
Ambrose Jennens		x
Bowyers (longbows, livery bows and crossbows)		
Richard Boulte	x	
Jonas Keifar	x	
John Jefferson		x

APPENDIX 2

Craftsmen	1593–1603	1620–5
Carpenters		
John Hedland	x	
John Edwards	x	
Mathew Banckes		x
William Wheatley		x
John Horton		x
Alice Horton (W)		x
Collarmaker (horse collars)		
George Graves	x	
Coopers (barrels, casks)		
Richard Goad	x	
Anne Goad (W)	x	
Humphrey Harrison		x
Alexander Norman		x
Cutlers (swords)		
Thomas Cale	x	
John Cooper	x	
Thomas Cheshire	x	
John Porter	x	
Robert Smith	x	
John Harmer	x	
William Cave		x
Robert South		x
Fletcher (arrows)		
John Powell	x	
Girdlers (sword belts, lanterns, cases of plate, bandoliers)		
Peter Wright	x	
Anne Wright (W)	x	
John Hambleton	x	
Tobias Bury	x	
William Hurt	x	
Robert Wright		x
John Smith		x
Gunfounders		
Henry Pitt	x	
Thomas Johnson	x	
John Philips	x	
Richard Philips	x	x
George Elkin	x	
Samuel Owen	x	
Peter Gill	x	
John Jacob	x	

CRAFTSMEN AND SUPPLIERS, 1593–1603, 1620–5

Craftsmen	1593–1603	1620–5
Thomas Browne	x	
John Browne		x
Richard Polhill	x	
Thomas Pitt		x
Richard Pitt		x
Gunmakers		
Walter Kue	x	
Philip Dier	x	
Gosson Harrison	x	
William Hoape	x	
Alexander Glendell	x	
William Shaw	x	
Richard Burnett	x	
Richard Parry	x	
Richard Berrowe	x	x
Jeffrie Staunton	x	
John Longworth	x	
Thomas Laverocke Sr	x	x
Thomas Parker	x	
Richard Shipping	x	
Christopher Bird	x	x
James Mitchell	x	
Vulcan Skynner	x	
Jane Staunton (W)	x	
Adam Swan	x	
John Gurre	x	
Robert Browning	x	
Melchezedicke Jonson	x	
Henry Bowers	x	
Thomas Addice	x	x
Robert Stephens	x	
James Thomas	x	
William Griffin	x	x
Cuthbert Thewe	x	
Peter Jones	x	
Robert Smith	x	
Thomas Daye		x
John Skynner	x	
Williame Catle (Kettle ?)	x	
James Burleighe	x	
John Woodruffe	x	
Jane Woodruffe (W)	x	
Isabel Hopkins (W)	x	
Mary Mythchel (W)	x	
Robert Bucke	x	
John Barboure	x	x
Thomas Laverocke, Jr	x	x

APPENDIX 2

Craftsmen	1593–1603	1620–5
Robert Humphrey	x	
John Crampe	x	
John Miller	x	
Sylvester Foster	x	
Roger Holder	x	
Maire Longworth (W)	x	
William Saunders		x
Henry Rowland		x
John Harrington		x
Edward Jones		x
John Cowch		x
John Silke		x
Izacher Spence		x
Christopher Fell		x
Edward Groffarn		x
William Groves		x
William Clare		x
John Eales		x
Thomas Southwicke		x
Wardner Pynne		x
George Brough		x
Richard Miller		x
John Cannon		x
Richard Pope		x
Thomas Locke		x
Richard Holder		x
Thomas Calerope (Caltrapp)		x
Henry Burras		x
Alice Laverocke (W)		x
Henry Coxe		x
John Ketle (Catle?)		x
Stephen Russell		x
John Birham		x
Richard Brante		x
John Cottrell		x
Constantine Bateson		x
John Forster		x
Alice Birham (W)		x

Suppliers	1593–1603	1620–5
Axes		
Edward Langton	x	
Thomas Manning	x	
Lewes Tayte		x

CRAFTSMEN AND SUPPLIERS, 1593–1603, 1620–5

Suppliers	1593–1603	1620–5
Brass		
Humphrey Liddell	x	
John Williams	x	
Mary Jonson (W)	x	
Canvas		
Samuel Garatt	x	
Andrea Bassano		x
Copper		
John Braddizel	x	
Joseph Hayes	x	
Emptions (miscellaneous ships' supplies)		
*William Smeaton	x	
George Smyth	x	
Richard Gossenhill	x	
Thomas Thorpe	x	
Robert Pawenir	x	
*Thomas Watte	x	
James Woodward	x	
William Hartes	x	
Roger Joyner	x	
*William Scott	x	
John Williams	x	
*Edward Partheriche	x	
Joshua Savour	x	
*Thomas Lincoln	x	
*Richard Haynes	x	
*William Forster	x	
*Robert Bevis	x	
*Edward Johnson	x	
*Simon Drawater	x	
Andrea Bassano		x
*William Barroway		x
*John Welles		x
*Richard Lenthall		x
Mathew Person		x
*John Squire		x
*Richard Paulfreyman		x
*Tristram Slader	x	x
Roger Esone		x
Charles Grosse		x
Nicholas Blague		x
Richard Burke (or Bucke)		x
John Jackson		x
Robert Bowerman		x
Richard Longe		x

APPENDIX 2

Suppliers	1593–1603	1620–5
George Outred		x
Robert Applebee		x
Henry Burnett		x
Iron		
Hugh Benson		x
Lead		
John Allen	x	
James Pilkington	x	
Edward Bagshott	x	
John Byche	x	
John Sibley	x	
John Squier	x	
Joseph Davy		x
Henry Deacon	x	
Leather		
William Legate	x	
John Luger	x	
Merchants		
Edmund Burton	x	
John Chapman	x	
Simeon Furner	x	
Thomas Thorpe	x	
Giles Fleming	x	
John Stockes	x	
Randolph Symmes	x	
William Shutte	x	
Thomas Blande	x	
William Bealle	x	
Richard Poyntell	x	
John Robinson	x	
Leonard Hardwode	x	
Richard Boune	x	
John Davis	x	
Richard Haynes	x	
William Ferrys	x	
Richard Paulfreyman	x	
Anthony Goddard	x	
Arthur Worlyshe	x	
George Chandler	x	
Robert Evelin	x	
Thomas Lincoln	x	
William Bloys	x	
John Paginton	x	
William Bardsey	x	

CRAFTSMEN AND SUPPLIERS, 1593–1603, 1620–5

Suppliers	1593–1603	1620–5
John Hawkins	x	
David Middleton	x	
John Trevor	x	
John Fletcher		x
James Younge		x
Thomas Horsell		x
Philip Burlamachi		x
James Paulfreyman		x
Petards		
Barnard Johnson		x
Thomas Pitt		x
Cornelius Drebbel (water petards and mines)		x
Arnold Rotsipen (ditto)		x
Saddles		
George Graves		x
Shovels and Spades		
Christopher Oswine	x	
Robert Cutts	x	
Thomas Wright	x	
Elizabeth Bennet (W)	x	
Barnaby Boston	x	
John Raybold	x	
John Turner	x	
Jerome Boynton	x	
Philippe Bingham	x	
Peter Shutter	x	
Richard Shepard	x	
John Watson	x	
Hester Jennens (W)		x
John Grace		x
Ambrose Jennings	x	x
Tin		
Humphrey Weams	x	
Stephen Sloane	x	
Richard Glover	x	

Source: Compiled from indenture books, PRO, WO 49/17–29, 49–55

W = Widow; * = known Ordnance office personnel

APPENDIX 3

Sample supply lists: army and navy

These two sample lists illustrate the wide range of supplies provided by the ordnance office. The first lists the contents of a 'typical' supply train to Ireland in 1601. The second is a list of naval supplies prepared for the *Vanguard* in 1594.

1. Supply train to Ireland
It took 43 carts to send all these items to Bristol and Chester for shipment, 38 carts to Bristol, 5 to Chester. The total cost of the shipment was £358 2s. 4d. and its value was approximately £2,900. Almost half of the cost, £1,400, was for gunpowder. The list is taken from PRO, WO 55/451 with the supplies sent from the ordnance office being based on a warrant dated 2 May 1601 from the queen to Sir George Carew, Mr George Harvey or any other ordnance officer. A copy of the warrant is also located in WO 55/451. The next warrant in this collection is one authorising payment of £1,005 15s. 7d. to Carew for supplies for Ireland (Dublin), £219 4s. 4d. for supplies for Munster, and £237 15s. 10d. for items for Lough Foyle, totalling £1,462 15s. 9d. This almost certainly refers to the shipment reproduced here since the powder was already paid for and taken from the store; it would not be listed again under this privy seal. The estimated £1,400 for powder, when added to the above sum, makes the total shipment worth approximately £2,862 15s. 9d. In the indenture book for the year, PRO, WO 49/26, John Allen, clerk of the ordnance in Ireland, is listed as being the conductor for this supply on 22 May with indentures for the other items of supply being filled out as late as 24 May. There is no information on when this train reached its destinations. However, a letter from the privy council to the mayor of Chester on 12 July 1601 referred to a shipment which had been sent out in early May for Lough Foyle, conducted by John Allen, but of which nothing had been heard since. The council was in the process of tracing that shipment and wanted the mayor to help. (*APC 1601–04*, 46–7, privy council to the mayor of Chester, 12 July 1601.)

The ordnance office was able to complete the complicated arrangements for the train and probably send it off, within approximately three weeks of the warrant authorising it. There is no way of establishing whether the officers anticipated the order and had begun to get it ready before the warrant on 2 May. Three weeks to prepare a large train for overseas shipment was a very good reaction time.

SAMPLE SUPPLY LISTS: ARMY AND NAVY

To Dublin via Bristol

Item	Quantity
Gunpowder	15 lasts
Match	12 tons
Lead	15 tons
Calivers (3½ ft. w/moulds)	300
Robinet shot (1¼ in.–¾ lbs.)	300 rounds
Light horsemans staves	200
Shovels and spades	2,000
Crows of iron	24
Pickaxes	500
Felling axes	300
Hedging bills	800
Reapehookes	500
Nails	2 barrels
Hande and draught rope	2,000 weight
Soape	200 weight
Linseed Oil	6 gallons
Rozen	100 weight
Pitch	100 weight
Marlin	50 pounds
Twine	50 pounds
Close lanterns	6
Lanterns	18
Chests for calivers	9
Chests for crows of iron and axes	11
Double casks for powder	15 lasts
Smiths forge with tools (includes bellows, anvil, tongs, vice etc.)	1
Carpenters tools (includes axes, hatchets, adzes, mallets, chest etc.)	misc.
Wheelers tools and spare axles	misc.
Tallow, canvas and rope for carts	misc.

For Sir George Bowcher to send on to Munster

Item	Quantity
Gunpowder	5 lasts
Match	5 tons
Lead	5 tons
Shovels and spades	2,000
Pickaxes	500
Crows of iron	50
Chests	6
Rope	misc.

For shipment to Lough Foyle via Chester

Item	Quantity
Shovels and spades	2,000

APPENDIX 3

Pickaxes	1,000
Chests	10
Carts (with canvas, rope and tallow)	5

2. Naval supplies

The ordnance office spent a great deal of time and money on the navy, even during times of peace for there were always some ships at sea consuming supplies. A 'typical' ship, in this case the *Vanguard*, was provided with the following items out of the ordnance office on 10 August 1594. This list is taken from PRO, WO 49/18, indenture book and book of deliveries for 1594. The office listed both the items they were supplying and the items of that type which were still on the ship from a previous supply. They were not consistent in this however.

Item	Remain	Supplied
Demi-cannon of brass	0	4
Culveringe	5	9
Demi-culveringe	5	10
Sacres	2	0
Minion	2	0
Ladles for demi-cannon	3	2
Ladles for culveringe	9	4
Ladles for demi-culveringe	11	4
Ladles for sacres	2	1
Ladles for minions	2	1
Ladlestaves	12	3 doz.
Cross-barred shot for demi-cannon	18	22
for culveringe	28	50
for demi-culveringe	34	56
for sacres	16	14
for minion	0	20
Round shot for demi-cannon	120	0
for culveringe	243	146 (of which 46 base shot)
for demi-culveringe	376	74
for sacres	60	40
for minion	30	70 (35 fawc. [falcon shot])
Basse and burre shot	400	600 (200 base)
Stone shot for cannon	15	0
Cannon corne powder	150 pounds	2 lasts, 1,800 pounds
Musketes, furnished	19	161
Calivers, complete	4	26
Match	220 pounds	354 pounds
Lead for shot	150 pounds	466 pounds
Long pikes	60	20
Short pikes	20	20

SAMPLE SUPPLY LISTS: ARMY AND NAVY

Item	Remain	Supplied
Black bills	88	0
Longebowes	28	0
Arrowes	69 sheaves	0
Bowstrings	3 doz.	2 doz.
Glue	0	½ pound

The total cost of these emptions was £16 6s. 5½d. To this must be added £6 13s. 7d. for miscellaneous 'fireworks' for the *Vanguard* such as camphor, turpentine, rozen, pitch, tallow and various oils, probably used to create firearrows and firebombs to send against enemy ships. The total for this supply was then £23 0½d.

APPENDIX 4

Ordnance supply items: prices 1574, 1593, 1625

The price rises on many ordnance supplies were minimal; some items cost less in 1625 than they had in 1574. The rising cost of war was not, therefore, a result of the increased cost of war matériel. Other aspects of military supply — food which was tied to cost of living, salaries which increased slightly but as armies grew larger and more personnel were involved the bill was higher, and clothing which wore out quickly and often had to be replaced twice a year — were where the real increases in cost lay.

Item	1574		1593		1625	
Ordnance, brass	70s.	(cwt)	70s.	(cwt)	–	
Ordnance, iron	240s.	(ton)	200s.	(ton)	270s.	(ton)
Shot, round	160s.	(ton)	160s.	(ton)	200– 220s.	(ton)
Gunpowder, corn	9d.	(lb.)	8d.	(lb.)	8s. 5d.	(lb.)
Match	30s.	(cwt)	19s.	(cwt)	4s.	(cwt)
Calivers (each)	20s.		9s. 6d. – 12s.		2s.	
Muskets (each)	–		16s. 8d. – 1s.8d.		18s. 6d. – 20s.	
Bandoliers (each)	–		4s.		4s.	
Pikes, long (each)	2s.6d.		2s. 6d.		3s. 2d.	
Pikes, short (each)	–		2s. 0d.		–	
Swords (each)	–		6s. 8d.		6s. 2d. – 8s.	
Corslets (each)	30s.		*18s.		*18s.	

* The dramatically lower price in 1593 and 1625 probably indicates that the 'bare' corslet is being provided, consisting simply of the back and front pieces rather than the entire outfit of front, back, gorget (collar) and greaves for the legs.

APPENDIX 5

Estimated ordnance office expenses in selected years

All sums are in pounds sterling to the nearest £100. The figure for gunpowder is provided for comparison in order to show the high percentage of the ordnance office budget which was spent on this one item.

Year	Indenture books	Lieutenants accounts		Gunpowder	
1578	–	7,300		2,300	
1581	–	21,700		16,400	
1587	–	7,000		400	
1593	8,700	15,300	(av.)	8,000	(av.)
1594	10,000	15,300	(av.)	8,000	(av.)
1595	14,900	15,500		5,900	
1596	25,900	29,500		20,300	
1597	–	18,000		9,200	
1598	12,500	18,000		9,100	
1599	19,400	21,600		3,500	
1600	14,500	15,800		7,000	
1601	15,700	17,200		7,000	
1602	17,300	16,300		7,000	
1603	7,800	10,300		6,300	
1604	5,000	6,400		–	
1605	5,100	6,300		1,500	
1606	–	10,300		3,200	
1607	–	13,300		6,100	
1608	–	12,300		5,900	
1609	–	8,800		2,400	
1610	6,800	9,000		2,400	
1611	–	11,900		5,100	
1612	–	9,400		3,200	
1613	–	10,500		–	
1614	–	7,900		–	
1615	–	5,600		–	
1616	–	7,500		2,000	(av.)
1617	–	5,300		2,000	(av.)
1618	–	3,200		2,000	(av.)
1619	4,600	5,100		2,000	(av.)
1620	4,700	#16,900		2,000	(av.)

\# Includes £13,000 allowed to pay Dallison's debts in that year.

APPENDIX 5

Year	Indenture books	Lieutenants accounts	Gunpowder
1621	14,300	*19,400	2,950
1622	4,500	*13,200	2,600
1623	8,500	*5,500	2,800
1624	16,900	*1,200	13,600
1625	49,400	*29,500	5,100

* Years between 1621 and 1625 do not include some £12,357 paid to the lieutenant not for supplies but to pay Dallison's debts. This sum cannot be traced to any one year as is possible in 1620. The total cost of reducing Dallison's debt may even have been in excess of £25,000.

The indenture books did not exist before 1593, so no figures are available before that date. It has therefore been difficult to assess the cost or quantity of supplies used in war before 1593. Figures in the lieutenants' accounts are often averages since the taking of yearly accounts, which was the norm (except for 1593–4) before 1613, stopped in that year. Subsequently Dallison's accounts were taken from January 1613 to June 1615 and Sir Richard Morrison's from April 1614 to March 1621 and then from April 1621 to July 1625. The overlap with Dallison is puzzling, since no money seems to be credited to Morrison before 1616. The inclusion of accounts since April 1614 was probably an accountant's measure to cover the period when Dallison was relieved of daily management of the office while still allowing the money owed to suppliers who brought in items to the office to be paid correctly. Certainly a key element in Morrison's accounts from 1614 to 1621 was the sum of £13,062 paid to him as part of an estimated £23,848 in debts left over since 1608. The remainder of that debt was paid off in his next account covering the years 1621–5. Still, no ordinary payments or payments under privy seal are listed earlier than Easter term 14 James (1616). It has been difficult to determine the years in which office expenditure actually took place, because of the division of Morrison's accounts into two batches.

Obvious discrepancies between the indenture books of the ordnance office and the lieutenants' accounts can be identified in this table. To a certain extent this was to be expected. Money that was sent to the lieutenant in one year was often not spent until the next and a certain amount of overlap would certainly explain such small differences as the £600 in 1595 or even, perhaps, the £2,200 in 1599. As a whole, the accounts for the Elizabethan period are not too divergent although the £5,500 difference between accounts in 1598 is inexplicable. It is also puzzling that Sir George Carew's first account as lieutenant of the ordnance in 1593–4 shows that he was paid and allowed about £30,600 whereas the supplies actually brought into the office only totalled, according to the books, around £18,700. Carew held a (deservedly) high reputation at the time, so he was either allowed a little extra for munitions which were not brought in, or else he had to pay some of the debts of the previous lieutenant – Robert Constable. The only record, however, of debts left unpaid by Constable is for just £1,707 0s. 2d. which seems to have been settled by seizing some of his lands. (*CSPD Add. Eliz. I and James I 1580–1625*, 452, [1604?].)

The discrepancies after 1620 can be explained by the unusual infusion of money into the office's accounts not for supplies but solely in order to pay Dallison's debts. The indenture books would not list any supplies for those years since none were brought in. This could only be corroborated by a detailed examination of all the indenture books from 1608 to 1615.

The patterns of expenditure in the ordnance office can be roughly divided into five phases: 1587–99, 1600–5, 1606–13, 1614–19 and 1620–5. During the first period, from 1587 to 1599, there was a gradual increase in the amount of money spent on ordnance, although the early figure of £21,700 spent in time of peace seems to indicate that more preparation was done before 1585 than might have been expected if the 1587 figure were taken as typical. The peak of expenditure was reached in 1599 when massive supply trains were being prepared for Essex's expedition to Ireland. From this point expenses fall off slightly, and the second phase of expenditure, from 1600 to 1605, shows a pattern of irregular decline with an occasional spurt of activity such as in 1601, possibly as a result of the Kinsale campaign. It is interesting to see that a sharp decline in expenditure on ordnance supplies took place between 1602 and 1604. It did not take the government long to bring Elizabeth's war-machine to a halt once the Irish situation had settled down. Carew's frugality, combined with the conclusion of peace with Spain in 1604 resulted in the lowest expenditure on military supplies until 1617.

The third phase, from 1606 to 1613, is characterised by the larger expenses resulting from a small rebellion in Ireland and a modest expedition to Kintyre. In addition, accounts for these peaceful years often list page after page of expenditure on fireworks, gifts for foreign princes and special pageants such as the elaborate display at the creation of Henry as Prince of Wales in 1610. This ceremony alone cost over £1,000 and included fees for carts, fireworks and labourers as well as an unusual item, a costume of Neptune to be worn by the actor who presented a poem of Ben Jonson's to the king. (PRO, WO 49/35, indentures 10–18 June 1610.) The peak of expenditure in this period was in 1607, if Dallison's untrustworthy accounts can be given credence to the extent of providing at least an indication of how much money the government thought was being spent on ordnance supplies. From that point, expenditure drops slightly, but fluctuates throughout the rest of the period at an average of around £10,000 per year.

The fourth period in ordnance office finances, from 1614 to 1619 shows the result of the Dallison scandal, with ordnance expenditure dropping from £7,900 in 1614 to a low of £3,200 in 1619. These are only tentative figures, since it has proved very difficult to break the lump sums listed by the auditors of the exchequer into their years of actual expenditure. This is particularly true in respect of gunpowder which is merely listed as costing £10,000 between 1616 and 1619: there is no indication of year-by-year expenditure.

APPENDIX 5

The indenture books exist for this period, but have not so far been examined; detailed investigation of each of them would help to clarify just when the money was spent.

The last phase of ordnance expenditure shows the increasing amounts of money spent on supplies from the first threat of continental intervention through to the beginning of the war with Spain in 1625. The rise was by no means constant, since the years 1620, 1621, and to a certain extent 1622, were followed by two years of very low outgoings. The interesting point about 1624 and 1625 is the large discrepancy between the amount of money actually spent on supplies as listed in the indenture books and the small amount, especially in 1624, which went through the hands of the lieutenant. Much of the money was spent by others, probably by Philip Burlamachi, buying supplies on the continent.

Bibliography

Unpublished Primary Sources

Bodleian Library, Oxford
MSS Rawlinson

British Library, London
MSS Additional
MSS Cotton
MSS Egerton
MSS Harleian
MSS Royal
MSS Sloane
MSS Stowe

Hampshire Record Office
MSS Herriard/Jervoise

House of Lords Record Office
Main Papers

Magdalene College Library, Cambridge
MSS Pepys

Public Record Office, Chancery Lane, London
C 66	Court of chancery, patent tolls
E 101	Exchequer, accounts, various
E 122	Exchequer, King's remembrancer, customs accounts
E 351	Exchequer, declared accounts
E 403	Exchequer, warrant books, pells
E 405	Exchequer, receipts and issues
E 407	Exchequer, miscellaneous
PROB 11	Prerogative court of Canterbury [PCC]
SP 9	State papers, miscellaneous
SP 12	State papers, domestic, Elizabeth I
SP 14	State papers, domestic, James I
SP 15	State papers, addenda, Edward VI–James I
SP 16	State papers, domestic, Charles I
SP 38	State papers, docquets
SP 39	State papers, warrants
SP 40	State papers, warrant books
SP 46	State papers, supplementary
SP 63	State papers, Ireland

ENGLISH ORDNANCE OFFICE

SP 78   State papers, foreign, France
SP 84   State papers, foreign, Holland

Public Record Office, Kew
AO 1   Audit office, declared accounts
WO 49   War office, ordnance office, debenture books
WO 54   War office, ordnance office, quarter books
WO 55   War office, ordnance office, warrants and issues

Yale Center for Parliamentary History
Diary of Sir Walter Erle, transcript of British Library, MS Additional 18579
Diary of Sir John Holland, transcript of British Library, MS Tanner 392
Diary of Sir William Spring, transcript of Houghton Library, Harvard, English MS 980
Diary of Bulstrode Whitelocke, transcript of Cambridge University Library, D. d. MS xii

Printed Primary Sources

Acts of the privy council, ed. J. R. Dasent, 32 vols, London 1890–1970
Calendar of the Carew manuscripts, ed. J. S. Brewer, 6 vols, London 1867–73
Calendar of state papers, addenda, Elizabeth I and James I 1580–1625
Calendar of state papers, domestic series, of the reigns of Edward VI, Mary, Elizabeth I, James I and Charles I, London 1857–
Calendar of state papers relating to Ireland, of the reigns of Henry VIII, Edward VI, Mary, and Elizabeth 1509–1603, ed. H. C. Hamilton, E. G. Atkinson and R. P. Mahaffy, 11 vols, London 1860–1912
Commons debates 1621, ed. Wallace Notestein, Francis H. Relf and Hartley Simpson, 7 vols, New Haven, Conn. 1935
A copy of papers relating to musters, beacons, subsidies, etc. in the county of Northampton A.D. 1586–1623, ed. Joan Wake (Northamptonshire Record Society iii, 1926)
D'Ewes, Sir Simondes, *A compleat journal of . . . the House of Lords and Commons throughout the whole reign of Queen Elizabeth of glorious memory*, London 1693
Earl of Hertford's lieutenancy papers: 1603–1612, ed. W. P. D. Murphy (Wiltshire Record Society xxiii, 1969)
Historical Manuscripts Commission, *Calendar of the most honourable the Marquess of Salisbury, preserved at Hatfield House, Hertfordshire*, 24 vols, London 1883–1976
―――― *Manuscripts of the duke of Buccleuch and Queensberry*, 3 vols, London 1899–1926
―――― *Third report of the royal commission on historical manuscripts*, London 1872
―――― *Fourth report of the royal commission on historical manuscripts*, London 1874
Jacobean commissions of enquiry, 1608 and 1618, ed. A. P. McGowan, London 1971
Journals of the House of Commons, London 1742–
Journals of the House of Lords, London 1767–

Lancashire lieutenancy under the Tudors and the Stuarts, ed. John Harland, 2 vols (Chetham Society xlix, l, 1859)
List and analysis of state papers foreign series, ed. Richard B. Wernham, 3 vols, London 1969
Montagu muster book 1602–23, ed. Joan Wake, Peterborough 1935
Naval tracts of Sir William Monson, ed. Michael Oppenheim, iii (Naval Records Society xxiv, 1913)
Northamptonshire lieutenancy papers and other documents 1580–1614, ed. Jeremy Goring and Joan Wake (Northamptonshire Record Society xxvii, 1975)
Norton, Robert, *The gunner*, London 1628
Notes of the debates in the House of Lords, ed. Francis Relf (Camden Society xlii, 1929)
Parliamentary diary of Robert Bowyer 1606–7, ed. D. H. Willson, Minneapolis 1931
Parliaments of Elizabeth I: 1558–1581, ed. T. E. Hartley, Wilmington, Del. 1981
Proceedings in parliament 1610, ed. Elizabeth Read Foster, 2 vols, New Haven – London 1966
Proceedings in parliament 1628, ed. Mary Keeler, Mary Frear, Maija Jansson Cole and William B. Bidwell, 6 vols, New Haven – London 1983
Royalist ordnance papers 1642–1646, ed. Ian Roy (Oxfordshire Records Society xliii, 1964)
State papers relating to the defeat of the Spanish Armada anno 1588, ed. J. K. Laughton, London 1894
Statutes of the realm, London 1810–28
Stuart royal proclamations, I: *The royal proclamations of King James I*, ed. James F. Larkin and Paul L. Hughes, Oxford 1973
Stuart royal proclamations, II: *Royal proclamations of King Charles I: 1625–1646*, ed. James F. Larkin, Oxford 1983
Tudor royal proclamations, III: *The later Tudors 1588–1603*, ed. James F. Larkin and Paul L. Hughes, New Haven – London 1969

Secondary Sources

Ashley, R., 'The organisation and administration of the Tudor office of the ordnance', unpublished BLitt diss. Oxford 1973
Ashton, Robert, 'The disbursing official under the early Stuarts: the cases of Sir William Russell and Philip Burlamachi', *Bulletin of the Institute of Historical Research* xxx (1957), 162–74
―――― *The English civil war: conservatism and revolution 1603–1649*, London 1978
Aylmer, G. E., 'Studies in the institutions and personnel of English central administration 1625–42', unpubl. DPhil diss. Oxford 1954
―――― 'Attempts at administrative reform 1625–40', *English Historical Review* lxxii (1957) 229–59
―――― *The king's servants: the civil service of Charles I, 1625–1642*, London – Boston 1974
Barnes, Thomas G., *Somerset 1625–1640: a county's government during the 'Personal Rule'*, Cambridge, Mass. 1961

────── 'The prerogative and environmental control of London building in the early seventeenth century: the lost opportunity', *California Law Review* lxviii (1970), 1332–63

Blackmore, H. L., *The armouries of the Tower of London, I: The ordnance*, London 1976

Boynton, L. O. J., 'The charter of the Company of Gunmakers, London', *Journal of the Society of Army Historical Research* vi (1927), 79–92

────── *The Elizabethan militia 1558–1638*, London 1967

Chaudhuri, K. N., *The English East India Company: the study of an early joint stock company 1600–1640*, New York 1965

Cockle, Maurice J. D., *A bibliography of English military books*, London 1900

Colvin, H. M. (ed.), *A history of the king's works*, iv, London 1982

Cruickshank, C. G., *Elizabeth's army*, Oxford 1946

Davies, C. S. L., 'Supply services of the English armed forces 1509–50', unpubl. DPhil. diss. Oxford 1963

The dictionary of national biography from the earliest times to 1900, 22 vols, London 1949–50

Dietz, Frederick, *English public finance 1558–1642*, New York – London 1932

Elton, G. R., *The Tudor revolution in government*, Cambridge 1953

────── *The Tudor constitution*, Cambridge 1960

Falls, Cyril, *Elizabeth's Irish wars*, London 1950

Ferris, J. P., 'The saltpetermen in Dorset 1638', *Proceedings of the Dorset Natural History and Archeological Society* lxxxv (1963), 158–63

Ffoulkes, Charles J., *The gun-founders of England*, 2nd edn, York, Penn. 1969

Firth, C. H., *Cromwell's army*, London 1902

Fissel, Mark Charles (ed.), *War and government in Britain, 1598–1650*, Manchester – New York 1991

Fletcher, Anthony, *A county community in peace and war: Sussex 1600–1660*, London – New York 1975

Fortescue, J. W., *The history of the British army*, 13 vols, London 1910

Gardiner, Samuel R., *The history of England from the accession of James I to the outbreak of the civil war 1603–1642*, London 1883

Hale, J. R., 'Tudor fortifications 1485–1558', in idem, *Renaissance war studies*, London 1983

Hasler, P. W., *The House of Commons 1558–1603*, 3 vols, London 1981

Hayes-McCoy, G. A., 'The completion of the Tudor conquest and the advance of the Counter-Reformation 1571–1603', in T. W. Moody, F. X. Martin and F. J. Byrne (eds), *A new history of Ireland, III: Early modern Ireland, 1534–1691*, Oxford 1976, 94–140

Hogg, O. F. G., *English artillery 1326–1716*, Woolwich 1963

────── *The royal arsenal: its background, origin and subsequent history*, 2 vols, London 1963

Hurstfield, Joel, *Freedom, corruption and government in Elizabethan England*, Cambridge, Mass. 1973

Jenkins, Rhys, 'Early gunfounding in England and Wales', *Transactions of the Newcomen Society* xlix (1971–2), 145–52

Keep, A. P. P., 'Star Chamber proceedings against the earl of Suffolk and others', *English Historical Review* xiii (1898), 716–29

BIBLIOGRAPHY

Loades, David, *The Tudor navy: an administrative, political and military history*, Aldershot 1992

MacCaffrey, Wallace T., 'Place and patronage in Elizabethan politics', in S. T. Bindoff, J. Hurstfield, and C. H. Williams (eds), *Elizabethan government and society: essays presented to Sir John Neale*, London 1961

Malden, H. E. (ed.), *Victoria county history of the county of Surrey*, 4 vols, Westminster 1902–12

Martin, Colin and Geoffrey Parker, *The Spanish Armada*, London – New York 1988

Mattingly, Garrett, *The Armada*, Boston, Mass. 1959

Merriman M. and John Summerson, 'The Scottish border', in Colvin, *A history of the king's works*

Neale, J. E., 'Elizabeth and the Netherlands 1586–87', in idem, *Essays in Elizabethan history*, London 1958, 170–201

Nef, J. U., *The rise of the British coal industry*, 2 vols, London 1932

—— *Industry and government in France and England 1540–1640*, Ithaca, New York – London 1969

Oppenheim, Michael, *A history of the administration of the royal navy and of merchant shipping in relation to the navy from MDLX to MDCLX with an introduction treating of the preceding period*, n.p. 1896, repr. 1961

Parker, Geoffrey, *The army of Flanders and the Spanish road 1567–1659*, Cambridge 1972

—— 'The "military revolution", 1560–1660 – a myth?', *Journal of Modern History* xlviii (1976), 195–214

—— *The military revolution: military innovation and the rise of the west, 1500–1800*, Cambridge 1988

Peck, Linda Levy, *Northampton: patronage and policy at the court of James I*, London 1982

—— *Court patronage and corruption in early Stuart England*, Boston, Mass. 1990

Power, M. J., 'London and the control of the "crisis" of the 1590s', *History* lxx (1985), 371–85

Prestwich, Menna, *Cranfield: politics and profits under the early Stuarts: the career of Lionel Cranfield, earl of Middlesex*, Oxford 1966

Price, William Hyde, *The English patents of monopoly*, Boston – New York 1906

Reid, R. R., *The king's council in the north*, London – New York 1921

Roberts, Michael, *The military revolution 1550–1660*, Belfast 1956

Rodger, N. A. M., 'Ordnance records and the Gunpowder Plot', *Bulletin of the Institute of Historical Research* lii (1980), 124–5

Rodriguez-Salgado, M. J. and Simon Adams, *England, Spain and the gran armada: 1585–1604*, Savage, Maryland 1991

Russell, C., *The crisis of parliaments*, London – New York 1971

—— *Parliaments and English politics 1621–1629*, Oxford 1979

Schubert, H. R., *History of the British iron and steel industry*, London 1957

Smith, A. Hassell, 'Militia rates and militia statutes', in Peter Clark, N. R. N. Tyacke and G. R. Alan (eds), *The English commonwealth 1547–1640: essays presented to Joel Hurstfield*, New York 1979, 93–110

Stearns, Stephan J., 'The Caroline military system, 1625–1627: the expeditions to Cadiz and Re', unpubl. PhD diss. Berkeley, Ca. 1967

Stern, Walter M., 'Gunmaking in seventeenth-century London', *Journal of the Arms and Armour Society* 1 (1954), 55–100

Stewart, Richard Winship, 'The "Irish Road": military supply and arms for Elizabeth's army during the O'Neill rebellion in Ireland, 1598–1601', in Fissel, *War and government in Britain, 1598–1650*

Straker, Ernest, *Wealden iron*, London 1931

Thompson, I. A. A., *War and government in Habsburg Spain 1560–1620*, London 1976

Thomson, G. Scott, *Lords lieutenants in the sixteenth century: a study in Tudor local administration*, London – New York 1923

Tomlinson, Edward. M., *A history of the Minories*, London 1907

Tomlinson, H. C., 'Wealden gunfounding: an analysis of its demise in the eighteenth century', *Economic History Review* xxix (1976), 383–400

―――― *Guns and government: the ordnance office under the later Stuarts*, London 1979

Weber, Max, *From Max Weber: essays in sociology*, ed. and trans. H. H. Gerth and C. Wright Mills, New York 1958

Wernham, R. B., 'Elizabethan war aims and strategy', in Bindoff, Hurstfield and Williams, *Elizabethan government and society: essays presented to Sir John Neale*, London 1961, 340–68

―――― *After the Armada: Elizabethan England and the struggle for western Europe 1588–1595*, Oxford 1984

Willcox, W. B., *Gloucestershire: a study in local government, 1590–1640*, New Haven, Conn. 1940

Young, Michael B., 'Illusions of grandeur and reform at the Jacobean court: Cranfield and the ordnance', *Historical Journal* xxii (1979), 53–73

―――― *Servility and service: the life and work of Sir John Coke*, London 1986

Index

Abbot, George (archbishop of Canterbury 28n.
Armada 1, 21, 55, 76, 86, 91, 92, 110, 118, 127, 136
armour 102, 103, 113, 116, 122–30, 133–7, 139
armouries, county 3, 128–33
Armoury 5, 6, 39, 40, 102–4, 109, 121–6, 128, 129, 137, 144
arms supply system 5, 27, 30, 142, 144, 148
artificers 6, 8, 9, 11, 18, 19, 23, 27, 28, 40, 48, 49, 52, 62, 112, 116
artillery 2, 11, 15, 16, 64, 67, 75, 76, 120. *See also* great ordnance
Ashton, John 136
Ashurst 67, 70
Aylmer, G. E. 35n., 39n., 41n., 44n.

Bacon, Sir Francis 28n.
bandoleers, musket 98, 102
Bath, earl of 138
Beale, William 105
Bedfordshire, county storehouse 130, 131
Bedwell, Thomas 16, 40n., 44n., 46
Bell House, Houndsditch 73
bell metal 72
Berwick 7, 111–15, 122
bills 11, 26, 27, 31, 48, 122, 128
blacksmiths 63, 99–101, 134
Boroughs, Sir John 136
Bourchier, Sir George 116
Bowland, Richard 50
Bowyer, Captain William 115
bowyers 63
Brenchley 65, 67
Bristol 69, 100, 108, 116, 134–6
bronze ordnance 71–6
Brown, John 65, 70, 71, 76, 78
Buckhurst, Lord (earl of Dorset) 11, 137
Buckingham, duke of 31, 87
Bull, Stephen 13, 15, 16n.
Bull, William 15
bureaucracy 2–4, 7, 14, 34–6, 42–4, 48, 63, 78, 143, 145, 147–9
Burghley, Lord *see* Cecil, Thomas and Cecil, William

Burlamachi, Phillip 79, 90, 91, 105

Cadiz xi, 10, 24n., 37, 68, 72n., 90, 93, 100, 104, 140, 142, 144
Caesar, Sir Julius 28n., 50n.
calivers 17, 86n., 93, 96–101, 107, 112, 115, 120, 128, 133, 139
Cardiff 69
Carew, Sir George (baron Carew of Clopton, earl of Totnes) 10–12, 16, 26, 36, 37, 39, 40, 46n., 52, 53, 56, 59, 67, 70, 75, 87, 98
Carlisle 112n., 113
Caron, Noel de 71
carpenters 9, 18, 63, 98, 101, 122
Carter, Francis 16n.
castles 7, 19, 53n., 79, 111, 113, 116–18, 120, 140. *See also* forts
Cecil, Sir Robert (viscount Cranbourne, earl of Salisbury) 10, 12, 20, 23n., 38n., 49n., 56, 57n., 72, 114, 115, 125, 128, 135 and *passim*
Cecil, Sir Thomas (Lord Burghley) 129
charcoal 67, 81
Charles I 3, 14n., 20n., 35, 78, 79, 140, 148
Chatham 7, 18, 19, 21, 38, 48, 111, 120, 121, 140
Cheshire 104, 138
Chester 100, 108, 116
clerk of the deliveries 9, 13–15, 17, 24, 40, 48, 50, 144
clerk of the ordnance 9, 13, 14, 16, 20, 38, 44, 46, 48, 50, 54
clerks 4, 6, 9, 13, 15–17, 19, 22, 45, 55, 104, 105, 112, 121, 143
Cocke, Sir Henry 129
Coke, Sir Edward 28n.
Coke, Sir John 22n., 41, 54, 94
Combe 70
Constable, George 85
Constable, Sir Robert 11n., 12, 25n., 27, 37n., 46n., 85n.
copper mine 72
corruption 3, 4, 7, 8, 11, 15, 21, 27, 29, 31–3, 42–6, 48, 49–52, 56–60, 62, 142
corslets 102, 111, 139

177

county storehouses 128–33
craftsmen 18, 23, 26–28, 48, 58, 62, 63, 68, 73–6, 96, 98, 99, 101–5, 109, 145
Cranfield, Sir Lionel (earl of Middlesex) 14n., 20n., 22, 24n., 25n., 28n., 30, 54, 58n.
Crowe, Sackville 70
Cudnor, William 17n.
Cumberland, earl of (George Clifford) 76
customs 51, 55, 61, 119
cutlers 102–4, 109

Dale, Henry 86
Dallison, Roger 12, 25–30, 52–7, 59, 62, 76, 77, 91
Davis (or Davies), Sir John 11, 23n., 37, 38, 40, 41
Davis, Sir John (attorney general) 11n.
Dawtry, Captain Nicholas 127n.
demi-lances 122, 128
Deptford 7, 18, 21, 111, 120, 121, 140
deputy lieutenant (ordnance office) 9, 13, 18, 37, 124, 129
deputy lieutenants (counties) 126, 127, 129, 133, 134, 136, 137
Dover 7
Dublin 7, 111, 116, 117
Dutch 79, 93, 141

East India Company 71, 81
East Smithfield 66, 100
Edwards, John 102
Elizabeth I xi, 1–3, 6, 16, 17, 20n., 26–9, 31, 33, 34, 51, 60, 64, 65, 68, 78, 80, 86–8, 92, 97, 103, 105, 109, 116, 122, 127, 134, 138, 141, 144–6, 148
Elkin, George 75
Elton, G. R. vii, viii, 34
emptions, supply of 45, 104, 109
Essex, earl of 8, 18, 20, 22n., 37, 38n., 40, 101, 117n., 118, 125
Evelyn, George 87, 95n.
Evelyn, John 58, 85, 86, 91, 94
Evelyn, Robert 85, 87
exchequer 10–13, 16, 19, 23n., 25, 46, 48, 49, 51–4, 56, 57, 60, 61, 62, 107, 111
Exeter, earl of 134, 135

finance, ordnance office 6, 24–32, 145, 167–70
firelocks 99n.
fireworks 50
Fissel, Mark C. viii, 116n.

flask 97, 126, 133
Fletcher, John 109
fletchers 63
forts 7, 16, 19, 53n., 73, 94, 111, 117–20, 140
Fowkes, (or Fookes) William 17
Fulke, Greville 28n.
furbishers 9, 17–19, 23, 40
furnaces, ironmaking 64–7, 70–1
Furner, Simeon (or Simon) 28, 85–7, 106

Gill, Peter 27, 28n., 74
Glamorgan 65, 69
Gore, Robert 16n.
Gorges, Sir Ferdinando 6, 118, 119
Gotobed, Henry 19
Greenwich 122–5, 134
Gresham, Sir Thomas 97n., 105
Grey, Henry 130
gunfounders, gunfounding 27, 64, 65, 66, 68, 69, 74–6, 101, 110
gunmakers, gunmaking 18, 74, 86, 96–101
Gunmakers' Company 99, 101
gunpowder xi, 2, 3, 6, 7, 15, 16, 19, 21–5, 30, 48–51, 58, 63, 68, 69, 78–98, 101n., 102, 105–7, 109, 110, 112–14, 116, 119, 130–4, 144–6
Gunpowder Plot 113, 131, 133

halberds 18, 24, 113, 122
Halder, Henry 17, 48
Hall, William 86
Hammond, William 15
Hampshire 128, 131, 132, 136
Hampton Court 122, 123
handguns 2, 16, 17, 95, 96, 100, 101, 107, 109
Harding, Richard 85, 87
harquebus 17, 97
Harvey, George 12, 13n., 37, 40, 74, 124
Hawkyns (or Hawkins), Sir John 26n.
Haynes, Richard 45, 76
Hereford 128
Hertfordshire 129, 139
Heybourne, John 28
Heydon, Sir John 29n.
Heydon, Sir William 29n.
Hill, Richard 85, 86
Hilliard, Thomas 83n.
Hogge, Brian 48
Hogge, George 48, 85n.
Hopkins, Martin 28, 40
Horsemonden 67

INDEX

Houndsditch 73, 74
Howard, Charles (earl of Nottingham, lord admiral) 1, 86n.
Howard, Thomas (earl of Suffolk, lord treasurer) 28, 31, 56, 57, 59, 62
Huntingdon, earl of 135
Hurstfield, Joel 43

Ireland 7–12, 19, 21, 31, 39, 52, 75, 76, 93n., 94, 97, 100, 101, 104, 105, 107, 108, 111, 116, 117, 124–6, 134, 135, 140–2
iron mills 67n. *See also* furnaces
Isle of Wight 128

James I xi, 27, 31, 33, 52, 55, 57, 60, 83, 103, 113, 114, 120, 125, 138
Jervoise, Sir Thomas 136
Johnson, Edward 40
Johnson, Sir Robert 15, 40

Kaye, Sir John 41–2
Kaye, Richard 41–2
keeper of the small guns 9, 13, 17, 39, 40, 48, 49, 96, 97
keeper of the stores 9, 13, 15, 16, 20, 23, 24, 36, 37, 40, 41, 44, 46, 47, 49, 50, 144
keeper of the rich weapons 9, 18
Kennedy, Mark 85n.

Lancashire 67, 72, 85, 131, 133, 134
Lee, Sir Henry 39, 40, 47n., 68, 123, 124n., 125
Lee, John 37, 39, 40, 46, 47, 48n., 125
levies 5, 104, 106, 107, 125, 126, 132, 138
lieutenant of the ordnance 5, 10–13, 23, 25, 26, 28, 36, 37, 50
Linewray, John 15, 23n., 44n., 45n., 47n., 49
London 6, 10, 18, 21, 66–8, 73, 85, 86, 98, 100–9, 111, 112, 114–16, 121, 124, 129, 130, 134–6, 138, 140
Lords, House of 58, 103
lords lieutenant 127, 129–30
Low Countries xi, 2, 71, 79, 86, 90, 102, 104, 125, 136, 137, 141. *See also* Dutch

MacCaffrey, Wallace T. 35, 36n., 43n
maces 122
Mansell, Sir Robert 26n.
Mansfield, Count 90, 109
Maresfield 67, 70

master gunner of England 9, 13, 15, 16, 18, 23, 68, 120
master of the ordnance 6–11, 15, 17, 22, 24, 26, 52, 53, 56, 66, 75, 111, 113, 114, 116, 122
master of the ordnance in the north 7, 111, 113
master of the armoury 6, 39, 40, 123–5
match 17, 23, 28, 48, 61, 98, 99, 105–7, 109, 120, 132, 137
matchlocks 98, 99n.
merchants 18, 21, 27, 28, 39, 48, 50–2, 61–3, 65, 68, 69, 76, 86, 96, 102, 104–9, 116, 135, 142, 145, 146
messenger 9, 18
Milhall 67, 68, 71
militia 3, 5, 100, 110, 126–32, 134–9
militia act (1558) 127
militia arms 127, 135
militia officers 137
militia rates 128, 136–8
Minories 6, 7, 19, 20, 23, 52, 100, 140
Mint, office of the 6, 19n.
monopolies 87, 110, 145–7
Morice, Francis 15, 54
morions (or morrions) 122, 137
Morrison (or Morison), Sir Richard 12, 26, 54, 125
Mountjoy, Lord, Charles Blount 10
Muscovy Company 105n.
Musgrave, Sir Richard 12n., 112, 113
Musgrave, Sir Simon 112
muskets 17, 23, 24, 86n., 96, 97–101, 103, 105, 109, 112, 113, 115, 118, 120, 123, 126, 128, 134, 135
musters 129, 131, 135

Naunton, Sir Robert 28n.
navy 28, 33, 44, 46, 54, 55, 60–2, 66, 70, 90, 92, 93, 117, 120–2, 141
Netherlands *see* Low Countries
Nicholson, Edmond 107–8, 116n
Northampton 35, 110n., 130, 132, 135
Northamptonshire 129–32, 134, 135
Notestein, Wallace 55n.
Nottingham, earl of *see* Howard, Charles

Oppenheim, Michael 44, 93n
ordinary allowance 11, 18, 22, 23, 25, 28–30, 52, 57, 124, 125, 126, 145
ordnance annexes 121
ordnance, brass (bronze or copper) 21, 22, 27, 63, 64, 66, 71, 73n., 112, 114, 117, 118, 145

179

ordnance, great 63–79
ordnance, iron 24, 51, 65–71, 73, 76, 78, 79, 121
ordnance office, officers 4–8, 10–23, 25–30, 32, 33, 36, 37, 39, 40–2, 44–7, 49–53, 55–63, 65, 67–70, 74, 76, 77, 78, 86, 88–93, 96, 97, 99–102, 104–9, 111, 112, 114, 116, 117, 118, 120–2, 125, 126, 142–5
ordnance office in Ireland 21, 116–17
overseas levies 125, 126, 138
Owen, Samuel 74

Palatinate 29, 78, 89, 90, 94, 102, 109, 144, 146
Parker, Geoffrey vii, 2, 4n., 79n., 116n., 147n.
parliament 3, 55, 69, 82, 84, 103, 114, 140, 148
patronage 34, 35, 37, 38, 40, 42–4
Paulfreyman, James 17
Paulfreyman (or Palfreyman), Richard 13, 17, 37, 39, 40, 47
Paynter, William 15, 16, 44n., 46, 50
Peck, Linda Levy vii, 15n., 26n., 35, 43, 60n.
petre, petremen *see* saltpetre, saltpetremen
Peyton, Sir John 20, 21n., 50, 99, 122n.
Phillips, Richard 75
pikes, pikemaker 24, 28, 95, 102, 103, 105–7, 109, 112, 113, 115, 116, 118, 123, 126, 130, 139, 147
Pitt, Henry 74n., 75
Pitt, Richard 75
plumber 9, 18, 97, 101
Plymouth 118, 119, 132
Portsmouth 7, 18, 20, 21, 111, 117, 119, 120, 123, 125
Poulet, Captain Hampden 128
Powell, John 46, 50
Prestwich, Menna 54n., 55n., 60n.
private arms 100, 127, 128
privy seal 23, 25, 28, 30, 58, 145
proclamation, gunpowder 94; saltpetre 83–4
proofmaster 9, 16, 18, 68

Raleigh, Sir Walter 9
recusant arms 133–4
reform, ordnance office proposals: 1598 report 47–9; 1601 report 49–52; 1618–19 commission 54–9
rests, musket 98
reversion, of offices 34, 39–42, 112

Reynolds, John 15, 129
Rhé xi, 24n., 90, 140, 142
Riddlesden, Sir Stephen 15, 48
Ridge, William 18
Riverhall 67
Roberts, Michael 4
Robinson, Robert 85
Robinson, Thomas 84
Rochester 7, 18, 19, 21, 48, 111, 120, 121, 140
rope 28, 45, 98, 105–7, 109
Roy, Ian 2, 69n., 81n.
Russell, Conrad vii, 55n., 72n.

saltpetre, saltpetremen 7, 63n., 80–5, 87, 90, 112, 145
Selby, William 112
Sheldon, Edward 139
shot 2, 18, 50, 63n., 65, 68–70, 77, 78, 92, 93, 96, 97, 101, 107, 109, 115, 118, 120, 126, 130, 131
Shropshire 68, 127
Sidney, Sir Philip 8
skulls 122
Smythe, Sir John 128
Somerset, militia in 127, 134, 137
Southwark 73, 100
Spain x, 1, 2, 6, 16, 51, 64, 66, 75, 76, 78, 80n., 84, 86, 90, 91, 93, 94, 98, 109, 110, 114, 118–20, 133, 141–3, 147, 148
staples (of arms) 20–2, 48, 58, 86, 91, 117, 132
Steward, James 76
Suffolk, county of 133
sulphur 105
Surrey 85, 87
surveyor of the ordnance 9, 13–15, 23, 24, 37, 40, 41, 46, 52, 54, 117, 144
Sussex 64–6, 70
Sutton, Thomas 111
swords 39, 103, 104, 107, 109, 124–6
Sydenham, Sir Ralph 41, 42
Symmes, Randall 28, 86, 100, 106

Thirty Years War 123n.
Thompson, I. A. A. 1, 80n., 147
Tower of London (White Tower) 6, 7, 13, 16, 18–21, 23, 53n., 83, 84, 86n., 91, 92, 94, 95, 99, 100, 102, 113n., 114–16, 120, 123–6, 134, 135, 140, 146
Tower Wharf 7, 66–8, 100
trained bands 108, 127, 128, 130, 133, 135, 136, 138

INDEX

Treasury, Commissioners of the 28–30
Tree, John 19
Tynemouth Castle 113
Tyrone, rebellion of 11, 97, 110, 141

VanderLew, Maximilian 76
Vauxhall 73
Vere, Sir Francis 119, 120n.

Wales 65, 66n., 67, 69, 100, 131
Walsingham, Sir Francis 1, 86n.
wardrobe, office of the 6, 28, 33, 46, 55, 60, 61, 122
Warwick, earl of (Ambrose Dudley) 8, 10n., 20n.
Weald, Sussex, iron production 64, 67–9
Weber, Max 34
Whitehall 9

Willoughby, Lord 115n.
Wiltshire 138
Winchell, Moses 18
Windsor Castle 123
Woolwich 7, 18, 120–3, 140
Wooten 87
Worcester 83, 87, 131
Worcester, earl of 83, 87
Worcestershire 131
Wright, Ann 102
Wright, Peter 98
Wright, Robert 102

yeoman 6, 13, 124
York 128, 129
York, Sir Edward 128
Yorkshire 85, 128, 135
Young, Michael 22n., 54n., 55n.